Teaching Diversity in Rural Schools

Teaching Diversity in Rural Schools

Attaining Understanding, Tolerance, and Respect Through Young Adult Literature

Lisa A. Hazlett

ROWMAN & LITTLEFIELD
Lanham • Boulder • New York • London

Published by Rowman & Littlefield
An imprint of The Rowman & Littlefield Publishing Group, Inc.
4501 Forbes Boulevard, Suite 200, Lanham, Maryland 20706
www.rowman.com

86–90 Paul Street, London EC2A 4NE, United Kingdom

Copyright © 2023 by Lisa A. Hazlett

All rights reserved. No part of this book may be reproduced in any form or by any electronic or mechanical means, including information storage and retrieval systems, without written permission from the publisher, except by a reviewer who may quote passages in a review.

British Library Cataloguing in Publication Information Available

Library of Congress Cataloging-in-Publication Data

Names: Hazlett, Lisa A., 1959– author.
Title: Teaching diversity in rural schools : attaining understanding, tolerance, and respect through young adult literature / Lisa A. Hazlett.
Description: Lanham, Maryland : Rowman & Littlefield, [2023] | Includes bibliographical references. | Summary: "The purpose of Teaching Diversity in Rural Schools is to assist secondary English Language Arts rural educators and students regarding diversity education by facilitating the development of understanding, tolerance, and respect toward those different from oneself through the use of rural, small town-themed young adult literature"— Provided by publisher.
Identifiers: LCCN 2022044441 (print) | LCCN 2022044442 (ebook) | ISBN 9781475859607 (Cloth) | ISBN 9781475859614 (Paperback) | ISBN 9781475859621 (epub)
Subjects: LCSH: Education, Rural—United States. | Rural Schools—Curricula—United States. | Young adult literature—Study and teaching (Secondary) | Rural conditions in literature. | Multiculturalism—Study and teaching (Secondary) | Language arts Teachers—In-service training—United States.
Classification: LCC LC5146.5 .H39 2023 (print) | LCC LC5146.5 (ebook) | DDC 371.009173/4—dc23/eng/20221021
LC record available at https://lccn.loc.gov/2022044441
LC ebook record available at https://lccn.loc.gov/2022044442

In Memory
Merrill D. Spiegel
1931–2019
J. Stephen Hazlett
1940–2006
John H. Bushman
1940–2020

Contents

Preface	ix
Introduction	xvii
Chapter 1: Introduction to Rurality	1
Chapter 2: Consideration of Canonical Adult Classics vs. Young Adult Literature	33
Chapter 3: Importance of Young Adult Literature With Upper Midwestern Settings, and Locating Titles	45
Chapter 4: Rural Public Education and Diversity Issues	61
Chapter 5: Rurality Denigration and Developing Lifestyle Pride	93
Chapter 6: Lesbian, Gay, Bisexual, Transgender, and Queer/Questioning (LGBTQ+) Students and Rural Communities	119
Chapter 7: Exceptional, Undocumented, and Homeless Students in Rural Schools and Communities	151
Chapter 8: Rural Death and Grief	173
Appendix A: Bibliography of Rural-Themed YAL Titles by Single State	199
Appendix B: Bibliography of Rural-Themed YAL Titles by Multiple States/Areas	227
Appendix C: YAL Bibliography of Settings Outside the United States	231

Appendix D: YAL Bibliography of Titles From Unidentified State
   or Unidentified State With Named Area/Region   235

About the Author   239

Preface

Teaching Diversity in Rural Schools: Attaining Understanding, Tolerance, and Respect Through Young Adult Literature was written because I finally snapped while riding a shuttle transporting National Council of Teachers of English (NCTE) 2019 Annual Convention in Baltimore, MD, attendees to conference hotels. Over the years of traveling elsewhere, my colleagues and I have been asked every conceivable question regarding living in South Dakota (SD), including my favorites:

- Do you have electricity and roads?
- What do you do with Mt. Rushmore in the winter?
- When you look out your window, do you see teepees?
- Oh, did you leave from Bismarck? (Bismarck is in North Dakota.)
- (From a publishing representative) Do you have enough people who read in South Dakota that you need to order books?
- (From a publishing representative) I didn't know you had schools there!

I've heard these and many more over the years, thankfully lessening, but while in the overfull shuttle, an ELA (English language arts) teacher next to me began this (verbatim), and continually recurring, conversation once identifying my state:

ELA Educator: Hi! I'm Lauren, from Pittsburgh. Where are you from?

Lisa: Hi, it's nice to meet you. I'm Lisa, from South Dakota.

Lauren: Reeaally!? How many *days of travel* did you have?

Lisa: Excuse me?

Lauren: I mean, how did you *get* here?

Lisa: Uh, I left from Sioux City, flew to Chicago, and then got on the plane for Baltimore.

Lauren: So how *many days* did all this *take*?

Lisa: Um, the airport's about half an hour from home. I leave from Sioux City because I have early flights and the Sioux Falls airport is an hour away.

Lauren: (Suspicious look) You did this *today*? But I don't understand how it took you less time as I'm from Pittsburgh.

Lisa: Well, my flight was at 6:30 a.m., so there wasn't much traffic, and the airport's really small, planes mostly go to Chicago and back.

Lauren: (Perplexed) Well, must be nice, I guess. (Turns to person on other side).

Welcome to living in a rural state. This exchange is one I've had too frequently to count, along with the microaggressions above and in Chapter 5. Had I been younger, I would've described my team of barking, slavering sled dogs at the ready, but now I attempt to educate others about South Dakota.

As the shuttle progressed, I mused that, aside from Poe's grave, Baltimore appeared largely the same as every other city. Remove the monuments/attractions (e.g., St. Louis's Arch, Chicago's Willis Tower) and welcome to Sioux Falls, home of snarled traffic, short-lived restaurants, and increasing urban sprawl.

I'm still amazed by so many having such absurd ideas regarding South Dakota, and presumably the other Upper Midwestern (UM) states of Iowa, Minnesota, Montana, Nebraska, North Dakota, and Wyoming as well. I don't imagine New York City residents living in tenements, hoping to board the next Orphan Train to the uncivilized West, or Kentuckians swilling moonshine in a holler, barefoot, and puffing on corncob pipes. Why is South Dakota viewed as living in the past, but not most other states?

Doubtless, two contributions to this idea are that most UM states are large with small populations (South Dakota's population is near 885,000 [U.S. Census Bureau, 2018]) and rurality's negative media portrayal as toothless farmers wearing overalls without shirts or survivalist families in camouflage with multiple guns (the baby's is in the diaper), railing against anything considered liberal.

Rural individuals are consistently depicted as religiously fundamental, judgmental, prejudiced, and homophobic, plus intellectually challenged, leery of higher education, speaking non-standard English, and uninterested or ignorant of sophisticated events and activities. We're overweight, awash in polyester, badly groomed, and with dated, unflattering hairstyles. Such illustrations are so predominant that it's daunting to attempt showing rural individuals realistically.

Regardless, by the time I reached the hotel, told Lauren I hoped she'd have a great convention (she narrowed her eyes slightly and nodded), and was handing my AMEX to the check-in person (You came *all the way* from South Dakota!?), I decided to start writing.

For this text's purposes, *rurality is determined as those areas of the country whose largest cities through smallest towns are so small and densely White that its residents have little to no personal contact with racially diverse individuals, with any area minorities living and/or viewed separately from the community.*

Indeed, statistics show the UM's uniqueness of overwhelmingly and nearly exclusively one race, White. Only western and northern Alaska's indigenous composition is also primarily single race (U.S. Census Bureau, 2018). In tandem, one is highly unlikely to have *personal* encounters or exchanges with those non-White (U.S. Census Bureau, 2018; World Population Review, 2020) within these states.

The UMs diversity percentage is approximately 17% (U.S. Census Bureau, 2018), but this number is derived from only *two* counties (Nobles, MN; Beadle, SD), with five additional counties from Minnesota showing high minority numbers (Countryahh.com, 2022). That is, the population of *seven* counties from *two* states have a diversity rate of 17%, with the rest having 16% to 0% non-White individuals (U.S. Census Bureau, 2018). SD's higher rates are from its nine Native American reservations, approximately 10% of the state's residents (Native-Americans.com, 2014), and Minnesota's distinctly higher population.

These states' largest cities are also small in comparison to others, with their approximate populations 755,000 for Minneapolis–St. Paul's metro area, followed by Omaha's 480,000 and dropping sharply to Des Moines' 208,000. Next is Sioux Falls' 193,000, Fargo's 126,000, Billings' 109,000, and Cheyenne's 65,000 (World Population Review, 2020).

The UM's lack of contact and connections with minorities seems unlikely, but consider Fargo, North Dakota's largest city; its 126,000 residents identifying as 85% White, 6% Black, 4% Asian, and 3% Hispanic/Latinx (U.S. Census Bureau, 2018). Its Asian population is approximately 50; how likely is one to encounter casually an individual from this group, or any other minority, as their combined population is some 160 persons? The UM's other states and largest cities show similar percentages, with smaller towns having few to no minorities.

Rural adolescents' educational system and their community's role within it is different from those of larger areas; schools are the town's social center, residents enthusiastically participating in and attending all events/activities regardless of whether their children are performing or long graduated.

These students and educators have distinct needs, issues, and concerns specific to their situation, but infrequently addressed. Rural ELA education is generally absent in mainstream educational research, usually relegated to a journal's special-themed issue, likewise missing from textbooks and articles. Similarly, conference/conventions have fewer rural speakers, attendees, and educator/researchers.

Professional educational methodologies, classroom practices, unit and lesson plans, discussion guides, and other materials are widely available on the Internet, but commonly tailored to larger suburban/urban schools and classrooms, making many inappropriate or otherwise incompatible to those rural. Yes, they could be adapted, but if taking longer to revise than create, inadvisable.

The responsibility to protect and support all children and adolescents in our lives, not just our own or those like ours, belongs to every adult in all communities. As secondary ELA educators, we're responsible for discussing diversity issues with teens, modeling tolerance and dignity toward those different, and protecting and defending students from harassment and discriminatory actions.

Such education, for students and adults, is vital in the UM, especially as most residents don't know what it's like to be different because they aren't. UM educators similarly mirror their students, as 80% are White, Blacks and Hispanics 7% and 9%, respectfully, Asians 2%, American Indian/Alaskan Natives 1%, Pacific Islanders fewer than 1%, and 2% claiming two or more races (National Center for Educational Statistics, 2021).

Authentic diversity education begins with students learning about and from those different, as true understanding of diversity, tolerance, and acceptance, cannot occur without others' experiences. Such education is more than using occasional texts by and about various minorities, or largely emphasizing one group during a celebratory month. Whatever we wish *learned* must be *taught*, with knowledge and understanding emerging by subsequent, continual discussion of the issues and concerns of those presented, their application/connection to community, US society, and past and current world events.

However, how do UM students learn knowledge/tolerance/acceptance of minorities when there are none (or few) within the area or community, those present consist of one group rather than many, meaningful exposure is infrequent, and some viewed with resentment or hostility?

This question's response and text's intent is to accurately portray rural, small-town lifestyles, especially those of the UM, through secondary ELA classrooms' young adult literature (YAL) use to evince students' understanding of diversity and its many issues. Carefully chosen titles can be extremely effective, providing the strong foundation needed for knowledgeable, accommodating adults respecting those different from themselves.

YAL was chosen for its suitability to students and portrayal of rural adolescents' contemporary lives, absent from canonical classics and other works.

White middle class teens have much to discover and enjoy from YAL (as do minority peers); perhaps the strongest lesson learned (or reminded) is that they, too, are minorities by their rurality, denigrated or misunderstood by those elsewhere, illustrated by the above conversation. Once possessing this understanding, their view of minority peers should shift, if only a bit, with students eventually considering themselves, and others, in different and more positive ways.

Next, teens and adults (as I) can become more active in combating others' rurality stereotypes and misconceptions; likewise, other minority students may also address specific negativities. Unchallenged inaccurate or offensive views remain and grow, and while I don't know if Lauren better understood South Dakota, I was vocal. Imagine her meeting others from the UM, each providing similar information or correcting erroneous beliefs, would her views then change?

All adolescents benefit from YAL, as they, regardless of place, share the same hopes, fears, desires, uncertainties, experiences, and needs. Reading novels reflecting their own lives (as rural-themed titles) provides assurance of hardly being alone, their problems and situations shared by many, both crucial to development and well-being. Teens must be equally able to read of characters *different* from them, as all need assistance in developing tolerance, understanding, and true friendships with those different.

Rural students are hardly ignorant, uninterested, or unconcerned regarding diversity; they're as intelligent and savvy as any other, their lifestyles largely the same as those elsewhere. Still, the Internet and other technological sources often provide much of their information regarding diversity, but not its corresponding personal experience and interaction, nor tolerance, understanding, sympathy, and empathy for individuals different from the majority.

However, YAL with rural, small-town settings can assist in achieving the above positives and help bridge the many gaps between rural white and minority adolescents, because unlike much of technology, its classroom use is not a solo activity. Instead, students ponder, question, discuss, challenge, reconsider, and otherwise share opinions and beliefs regarding novels read and connect them to their lives in safe environments. These activities, guided by educators, helps create and strengthen bonds among all.

Of course, this is hardly simple; rural adolescents need more than title lists or reading one or two like-themed titles; multiple discussions will be needed over time, and they will be uncomfortable, painful, hurtful, embarrassing, and challenging before purposeful or rewarding. Still, YAL features multiple instances of productive yet difficult conversations and situations, certainly a segue to initiating classroom talk, easing fears of beginning them.

We must all speak and act in ways that are respectful, fair, and dignified toward ourselves and others, and understand we may be vilified, lose friendships, anger families, or no be longer welcome in places or events long frequented by doing so. Students should be challenged to become unpopular for what is right and ponder the value of esteem from those discriminating; both also repeatedly featured in YAL.

There is currently much ugliness in the world and the United States, in all locations, over multiple issues large and small, with frightening and dangerous situations seemingly surrounding us and inching ever closer. The former majority of reasonable middle ground seems to have disappeared into only us vs. them, with once-close families and friends fractured by fierce disagreements, neither side seeing nuances or other options, opinions cemented as sole truth with those of differing views pilloried, or worse.

If adults are anxious, how much more are adolescents affected, without the maturity of those older and presumably not fully understanding various situations, their teachers or parents unwilling to elaborate? Many are doubtless attempting to learn more through peers, the Internet, or social media, imperfect sources at best, but how else to comprehend such issues or perhaps dispel anxieties regarding new home negativities?

If we wish to assist our students, we can do so by creating safe, comfortable classrooms in which all are welcome, all voices heard, and content taught appropriate for respective ages. We should be discussing *with* our students, not *to* them, considering and challenging meanings and opinions of literature read, rather than providing worksheets requesting one correct answer.

We must lead students to immerse themselves in their reading, imagining they are the protagonist or any character, and consider how what is read applies to them, others, and society. Educators and students must continually re-read, predict, and reconsider scenes and chapters, events and issues, with peers and educators, rather than using Internet summaries in lieu of reading a too-difficult text or because this allows answering packet questions more quickly.

Students and educators must analyze and critique together, speculating choices made by authors and how material would be different by other decisions, imagining future occurrences after the book's ending. As previous discussions have allowed students' thorough understanding of their reading, this knowledge permits predictions that are appropriate to characters and story.

We must enjoy what and how we teach, creating vibrant classrooms and students again interested in reading, pondering, and sharing themselves, instead of immediately finding summaries to parrot or movies to watch, novels unread. Our careful planning, preparation, and presentation allows our confident instruction, realized by students, and reassuring them their teacher is a knowledge adult, fully in control and capable.

Perhaps most importantly, this permits students to be the adolescents they are, leaving their problems and concerns at the classroom door, and upon leaving, possibly feeling they also have the strength to manage negative situations.

There is beauty everywhere and here; my part of the state (Vermillion, referred to as "The Miami of South Dakota") has endless miles of flat farmland and crops waving slightly in the breeze under brilliantly blue skies in utter silence. The earthy, crisp scents uniquely belonging to each season swath one in familiarity and security and were the same known to those before us and will call to those not yet born, their children and grandchildren, as time passes.

The feeling of peace is all-enveloping, with a closeness to those here before under unimaginably arduous conditions. Those long-ago individuals survived and thrived, creating foundations and paths for those like myself to follow, building them further, stronger, and welcoming my new creations before relinquishing to others, as I will soon do. It is hoped this text will inspire ELA rural educators and their students to continually flourish, together.

REFERENCES

Countryahh.com. (2022). List of all counties in Minnesota. https://www.countryaah.com/alphabetical-list-of-all-counties-in-minnesota/

National Center for Educational Statistics. (2022). *School local locations.* https://nces.ed.gov/surveys/ruraled/definitions.asp

Native-Americans.com. (2014, Feb. 25). *South Dakota Indian reservations.* https://native-americans.com/south-dakota-indian-reservations/

U.S. Census Bureau (2018). *United States quick facts.* https://www.census.gov/quickfacts/fact/table/US

World Population Review. (2020). *State demographics.* https://worldpopulationreview.com/states/

Introduction

This book's purpose is assisting secondary English Language Arts (ELA) rural educators and students, especially those of the Upper Midwest (UM), regarding diversity education, with the awareness that rurality is also a minority and an unfortunately denigrated one, much the same as other minorities, depending upon place and circumstances. Rural adolescents must embrace their rurality, work to remove its stereotypes and stigmas, and use these experiences in understanding and accepting others unlike them, whether racially, culturally, religiously, physically, mentally, or sexually different, as do many elsewhere in the country.

As in the Preface, the UMs isolated and less populated seven states of Iowa, Minnesota, Montana, Nebraska, North Dakota, South Dakota, and Wyoming are unique in their predominantly White populations, consistently holding few to no racial and cultural minorities in even its largest cities, and most certainly its smaller ones. All states have rural, small towns, but seldom solely of one race/culture, but if so, their states are far more densely populated with communities housing more diverse individuals near those rural. While this book may be used for any rural/small town location, its focus is on the UM states.

Many UM adults have at best only transitory contacts with minorities (e.g., a business employee or co-worker) and fewer, if any, personal friendships with frequent extended conversations and shared activities. Adolescents' contacts and exposure to minorities during their daily lives are likewise equivalent, largely from members residing in hometowns or shared connections with parents or other adults.

Teaching our students (and reminding adults) about our many minorities, assisting in developing understanding, tolerance, and respect toward those different is difficult when communities are without such individuals. Other minorities present, as Hutterites and Native Americans, this region's largest minority groups, overwhelmingly reside separately in communities and reservations, attending their own schools and colleges.

Technology is a great equalizer regarding exposure to those different but not a substitute for individuals, and rather than focusing upon what is missing, educators must first work with that present in their schools, classrooms, and communities. I believe there are six concepts tantamount regarding students and successfully connecting them to minorities via classrooms:

- rural students' understanding that they are also a denigrated minority;
- emphasizing that everyone is a minority, depending upon where and with whom one happens to be at the time;
- engaging in frank, honest, and factually correct discussions concerning minorities;
- including curricular study and other representation of minorities in classrooms;
- welcoming and protecting minorities in schools and classrooms; and most importantly,
- connecting the above to quality, rural-themed young adult literature (YAL) featuring contemporary minority protagonists and characters

We cannot change the world, but we can effect change in our ELA classrooms, with those students in them, using what we have available at the time. Surely the message, and truth, conveyed by these points and practices is that we are all more alike than different, and all individuals are of value.

CHAPTER AND TEXT COMPONENTS

- information regarding its particular topic and specific relation and importance to rurality
- rural-themed YAL applicable to topic presented, their annotations, and suggested discussion questions/activities
- discussion questions enhancing the chapter topic, connection to diversity/minorities, and applied to the featured YAL
- bibliography of suggested titles (those annotated in each chapter)
- some chapters contain additional suggested projects or guides
- a bibliography of rural-themed YAL titles of quality at the text's end

SUGGESTIONS FOR CLASSROOM USE

It is presumed that ELA educators are versed in YAL; but if not, the titles and corresponding information provide necessary information. While these titles are not a listing of all rural-themed YAL titles available, they represent as many as could be reasonably located, with each of sufficient quality and interest to secondary students.

As for separate themed questions/activities, they may be used as desired—either for class discussion or turned into longer assignments or projects. It is also presumed that ELA educators need fewer activity ideas and more information for those activities. That is, educators can easily consider Venn diagrams, concept maps, bullet lists, various listing/labeling strategies, and more regarding activities.

More necessary is the information to be used within the methodology selected; specific suggestions are generally not included to allow for educator selection of discussion or activity, and if activity, the form most applicable to their students. Likewise, the same presumption and expectation was used for those questions embedded within the text, based upon selected YAL titles. Additional activities and other projects may be used, or not.

Regardless of selection, it is intended that these items elicit classroom discussion among students *and* educators, rather than placed on worksheets requiring individual written responses without peer or other input. It is believed we learn best by discussing, predicting, considering, listening and applying others' views, reconsidering, analyzing, imagining ourselves as the characters or in like situations, examining and questioning the author's choices and style, and determining what might occur to protagonists and other characters once the novel ends: What happens next? What will the character be like in five or ten years?

Novel discussion is rich and enjoyable, allowing students to determine meaning and otherwise understand and learn from the text, with it remembered and referenced to additional works, producing the critical thinking skills so crucial for developing discernment, insight, inferences, implications, and independent interpretations. With each novel read these skills are honed and applied not only to other novels, but various life events and situations; students graduating with confidence regarding their communicative skills and the ability to use them successfully.

In tandem, it is also presumed educators desire the promotion and emergence of such development and thought, rather than narrowing novels to questions requiring information directly stated in the novel, only one correct answer, and the unspoken reality of one student supplying answers to many or copied from the Internet, never having read the material (if nothing else, discussion eliminates the horror of trade-and-grade, always culminating in educator re-grading).

NOTE TO EDUCATORS

As stated, there are few racial minorities in the UM, but regardless of an individual's minority status, discretion, understanding, and availability should be modeled or otherwise communicated to students. A discussion concerning Blacks when there is only one Black student in the room should be considered beforehand, rather than the individual becoming a target or otherwise subjected to discussions that appear, or are, about the *student*, rather than the minority group *in general*.

Individuals should not be expected to serve as spokesperson for their group, nor should educators assume minority students only desire reading novels about their particular group, from like authors. Moreover, novels should never be selected by presumption, as larger students given titles with protagonists wishing to lose weight, Latinx teens only seeing migrant workers, or a student whose father recently died offered books mirroring his/her situation.

A variety of novels should be available to all and naturally students enjoy reading of characters like themselves, but automatically or continually providing YAL with characters or authors of the same minority as the student without asking for preferences is also discrimination. Titles used for whole-class teaching should represent diverse characters and authors as applicable, with educators providing suggestions for personal reading, allowing student choice.

Additionally, discussions about a minority group not present in the classroom or school should be conducted as thoughtfully and discreetly as any other; speaking of Asian Americans while allowing various denigrations or other negative commentary is naturally unacceptable.

LGBTQ+ students should be especially respected; many are hiding their sexuality by fear of parental reaction, others desire privacy. Obviously, these students should never be outed or otherwise exposed; some may not wish to even be seen with an LGBTQ+-themed novel. For these students, and all others who would otherwise feel uncomfortable during various discussions, ELA educators should serve as private resources.

That is, students may meet and discuss concerns and other issues with educators separately from the class, be given additional resources, information, and contacts as needed, allowed to read novels, conduct Internet searches, and/or use various social media privately. Further appreciated assistance might be providing a secure, and unseen by other students, storage place for such materials.

Introduction   xxi

CHAPTER COMPONENTS

Chapter 1 is an introduction to rurality, with definitions of "rural" dependent upon the source, most multifaceted, conflicting, and confusing. The most indisputable is from the U.S. Census Bureau (2018), of "rural" being anything not suburban or urban. Of course, and as above, having so few minorities is a diversity, as is rurality. Also explored are its residents, rural lifestyles, prominent situations and issues, and overall positives and negatives. Essentially, rural residents and their lifestyles are the same as elsewhere.

Chapter 2 discusses the importance of using YAL as opposed to canonical classics only; obviously, rural-themed YAL should be used for diversity and minority discussions, as titles represent contemporary students, definitely absent from literature written long ago. Further, ELA educators should teach literature that students can comprehend from reading, class instruction, and discussion. Titles ill-fitting to particular students are spoon-fed by instructors continually summarizing sections, providing packets and worksheets, and/or students resorting to Internet summaries instead of reading the text.

Classics indeed rule, but many wonderful titles are torpedoed by too-quick discussions, students reading aloud, excruciating whether in front of the class or at their desks, and packets/worksheets/quizzes assigned. Students use the Internet for summaries and other information required of the above tasks, with viewing the movie after the unit allowing students to visualize what wasn't read.

A particularly dreadful assignment is scene reenactments, the finished video mostly students snickering at one another while demolishing something abandoned or nabbing hapless pedestrians in a public place and using as a character. Siblings and parents are also recruited, siblings' sabotaging when backs are turned, and parents ad-libbing how the video is clearly A+ work. Reconsider, please.

Chapter 3 examines rural-themed YAL, components necessary for evaluating its quality, common themes, and resources for locating novels, reviews, and supplemental materials. The importance of place is considered, and ways to find title's state locations (maddeningly difficult and time-consuming). Unfortunately, relatively few novels are set in the UM; of the approximately 650 titles used within, only 67 were set in in these states (10%) with an additional 7 in more than one state but including an UM one, for a total of 11%.

Specifically, titles with UM settings included 10 from Iowa and Nebraska, 24 from Minnesota, Montana with 14, 1 from North Dakota, South Dakota having 5, and Wyoming, 3. Of these, most were older (10+ years) or historical fiction and while of quality, students should be able to read contemporary novels set in their state as well as others. How are students to learn of these states and their rurality without YAL settings from them?

Chapter 4 examines typical rural schools, students, ELA teachers, and the community, different from most places. Schools range from one K-12 building, two buildings connected to another with one holding elementary, the other middle/secondary, or a separate elementary, middle, and high school.

Only larger cities have multiple schools (South Dakota's two largest cities, Sioux Falls and Rapid City, for example, are the only ones in the state having more than one public high school; Sioux Falls has three, Rapid City, two). Rural students, their classes, activities, and social lives are also reviewed.

Educator shortages, especially post-COVID are seemingly everywhere, including those rural. It is becoming increasingly harder to find teachers for UM states, their often strikingly lower salaries and locations without the amenities many desire definitely contributing factors. Rural ELA public school and post-secondary educators generally remain for their career or leave after two or three years without much in between. One either likes it here, or not.

Chapter 5 considers being rural from others' views, its many media denigrations, microaggressions, and stereotypes used in depicting rurality identified and examined. Likewise, negative comments addressed to students are considered, with accompanying specific activities assisting students in responding respectfully yet instructively.

There is also a longer activity for developing, or increasing, student's hometown pride and knowledge of town history that can used as applicable. If wishing to expand, it can include the entire school and students' parents or other family members, always a winner, but regardless, the activity is productive and enjoyable.

Students identifying as LGBTQ+ are the subject of Chapter 6, with their fears, concerns, issues, and situations, positive and negative, addressed, plus additional difficulties associated with being rural discussed. These students from the smallest towns can be achingly isolated; for example, a junior lesbian female's school may have two male gay students, another like student much younger, and a senior happily in a relationship with an individual from another town.

These students are much more likely to be hiding their sexuality, receive little to no LGBTQ+ information or resources in classes, and remain unwelcome in home, school, church, or community. Using Readers Theater as one teaching method for like-themed YAL novels is included with full instructions and examples.

Too many ELA educators do not use these titles, fearing parental disapproval and censorship, but this is a worry and not a reality. Why not teach a fantastic novel and deal with the phone call if and when it comes? Unfortunately, recent legislation promoting numerous anti-LGBTQ+ bills may cause superintendents and principals to restrict works used, not necessarily legal, but few formally object.

It should, however, be noted that these titles can be life-changing for LGBTQ+ students and necessary for all; many titles are simply worth the effort with educators encouraged to use, teach, and create lists of titles for reading suggestions.

Chapter 7 discusses rural students who are exceptional (EXCP), either cognitively or physically, along with those having other conditions and illnesses, such as cancer or Tourette's. Media representation of those cognitively challenged continually depicts individuals at the highest levels, but there are many much lower, yet unseen. These individuals' community and school lives are included, as are those of higher levels, plus living and work options beyond high school graduation.

Homelessness is also covered, increasingly seen in rural areas, and often from smaller towns' economic difficulties and lack of available jobs paying above minimum wage. Situations are currently worsening by heightened inflation, especially gasoline and grocery costs, and large numbers of those without medical insurance are also seeing increasing debt. The nation's opioid epidemic seemingly favors smaller towns, also causing instability.

Individuals without documentation are included here, increasing due to recruitment by the area's many meat-packing plants and other factory work. North Dakota's oil fields have peaked, but many individuals remained, some documented, others not.

Chapter 8 considers rural death, loss, and grief, something needing far more attention and discussion. Death and loss are different in rural communities, their occurrences deeply affecting most in town by small populations. Bluntly put, a student's death from a graduating 15-student class has, presumably, a more significant impact upon students than one from a 200-student one.

Regardless, schools and teachers become a center for grief expression, with educators expected to lead students, and by extension siblings and parents, through the grief process. It is easy for students to become overwhelmed by the many shrines, memorials, dedications, and other events occurring throughout the school year, grieving multiplying and interfering with teaching, unhelpful to all.

Parents are also ill-equipped for their child's friends no longer appearing at their home, being on a prom committee, now without a son or daughter attending, seeing boy/girlfriends forming relationships with others, peers graduating and leaving, their child eternally 16.

Instructions for forming a school or district grief plan is included, providing step-by-step information for educators regarding managing student losses and death from first notice to moving forward from grieving, including parents, siblings, and those having differing religions and practices than the majority.

Last, a bibliography of rural-themed YAL is included, titles listed by individual state, and a short theme annotation. It is hoped that by truly embracing all those considered minorities in our classrooms and communities, regardless of location, this effort will be felt by students and increasingly extended to more individuals in our contemporary, and often insensitive, society.

REFERENCES

U.S. Census Bureau (2018). *United States quick facts.* https://www.census.gov/quickfacts/fact/table/US

Chapter 1

Introduction to Rurality

All states have rural areas; however, Midwestern/Upper Midwestern (UM) states are unique in large size with scattered, smaller populations that are particularly insulated and homogenous. These residents have no or few personal encounters with those of different races and cultures and are also a minority.

RURAL DEFINITIONS AND LOCATIONS

Although many may consider *rural* as referring to the Midwest or perhaps the deep South, every state has such areas, and unfortunately defined differently by numerous governmental and other organizations. Identifications and classifications can depend upon an area's total population, population by square mile, distance from a larger city and its population, travel time necessary for consumer needs and more, and as various official definitions are combinations of these, determiners for rural are conflicting and confusing.

The U.S. Census Bureau's superbly simple yet vague definition of "rural" being those areas not urban/suburban (Ratcliffe et al., 2016/2021), presuming individuals comprehend the distinctions between urban, suburban, and rural locales. The National Center for Educational Statistics' (NCES; 2022) description also ascertains rural areas as small and remote from larger populations, whether urban or suburban, as do numerous other professional statistical sites. For those enjoying distinctive definitions, Wilger (2016) used "frontier" for states having 50% or more counties averaging a population density of six people per square mile or fewer, with these currently Alaska, Montana, Nevada, North Dakota, South Dakota, and Wyoming.

Most individuals, after examining the multiple complicated formulas with their differing and contradictory designations for *rural*, would find their certainty wavering regarding whether still living in a rural, suburban, or urban area. Frankly, a simpler and more accurate determination could be made by merely looking out a window or using this age-old quip:

What is the difference between rural, suburban, and urban areas?
If you're standing naked on the front porch and the neighbors can't see you, it's rural.
If you're standing naked on the front porch and the neighbors call the police, it's suburban.
If you're standing naked on the front porch and the neighbors ignore you, it's urban.

Regardless, rural definitions depend upon population, with the USCB (2018) stating approximately 20% of the U.S. population lives in a rural area.

United States Population Composition

The USCB (2018) reported the U.S. population as 76.3% White, then dropping sharply to 18.5% Hispanic/Latino and 13.4% African American. The smallest resident percentages are Asians at 5.9%, Two or More Races at 2.8%, American Indian and Alaska Natives at 1.3%, and Native Hawaiian and Other Pacific Islanders at 0.2%. However, while U.S. minorities represent 24% of the population, they are not evenly distributed throughout the country, with rural areas least diverse.

UPPER MIDWESTERN DIVERSITY

Rural minority populations differ by state, but the USCB (2018) reported that this group comprised approximately 17% of the Upper Midwest (UM), the least of the country. Its states of Iowa (IA), Minnesota (MN), Montana (MT), Nebraska (NE), North Dakota (ND), South Dakota (SD), and Wyoming (WY) are sizeable with small, widely scattered towns, far from their few largest cities, most having significantly lower populations than those elsewhere.

Further, this percentage of 17 is reached by only seven counties (six from MN and one from SD) across these seven states (Countryahh.com, 2022), assisted by their meat packing plants and/or livestock farms and active recruitment of people of color, immigrants, and those of low-income. Almost half (44.4%) of meatpacking workers are Hispanic, and one-quarter (25.2%) Black (Rho et al., 2020). The rest of these seven states' counties (477 total) house anywhere from 16% to 0 non-White individuals (USCB, 2018).

Aside from the above industries, South Dakota's nine Native American reservations comprising approximately 10% of the state's population (NativeAmericans.com, 2014), and Minnesota's distinctly higher, and denser, population than other UM states boosts this diversity percentage. For comparison, Minnesota's population is approximately 5,700,700, then Iowa with

3,180,000, and Wyoming last at 567,000. The same is true for the UM's largest cities: Minneapolis–St. Paul, MN's population is about 750,000; then Omaha, NE, at 471,000; and Cheyenne, WY, smallest at 64,000 (USCB, 2018).

All these states are so densely White even residents of their most diverse areas are highly unlikely to have *personal* encounters or exchanges with a non-White individual unless intentional (USCB, 2018; World Population Review, 2020). The one other U.S. area nearly exclusively single race is western and northern Alaska with its indigenous peoples (USCB, 2018).

This lack of minority contact may seem unlikely but relies upon scarcity. An example is Fargo, North Dakota's largest city: its population is approximately 124,000 with residents 85% White, 6% Black, 4% Asian, and 3% Hispanic/Latinx (USCB, 2018). Transforming percentages to numbers shows its entire minority population totaling some 160 individuals, certainly low for interactions.

RURALITY CHARACTERISTICS

What is it like, living in a rural area? Contemporary rural lifestyles are similar to those elsewhere, but there are particular concerns, issues, and situations more applicable here, the same as all other locations.

Income and Employment Issues

These are interconnected and create continuous circumstances, whether negative, positive, or something in between and vary depending upon individuals and place. However, rural poverty is an unfortunate reality; the national rate is near 11% with rural a much higher 17%. This percentage is doubtless affected by fewer jobs available, low-paying industry and other employment, more elderly/retired adults with lesser incomes, and large Native American clusters. South Dakota's Native population is 8%, with their poverty rate currently 25%, highest of all minorities, and its Pine Ridge reservation is the nation's poorest (USCB, 2018).

Farming/ranching remains a graying occupation, with institutional investors purchasing farmland (especially from those eager to retire), with corporations, domestic and abroad, now owning approximately 30% of American farmland. Such acquisitions are expected to continue, making land less available and affordable for younger individuals wishing to farm but not inheriting land (Keiffer, 2017).

Naturally, smaller areas have far fewer positions; like farming, most young adults returning to these hometowns are assuming family businesses, dental/medical/law practices, or teaching. Larger cities and towns and those having post-secondary institutions, state capital, penitentiaries and other state facilities, or famed attraction have more employment opportunities, but their location remain unattractive to many.

Rural salaries are lower regardless of occupation; residents earn approximately $35,000 yearly compared to the national average of $49,000 (USCB, 2018). Although rural natives anticipate such incomes, those moving into an area will doubtless face a financial loss. Naturally, rural graduates not particularly desiring to return to their state presumably find others' salaries more attractive, and those in majors with corresponding small-town employment nonexistent will hardly return, draining population and talent and continuing lower wages.

Rural costs of living are complicated; the days of small towns meeting their populations' needs are over. Like elsewhere, residents shop online and at big box/discount stores for convenience and lower prices, hurting downtown businesses. If these close, one must drive to the next larger town with longer commutes requiring more time and gasoline; regardless, vehicles are mandatory and should be winter weather-equipped, also costly.

Most services (hair salons, house cleaning, electricians) are less expensive than those suburban/urban, but fewer people equal less state income and higher taxes, and shipping distances raise prices of gasoline, food, and multiple other necessary items. Surprisingly costly are housing and apartments; both are limited with selection often between a high mortgage/rent for a newer dwelling, or much lower but expensive repairs/updates required for livability. These essentially equal the same amount, which is frustratingly high for younger residents.

Education Issues

Lower educational attainment is another negative, connected to income and employment opportunities. The national average for individuals with a bachelor's degree or higher is 34%. While 19% of UM residents have a post-secondary degree, only 14% of Native Americans do (USCB, 2018). However, smaller towns have commensurate class sizes; their graduating classes of 15, 30, or 50 are much lower than urban/suburban, and more rural residents have two-year degrees/vocational certificates than those elsewhere (U.S. Department of Agriculture, 2020), representing employment necessary to rural areas.

Crime and Safety Issues

Small populations report less crime; residents feel safe and secure, doubtless from 63% having lived in their local community for 11-plus years and more likely than those elsewhere to say they know all or most of their neighbors and are more trusting of them, according to the Pew Research Center's (PRC) 2018 study.

Indeed, rural areas see an average of 3,883 offenses per 100,000 people, below the national rate of 4,118, with theft, vandalism, and drug possession most frequent (Best Places, n.d.). The one state showing a violent crime increase is North Dakota (Governing, 2020), presumably attributed to their influx of transient oil field workers. Otherwise, life-threatening crime, gangs, shootings, and so on are virtually nonexistent.

Weather Issues

The National Geographic Society (2017) reported the UM as having the most unpredictable, erratic weather in the United States and as elsewhere, climate change has affected the region. Increased temperatures bring warmer and wetter winters with earlier springs, also with heavier precipitation and more intense storms. Summers are longer and becoming dangerously hot with higher humidity; all variations are particularly critical to farming/ranching, as they decrease yields and negatively affect animals (Union of Concerned Scientists, 2019).

Weather conditions disturb rural transportation; snow, ice, and fog create difficult driving, but residents and towns (fast snow removal/emergency routes) are prepared. Rural residents, as elsewhere, relish complaining about whatever is occurring outside.

Distance Issues

Dense (or any) substantial traffic is present only in the UMs largest cities, as are buses and taxis. Other transit is nonexistent, but Lyft and Uber are becoming more common. Zoom, FaceTime, and other technologies are increasingly used professionally and personally, although naturally travel is necessary.

Long drives are part of the rural lifestyle, and many travel with relatives/friends for shopping and use a weekend as a mini-vacation, staying in family-friendly motels that cater to this common UM practice. While nothing will assuage those disliking drives, highways are appealing and provide breaks with quirky tourist attractions, shops, sculpture parks, and restaurants with specialties, all of which accommodate travelers.

Political Issues

Rural states are portrayed as bastions of extreme right-wing politics, but as elsewhere individual views vary. The UM votes Republican in presidential elections; 63% in 2020 (ABC News, 2020). However, financial dependence upon tourism and residents' disliking laws concerning personal lives cause veering from conservative platforms regarding proposed state laws.

Summer tourism funds many UM states: Yellowstone National Park and Mt. Rushmore, among many others, each bring millions of dollars yearly to their respective states. As governors fear reducing already-lean budgets, prospective bills are usually tabled or vetoed if passage would negatively affect tourism or if bringing lawsuits in other states. Only one example was South Dakota's then-governor vetoing a popular 2016 bill restricting bathrooms for transgender people, fearing boycotts like North Carolina's passage, costing their state over three billion dollars (Jenkins & Trotta, 2017).

Personal lifestyle examples range from several states' 80–85 highway speed limits and Montana's ambiguous ticketing policies (Carter, 2015; Insurance Institute for Highway Safety, 2022) to voters' continual rejection (most recently in ND and SD) of anti-abortion bills (Ballotpedia, n.d.a, n.d.b, n.d.c), and South Dakota's 2020 approval of medical and recreational marijuana (O'Bryan, 2020). However, with the recent reversal of *Roe v. Wade*, most UM states are poised for strictest policies possible or complete banning, voters will determine outcomes with other recent passages of anything LGBTQ+ also questionable.

Ironically, while UM state governments are solidly conservative, surely frustrating those more liberal, tourism dollars' necessity halts passage of many conservative bills, equally dissatisfying for this group, something both can ponder while sailing on their highway of choice.

Religious Issues

Although the entire midwestern area is presumed as intolerant and fundamentalist Christian, its religious denominations and services attendance closely resemble the rest of the United States. Protestantism is the largest U.S. denomination (65%), and 67% of the UM. Non-Christian faiths (Jewish, Muslim, Buddhist, Hindu) represent 7%/5%, respectively, and those stating no affiliation were 26%. Individuals attending services once a month or more were 45% for both, and a few times a year or less were 54%, respectively (PRC, 2019).

Unfortunately, pastors' frequent relocating to larger places and shrinking congregations result in closures or one pastor serving several churches (PRC, 2019), both disheartening, but congregations are vibrant and welcoming; attendance or absence are individual decisions and respected. As elsewhere, some are particularly strident regarding piousness, leaving others free to ignore or ponder whether murky circumstances are spurring such virtue.

Entertainment/Social Issues

A common misconception of rural residents is unsophistication and uninterest in cultural opportunities, but according to the National Endowment for the Arts (NEA), so is most of the United States (2017a). Only 9% reported seeing a play, 8% a symphony, 3% a ballet, and 2% an opera, with those attending at least one visual or performing arts activity during the year approximately 54%, live performances 43%.

In surveying rural arts attendance, the NEA (2017b), found their offerings attracted nonlocal audiences at higher rates than urban ones, and 31% of rural audiences traveled farther to attend events than those in cities (19%). Rural events also showed more international individuals in audiences than urban ones (6% and 2%, respectively), and that populations of rural counties hosting performing arts companies grew faster than others.

Rural areas also offer safe holiday and other celebrations including the entire town, such as a New Year's Eve party for couples and another for families. Summers offer multiple activities for children and teens, clubs and organizations fill rural calendars, and school activities are attended by most residents.

A particular rural shortcoming is accommodating singles; although the percentage of marrieds and singles in the UM is essentially the same as the rest of the U.S. population (USCB, 2018), singles can feel distinctly alone. While singles attend the above activities, many are tailored for couples and families and are therefore unwelcoming by design.

Singles' groups are largely nonexistent due to small numbers; even in the largest state cities, online dating is impractical. Fewer organizations are available with distance and numbers resulting in less matches, most being hours away and from neighboring states. While FaceTime and other communications are used, they remain impersonal and unsafe; one could be speaking to anyone online. Driving 15 or 20 minutes for lunch or drinks is easy in cities; traveling three hours one-way or even agreeing to meet halfway is considerable for those rural.

However, single rural adults still have tight social networks and other activities may easily substitute for *Farmer's Only* and *Christian Mingle*, the most popular sites for the UM (HighSpeedInternet.com, 2017).

Technological Issues

Internet and other technological accessibility are minor problems for 58% of rural residents and a major one for 24% (PRC, 2018), depending upon location; those nearest largest cities and universities usually have few, if any, difficulties. School and library performance capabilities are generally higher than those residential with students welcome and assistance provided. Although sparse populations and geographic features can hinder reliable access, technological services are constantly improving, and while not the desired solution, it is recognized remote locations have inherent issues.

Medical Issues

Medical care is particularly serious for rural residents not living in their state's largest cities (and locations of hospitals associated with university medical schools), with two-thirds of residents indicating this a definite difficulty (PRC, 2018). Residents face the largest lack of physicians, services, and distance between providers (American Hospital Association [AHA], 2019), and practitioners assist many, but qualifications restrict full services. Most hospitals or clinics have specialists available on rotation, although travel is necessary for various needs.

Lengthy waits for EMT or other assistance in sparsely populated areas is common, with most hospitals small and generally equipped for least serious conditions (stitches, broken limbs, low-risk deliveries). Emergency patients must transfer by air or ambulance to another, but time taken for the majority reaching appropriate care can lead to additional complications or negative outcomes.

Like other rural professionals, turnover is frequent as many physicians are beginning careers and intending to leave soon (AHA, 2019), with residents continually seeing different individuals (with time between hires varying) without developing relationships necessary for comprehensive care.

Another missing but crucial service is behavioral/mental health care (AHA, 2019); rural psychiatric services and crisis centers, even in larger cities, are few and often led by laypersons, and while not necessarily negative, terminal degrees are needed.

Similarly, all rural support groups (AA, weight loss, cancer, depression) are fewer or nonexistent outside of large cities or one group (grief sessions holding widowers, divorcees, loss of employment) rather than those specific to a single issue. For various supports, wealthier rural residents are frequenting Telehealth services (online consultation), especially for mental health (AHA, 2019).

However, rural social networks are tight, and absence of such services does not leave unassisted individuals; physicians, ministers, educators, and others will provide professional supports and assist with transportation and other logistics. Residents understand the importance of such connections and work to meet needs, often nontraditionally.

Privacy Issues

Perhaps the most common rural denigration is residents knowing nearly everything about their neighbors and endlessly gossiping about them, but as with everywhere in the United States, people speak of one another, with rural talk magnified by small populations. Those in larger cities have multiple social circles with differing individuals in each; rural residents have one—the entire town.

Personal privacy is not any one location's domain, yet gossip seems forever attached to small towns. Still, residents are free to ignore, contradict, create irresistibly juicy stories for amusement, or to otherwise avoid being unnoticed, perhaps worse than gossip.

Lifestyle Satisfaction Issues

As rurality has so many adverse associations it's unsurprising that 70% of its population felt nonresidents viewed them negatively and failed to understand their lifestyle, but neither is it startling that approximately 75% indicated if given the opportunity they wouldn't live elsewhere and are satisfied with their location, lifestyle, and having family nearby (PRC, 2018).

However, only 22% of all Americans stated it particularly important to reside in racially and ethnically diverse communities, with 59% (52% rural) believing it somewhat important (PRC, 2018). All areas have intolerant and welcoming individuals, but this lower rural number is presumably influenced by overall lack of minority residents.

RURAL INDIVIDUALS AS MINORITIES

Ruralism is *itself* a minority, not necessarily recognized as such by residents, and continually misunderstood, mispresented, and usually denigrated by the media and others nonrural. Naturally, every location has positives and negatives, but an attitude overwhelmingly expressed toward those rural can be summarized by this too-familiar view of, "If living in a small town one lacks the ability to go elsewhere, and if liking it, stupid."

As most things rural are continually portrayed demeaningly, its reality and benefits are unknown to most, effectively causing residents, especially adolescents, to feel lesser than others. Everyone should be knowledgeable of where they and others live, respect themselves, and those within their community.

True understanding of the rural lifestyle is only attained from living there, but such areas attract few, especially those diverse. Who wants to be the only

Black or Asian family in town? What Jewish or Buddhist family will move to a place where the nearest worship congregation is 200 miles away? Such situations prevent minorities moving to or remaining in rural areas, effectively retaining White predominancy. Other rural minorities (e.g., Native Americans) are also disparaged, and live as a separate community rather than integrated into the town.

How can rural adolescents comprehend the many facets of diversity and minority individuals when there are no, or few, minorities in their town or school, and how can they, whether they are a racial/cultural minority or not, express who they are to peers and adults when disregarded or worse by others?

Thankfully, all rural adolescents can experience and learn of diversity through using young adult literature (YAL) in English/language arts (ELA) classes, covered further in upcoming chapters and providing students with questions and activities for learning more about rurality.

GENERAL SUGGESTIONS FOR DISCUSSION REGARDING DIVERSITIES

Question/Comment for YAL	Rationale
Where are YOU in the story?	This connects students to the text; instead of seeing characters *unlike* them, it allows one to focus on the feelings, emotions, beliefs, and actions that they have *in common* with those portrayed.
We are all diverse, depending upon where, or with whom, we happen to be at the time.	Rural White students are rarely a minority in their community, but they can be. Teens are minorities in a senior citizens' center, teaching summer bible study, or at a VFW. Where else may this occur? Students can explore like situations and consider what it means to be a minority.
How do you want YOUR story told, and by whom?	Textual interpretations depend upon the author, not necessarily truth; how would others' treatments differ with accuracy? What does it mean to be wrongly portrayed?
Determine accuracy for actual events, people, etc. portrayed. Classroom information should be correct; long-held beliefs may be myths or largely erroneous.	We have the right to our own *opinions*, but not our own *facts*. What preconceived beliefs have caused others' mistreatment?

For historical fiction (or any text as applicable) ask, *What might have been left out, or portrayed differently for accuracy?*	Students should be taught accurate information, regardless of how unfamiliar or unpopular.
Compare novel issues and situations to current contemporary ones, regardless of how minor (Who would or would not have been invited to the character's party?).	History and human nature change little; past and present textual events and problems are seen today. This is especially true for minorities, allowing students to recognize many inequities and treatment differences.
For classroom scenes, have students consider their own classroom by asking *Who was in your desk 10, 15, 20, and 30 years ago? About what were they thinking? How did their daily lives compare to yours?*	Popular culture changes, but people, not as much. Have students consider older buildings/places. (Who sat in this church pew 100 years ago? Who played softball in the park 75 years ago? Who was not allowed there, and what is the current situation?) Such thoughts connect us to others and allow consideration of what changes, and not.
Define terminology and slang used in text, and its pronunciation.	All groups have specific terminology that should be used correctly and appropriately. What misconceptions and attitudes have occurred from misinterpretations?
Food is an equalizer and shows differences, whether cultural or designating wealth and leisure. Have students examine how characters' meals are prepared, what is eaten, when, why, etc. What does this indicate about the characters and their lifestyles? Discuss and question all students about the foods special to their families. Share in the classroom when possible.	*Why does XXX's family eat XXX during Passover?* *What is eaten during your holidays?* *XXX's family follows a vegan lifestyle. What does this imply regarding their education and finances?* *XXX and friends laugh at those bringing lunches from home but toss most of their school-purchased ones without eating. What does this say about family backgrounds and entitlement?* *The characters argue about how X is prepared? What is your preference?* *What meals are special to your family, and why?*
Consider more provocative uses of food, and implications.	Although we have Thanksgiving and Christmas dinners for those less fortunate, how does this assuage hunger the other 363 days of the year? Who are these dinners for, those serving or eating?
Never self-censor.	If fearing a book will be banned or challenged, self-censorship assures its removal. Use the work without fear of the call that may never come, and many are worth any possible difficulties.

Question/Comment for YAL	Rationale
Hide personal biases.	Every group is multifaceted and should be depicted as such. Groups and various situations should not be misrepresented, whether positively or negatively.
Do not introduce novels having sensitive topics with a special introduction.	Students do not need to be *prepared* for a novel; its reading and discussion is enough. Introduce all novels the same and as appropriate to the story. Unequal preparation extends to various groups characters represent.
Never presume minority students only wish to read about their group, and never consider as their representative.	Why select only Asian-themed YAL for Asian Americans, and why presume they are familiar with specific customs and practices? What about those who want to read mystery/suspense? The same is true for any student, whether majority or minority.
Use correct distinctions regarding any racial or cultural group.	Too often, minorities are defined by collectives, as *Native American*, rather than Navajo, Apache, or Lakota; *Jewish*, rather than Hasidic and Orthodox. Neither minorities nor majorities are the same with such implication demeaning and denying individuality.
Unsure of the above? Ask any student about their lifestyle and compare similarities/differences among classroom peers.	*How is Hanukkah celebrated in your home?* *What is a sweat lodge?* *What does "soul sleep" mean to 7th Day Adventists?* *How do you celebrate Christmas?* *What are your birthday traditions?* *What Native American symbols are used incorrectly in school or elsewhere?*
All students should see themselves in YAL, including science fiction, fantasy, mystery/suspense, etc.	Students must see themselves depicted in all genres, rather than largely contemporary or historical fiction.

- Considerations regarding reading of those unfamiliar or viewed with antipathy by students, whether majority or not.
- Students should ponder how *Reading of others prepares individuals for life after high school* applies to themselves and others. Will individuals always be in situations with only those like them, and is this possible? What does this mean? If critical of a particular group not distinguishable by race (e.g., LGBTQ+, various religions), how will friendships or other connections be made? Does one revoke a friendship if learning later an individual is a member of that group?
- Contemplating *How does this affect you personally?* is particularly relevant to situations/issues/laws particularly opposed by some students. If not affecting an individual, why is denying such a choice to others so important? What preferred lifestyle components would students allow others to determine (especially those of opposing views)?

It can be difficult for middle-class+ students having caring, comfortable families, and the ability to attend college without crippling (or any) student loan debt, to understand not all have such privileges. Simply *working hard* is not necessarily enough to affect change for one raised in far less fortunate situations. Ask students to remove or add three things from/to their lives (e.g., having to work after school, with salary going to family, no extracurricular activities, parents without college degrees and much lower-paying jobs, being raised by one parent rather than two, having an addicted parent who continually disappears for several days, then returns) and then determine the difficulties and changes such a different lifestyle would bring.

Many envy those having expensive clothes, cars, large houses, ability to travel, and so on. What might change with less envy of a student's individual life, and what does this mean?

Have students define the difference between a *need* and a *want*. What are essential needs for future happiness and security, and why? Can they be achieved by everyone, and why or why not? What role does society play in needs and wants?

Stereotypes, misunderstandings, and incorrect information should be boldly addressed with facts provided. A sample short activity is below.

Students list the stereotypes associated with different groups; the teacher having researched commonly associated facts. Impersonal discussion allows viewing of all groups as portrayed in various venues and by individuals.

When *all* stereotypes are addressed rather than a single group, the discussion becomes nonpersonal, entertaining and informative. If desirous of tolerance and acceptance of others, they must be understood first, achieved by honest, frank, and factual discussion.

Group	Main Stereotypes	*How/Why Does This Prevent Individuals From Interacting With This Group?*	Facts
African Americans	Males in prison Gun, gang culture On welfare Slavery reparation Irresponsible fathers	Individual responses	How is welfare defined, and how much does it cost? Student/resident definitions should be compared to federal ones, with variances and new information discussed before researching expenses.
Rural Americans	Not intelligent Overweight Receive federal funds not to farm Live in squalor		
LGBTQ+	Predators Lifestyle choice The Christian Bible in opposition Desirous of recruiting children to LGBTQ+		

DISCUSSION QUESTIONS AND SUGGESTED ACTIVITIES

Discussion Questions	Sample Activities; Students Will . . .	Key Diversity Points
The U.S. Census Bureau's definition of *Rural* is vague. How would you describe rural?	Individual definitions are composed and discussed; the class may select the most representative or create a new one by adapting those presented.	Definitions will vary, i.e., diversity, likewise, those rural are also diverse. Creating a new definition from those offered suggests working together for a description fitting all.
How is living in rural areas different from elsewhere aside from size/location, and how much has technology affected rurality?	Differences seen are listed, then reviewed and revised to include those distinctly rural (e.g., farming or ranching are rural-only occupations). Next, those items once distinctly rural but changed by technology (e.g., rural areas have less shopping opportunities, but one may purchase online) can be categorized and discussed. This may lead to considering technology's positives and negatives (e.g., shopping online hurts small town businesses; Zoom allows meetings without long drives), and whether technology has truly changed rural culture, or if a convenience, as elsewhere.	Contemporary students, rural or elsewhere, don't have pre-technology experience but can discuss its affects upon rural lifestyles with those older (e.g., grandparents, other residents). Also pondered is whether teens' lifestyles would be considered as rural compared to earlier years of those older? Rurality is also a diversity, but technology is lessening differences between those rural and elsewhere. What does it mean to be rural now?
Why are rural areas, and those living in them, continually denigrated in the media and by multiple other sources? What truths do these opinions hold?	The most ubiquitous and/or disliked examples are listed on the left side of a four-column table. The middle holds student opinions of statements and accuracy, with the third documenting the stereotype's origin, history, etc. Last is ways to shatter stereotypes.	Stereotypes misrepresent rural students, but what incorrect and negative views do these teens have of others that are equally harmful and untrue?

Positive stereotypes regarding rural areas and its residents are also, and what is their accuracy? How are they beneficial or harmful?	These (e.g., rural residents work harder than others, are scrupulously honest) can also be charted, talk focused on burdens and positives.	Positive stereotypes also misrepresent rural students, and others. What equally false and hurtful opinions of others are held by rural teens?
What is one negative situation most needing change regarding living in a rural area?	Every place has disadvantages, harmful in various ways. Rural communities offer a strong sense of belonging, for example, but not for all residents. Students can discuss views, rationale, and potential actions for change.	Would negative situations, or those not fully belonging, be received well elsewhere? How do they define rural? Are such positives and negatives inherent in all communities, dependent upon place and size? What does this mean, and does change cause identity loss?
Rural diversity populations are unlikely to change, for multiple reasons. A main one is absence of support systems; for example, few desire being the only Black family in town, and Jewish families would presumably dislike driving an hour to the nearest synagogue. How does this affect rural communities and how can their few minorities be assisted?	Students can discuss this topic in many ways. What groups are in the area, and not? What incentives are available for minorities to live in the community? Is it impossible for some minorities to have positive lifestyles in many rural places? What is the effect upon a community of any group's absence?	How are knowledge, tolerance, and acceptance of others acquired with few, or no, residents different from the majority?

Discussion Questions	Sample Activities; Students Will . . .	Key Diversity Points
Rural areas have few, or no, minorities, but individuals interact and are personal friends with those most like them, encountered where living and working. Because no one place holds multiple minorities, deep friendships among numerous groups are unlikely. Still, lacking friends from a group does not mean prejudicial views toward them. Does a diverse society have members of many different groups but viewed as one, or members without biases regarding those different?	Discussion can focus upon with whom students interact, or not, and why, and considering a definition of a positive diverse society. Are prejudice and biases always present, regardless, and why?	Prejudice and biases are learned and present everywhere. How can they be lessened?
Regarding living in a rural area, what is most needed to be experienced by those living in suburban or urban places?	Opinions and rationales are discussed, ending with defining what is most valuable and unique regarding rurality.	Where did diversity fit here, and what does it mean if unmentioned or its absence positive?
Do you feel embarrassment or pride when relaying a rural hometown to others from much larger ones?	Responses are placed in positive/negative categories with rationales discussed. Emotions felt upon hearing the question is also considered. Hearing others' opinions may change views.	Discussion has the power of changing views, but both positive and negative ones. The most influential voices are not necessarily espousing opinions of quality. For some, following the group is more attractive than opposing.

Question	Suggestions	Discussion
What are your greatest fears regarding the rural lifestyle for the future?	Students can research various expected changes for their area, and other rural ones throughout the country and compare/discuss. What commonalities and differences were expressed? What do such fears mean, and how can they be connected to rural minority students and others?	Feeling powerless to affect change echoes that of many minority students. Discussion among all assists worries by providing preparation and coping suggestions regarding management. Working together strengthens all.
After graduation, do you wish to leave your hometown to live and work, and how will this be received by families? Will such reactions affect your decision?	Students consider their town and personal needs objectively. Choices and rationale are noted, such as those not desirous of leaving but must from career choice (e.g., no advertising agencies near). How many are similar? Discussion follows, with coping or other suggestions specific to individual situations.	Realities must sometimes be placed before desires, as some may not have choices regarding leaving/remaining. As above, this mirrors some minority teens, also without choices. Still, all working together can assist lifestyle improvements.

Note: These questions and suggestions, and those for all chapters, are suitable for both K-12 and post-secondary students with educator modification as applicable. They may be used for individual responses, with partners, groups, or whole class discussion. Topics should be applied to individuals' situations.

CREATING EDUCATOR DISCUSSION GUIDES

Introduction

Dynamic classrooms are those in which both educators and students discuss and share what they are reading, rather than the educator providing all information with little or no student commentary. Rosenblatt (1938/1985) stated characteristics of such classrooms, with teachers responsible for the following:

- creating a classroom community in which students explore texts for meaning and understanding
- encouraging students to talk/discuss/question extensively with peers and the teacher
- asking, discussing, and questioning the text studied, rather than tell students about it
- having students link personal experiences to their reading/writing/interpretation of the text read
- affirming student responses, allowing multiple interpretations, and guiding students toward the most applicable or appropriate responses/interpretations/meanings as necessary
- guiding students in recognizing and understanding literature conventions (i.e., simile, metaphor, hyperbole) and evaluating author writing style and choices made in the text

However, when using YAL or any reading material, *what* should be emphasized in discussion? How does one discuss without getting off the subject, spending too little or too much time on a topic, cover its most important aspects and literary elements, be sure students are understanding, contributing, and connecting reading to other works, *and* accomplish all these items within fifty-five-minute classes and two weeks or less for unit timeframes?

A particularly effective way is through the creation of *Educator Discussion Guides*, which are used for all texts (novels, short stories, plays, etc.) read and discussed by students. While these take some time to complete, they should not be done in one sitting and once finished it can be re-used. However, with each discussion of the text, educators will continually revise their guides as they note additional textual aspects, change various opinions, hear new views through student discussion, and so on.

Instructions for Creating an Educator Discussion Guide

1. Create a two-column table in a computer document.
2. Open novel (or other textual form) to Page 1.

3. Read each sentence; while reading, when seeing places to ask questions, points for students to notice, literary devices, vocabulary or other items needing clarification or emphasis, author's writing style/choices, and so on, record the page number and its corresponding information.
    a. For literary devices, vocabulary, items needing clarification (victrola, *The Butterfly Effect*) or other items that can be difficult to locate, record its page number and text placement:
    Swimming Metaphor on Pg. 5, 1st paragraph
    Alliteration on Pg. 7, lines 8–9
    Bird and flying imagery on Pg. 22, 3rd paragraph
    This allows for quick retrieval and eliminates fumbling and flipping pages, attempting to locate a phrase, sentence, or word, which can be remarkably difficult to do if not marked, and especially in front of a class. Never be unprepared for discussion, and these kinds of pauses disrupt educator concentration and student attention, neither fast nor easy to regain.
4. For the most important points, one can highlight text, use colored fonts, bold, italics, and so on. One's own notes of reminders and other similar items should also be recorded. Below is a short example from Cormier's (2001) *The Rag and Bone Shop*, with its complete guide included.

Pages	Commentary
3	Discussion of sin and how to erase, foreshadowing. Carl: *"Supposed to say I'm sorry now."* Appears more worried of the *sin* of his act over what he did.
3–4	Difference between *confession* and *absolution*. Trent serves as a priest. Foreshadowing, note four hours for Carl's confession and room set-up. (Jason's confession took far more time.)
5–7	Carl felt like God with gun—does whatever he wants with family. Enjoys the power to destroy. Turns killing boy into act of kindness so won't have to wake up to see murdered parents. Connect to Trent twisting Jason's statements. Carl only 17, first surprise.
7–8	Trent feeling illness, regret, rethinking role. Lottie is gone, no moral grounding. Defensiveness with, *"Only doing my job."*

Rationale and Use for Guides

Student discussion provides items one has missed, or questions not previously considered, so these are added to the guide.

One will not use every item on the guide, but each class discussion will move in different directions and the most important material will always be covered. This serves as the educator's personal guide of what to ask/discuss and allows for a focused, thorough discussion.

If an educator plans to teach a text, then he/she must be its expert. This means one must do more than reading the work once and using a supplement's (or other) analysis. There are numerous items one must know and do beforehand to teach/discuss any text well, with these recommended:

1. Re-read the work before teaching, every time it is taught. Knowledge of the work must be current, and re-reading allows for new details seen, different interpretations and options formed.
2. One must know pertinent details regarding the author, their other works, writing style, and critical analyses of the from several sources, not just one.
3. The timeframe of the work is important, as one must know central events/people/lifestyles of the time. If dollar amounts are mentioned, they should be entered into an inflation calculator to determine contemporary equivalent prices ($500.00 in 1921 equals $7725.00 today).
4. Students will need to understand the absence of technology and other items. For example, when *The Rag and Bone Shop* was written, the Internet and emails were just beginning to be used and cell phones were still in the future (the novel was written before its publication). Technology is not mentioned in the novel.
5. Knowing the above information, and more, allows for creation of discussion questions and other points.
6. A guide also allows for the discussion of the entire piece, having parameters regarding meaning, interpretation, etc.
7. Again, it assures the discussion remains on point, rather than veering off the topic and wasting time, and provides a focus for what is most important for students to know about the work, its author, era, and so on.
8. Guides provide the opportunity for educators to think critically and learn with their students.

Without a guide, it is difficult to discuss well, period. Unfortunately, good questions don't automatically occur when in front of a class, regardless of how familiar the material. Without notes it is easy to lose one's way and we are far more likely to ask questions that are clearly stated in the work, requiring one response, and/or not particularly important. Some examples of these questions are below:

What does Jason do during recess?
How old is Emma?
How does Alicia dress?
Where is Jason's father throughout most of the story?

A completed discussion guide for *The Rag and Bone Shop* is below.

Educator Discussion Guide for *The Rag and Bone Shop*
PP 38-39   Alicia speaks ONCE
PP 71, 123   Yeats' Poem
ABUSE re Brad and Alicia

Pages	Comment
3	Sin erased. Foreshadowing. Not worried about act, just the sin of it. *"Supposed to say I'm sorry now."* Discussion of sin and how to erase, foreshadowing. Carl.
3–4	Difference between *confession* and *absolution*. Trent serves as a priest. Foreshadowing, note four hours for Carl's confession and room set-up. (Jason's confession took far more time.)
5–7	Carl felt like God with gun—does whatever he wants with family. Enjoys the power to destroy. Turns killing boy into act of kindness so won't have to wake up to see murdered parents. Connect to Trent twisting Jason's statements. Carl only 17, first surprise.
7–8	Trent feeling illness, regret, rethinking role. Lottie is gone, no moral grounding. Defensiveness with, *"Only doing my job."*
12	Why did Jason have to work so hard for his grades? Manages to *sneak* on honor roll, due to *luck*. *Summer vacation—feeling of RELEASE.*
13	Jason had no friends. EVERYONE has at least one friend. Why NONE? What is so creepy about him that he has none? *No real desire to make friends, fit in. Deliberately does things to set himself apart and create attention and ridicule.* Like the attention of younger girls. Watches the 3rd and 4th graders at recess. Why don't the teachers say something? Reading Stephen King—not an easy read. See above for grades. Emma is 8.
14	Hates sports—especially contact ones. Father takes him to games. How well do his parents know him? *Connect to father taking him to game at end of book.*
17–18	Alicia's body found. *Why first when no time spent with her? Frequent Cormier technique.* She had been laid down with tenderness. Expression on face is horror and surprise. Not raped/molested/taken. No resistance to attacker.
19	Is Alicia a female Jason? Did Jason NEED Alicia, or did she need HIM? *Alicia's mother not seen, but suggested she wear shorts and brief halter. Utterly feminine girl. Wearing long dresses in heat. Page 37—dainty little girl.*
21	Braxton thinking about solving "finishing case" not "solving" case.
22	Jason promises not to cry anymore.
23	Jason's fight with Bobo. Stronger than he seems? *"Shock on his face had been terrific to see."*
24	Prided himself on powers of observation.
25	Unprovoked. Knew what word meant, although never heard it before. Jason seems mild, but slams Bobo early in story—p. 23, a *sweet and beautiful blow,* and felt a *thrilling sense of triumph*. Rams into Bobo the next day, not the one where he touched Rebecca *Connects Bobo with not crying again--*

Pages	Comment
28	Why didn't Emma like Alicia?
30	Scared when learns he was the last person to see her alive.
31	Hadn't told everything to police—and gave quick answers.
31	*Jigsaw scene told by Jason. Repeated on PP 38.*
32	Brad is mean to Alicia. If Jason had told police about Brad, would things have changed?
34	Says "lived" rather than "lives." Quick for a kid.
36	Jason suspects Brad, but why protect him?
	Alicia says "How the hell can I concentrate…" Language.
38	*Brad "accidentally" knocks over puzzle. Isn't asking, is telling. Piece missing. Alicia's withering look, haven't you done enough damage today? Voice as cold as icicle. You wouldn't want to know. Slaps puzzle off table. Contrast with dainty little girl.*
42–43	Killer on loose, killer of child. Get Trent to work on Jason. Why never consider Brad?
	How are Trent and Jason alike?
47	Catches people off-guard and vulnerable.
49	"Is the scenario in place?"
50	Made sure Jason's parents are away.
53	Jason wonders if going to station was a mistake.
55	Why did Jason want to be part of the investigation?
56	*Mother manipulated. "Little girl"*
59	One of the last to see her alive.
62	Sarah—replaces Lottie. Doesn't think Jason is guilty. Trent's conscience.
66	*Difference between truth and confession. CARL.*
68	Lottie—*You are what you do.*
70–71	*Trent = priest. Carl.*
74	Senator buying an arrest.
75–76	*Room set-up, lengthy description.*
79	Interrogation techniques.
84	Only stories. Not real, when asked about what he read, watched on TV. *First realized words were being twisted.*
87	Clarifies a question.
90	*Knows meaning of "context." like other words known.*
91	Thinks about lying.
99	Jason tells himself he had better be careful.
100	Jason starts to leave.
102	Trent needs Jason to confess.
104	Uses "escape."
110	*Jason asks Trent if he'd gotten himself a Coke. First time treated like person.*
115–16	Mentions Brad and Alicia fighting. Did he do wrong? Trent thinks about Brad but discounts him.
117–18	Says Alicia "way smarter." Trent asks about her making fun of him, Jason doubts friendship.
120	Says Brad his friend. Asked if attracted to Alicia.
123	Last line of Yeats poem.
124	"Premeditated".
127	"Sly"—realizes what Trent is doing.

128	Trent twists everything around.
131	*Trent knows Jason is innocent.*
132	Trent keeps on going.
134	Jason—what you SAY he did.
136	Not there to help the police, realizes.
137	*Confession—Absolution. Trent becomes a priest again. Confess vs. Confession.*
139	Says he can't confess. Strong. Says it TWICE.
140	Says he didn't kill her.
141	Trent realizes betrayal of Jason.
	Talks about silence in the hallway. *A terrible kind of silence.*
142	Bruised/broken voice. *Why did he confess?*
146	DA Alvin Dark—black bug?
146	Jason broken. Disbelief in his eyes.
147	Sarah says Trent made Jason confess. *Victory snatched from him. Offers cassette as a gift.*
148	*Broken—taken down from cross. CHRIST IMAGE.*
	Trent's career failed. No one returning calls. Appt. with Chief. Trent also broken.
149	*You are what you do. Applies to Jason and Trent.*
151	"Specific and Context" is thinking about his confession.
	Romans Chapter 7, vs. 15-21 similarity.
152–53	*If he said it, then maybe he can do it. Mind wanders to who he could kill.*
	Right vs. wrong. Must kill to be right, honest, in a mixed-up way. Has reversed the two by confessing, so must kill to make it right again. Honor, honesty.
	Drugged. Ask if ok. Hot in house. Resisted thinking about the heat/evil, hell images. Parents still gone.
154	Absolution. Like Carl. Takes the knife out.
	How has Jason's family contributed to his problems? Do they love him? So different from Emma.
	Which family cares more for their children—Jason's, or Brad's?

References

Cormier, R. (2001). *The rag and bone shop*. Dell Laurel Leaf/Random House.

Rosenblatt, L. (1995). *Literature as exploration*. MLA. (Original work published 1938).

GUIDELINES FOR WRITING DISCUSSION QUESTIONS

Introduction

Discussing a text with students is one of the best methods of determining understanding, using critical thinking skills, differentiation, reviewing and critiquing the work, learning about author writing style and choices, and more. By answering questions either individually or during class discussion, students are actively learning and practicing these skills, rather than being *told* information by the teacher.

Students glean little from worksheets; instead, they learn by discussion and being engaged with the text, their teacher, and peers. Discussion should allow students to project and ponder and use the text's information and what they have learned about a character or event to create a reasonable yet individual response. Quality discussions are thoughtful, invigorating, productive, and enjoyable for both students and educators.

A good discussion means the student will understand and remember the work—it won't be quickly forgotten. However, writing quality questions takes time and practice, with instructions and examples below.

Instructions and Examples of Quality and Poor Questions

Quality questions *must* have these three elements:

1. The student must have read/understand the work to answer the question.
2. The question's answer is *not* directly in the text.
3. The student must think/project/infer to answer the question.

Of course, one wants students to know the basic facts from the work, but if the piece has been read, they already should. Whatever is missing can be supplied during discussion with a quick reminder, either by the teacher or classmates. One way to give students greater ability regarding locating material is by using a scenario like the one below:

. . . *does anyone remember?* or

. . . *look on page XX, that's where XXX first appears;* would anyone like to comment on the scene? or

. . . XXX is seen first here, note how shy and quiet XXX seems compared to later—what happened?

The point is to presume the students will gain the basic facts by reading the material (no one grasps everything, including educators), and class discussion. Missed facts and points are *part of* the discussion, not the *focus* of it. One cannot discuss by asking *only* literal questions. If asking the year the novel takes place, its setting or main characters, and then continuing with additional similar questions, what can be discussed? *Discussion can only occur with student and teacher opinions.*

Examples of Quality and Poor Questions

Examples are from Cormier's *The Rag and Bone Shop* (2001).

Questions Directly From the Novel The answers to these are already known by reading the book and are essentially verbal worksheets.	In what town does this story occur? What did Emma think of Alicia? What happened in Trent's office? What did Jason do each day at recess?
Re-Writing Questions Any question can be changed into a quality one by re-wording it.	Describe a three ways Jason's town is like yours: Why do you think Emma didn't like Alicia? Explain: Which was the worst method of manipulation Trent used on Jason, and why? **or** Describe three ways grocery stores manipulate their customers: Is it realistic that Jason's teachers allowed him to stand at the fence every day? Why or why not?
Irrelevant Questions and Those With Obvious Answers	Was Trent upset when he learned Jason was innocent? Did Trent's interrogation harm Jason? Does Jason's mother enjoy driving?
Re-Writing Questions	Was Trent more upset for himself or Jason when discovering Jason's innocence? Explain: Will Jason be able to recover from Trent's interrogation? Explain: How did Jason's mother's busy schedule contribute to his problems before the interrogation? Explain:
Avoid One-Word Answers by Using Why, How, Describe, Explain, etc.	Was Alicia hot wearing long dresses during the summer? (Presumably yes) Should Jason's mother have gone to the police station after he was there for hours? (Presumably yes) Could Jason have stayed home by himself rather than being taken to Brad and Alicia's house? (Presumably yes)
Re-Writing Questions	Why did Alicia wear long dresses during the summer? Explain: Why didn't Jason's mother go to the police station after he was there for hours? Explain: Describe two or three reasons why Jason's mother didn't want him home by himself:
Avoid Questions With Multiple Replies by Stating the Type of Response Expected	How did Trent arrange his interrogation room? What questions did Trent ask Jason during his interrogation? How did Jason show his intelligence during his interrogation?

Re-Writing Questions	What was Trent's most effective room arrangement for Jason's interrogation, and why?
	What were the three most upsetting questions Trent asked Jason during his interrogation, and why?
	Describe two ways in which Jason showed his intelligence during his interrogation:
Ask One Question at a Time, Not Several at a Time	Who was Carl, and what does he foreshadow in the story?
	Does Trent miss Lottie, and does Sarah resemble her?
	Should the police have questioned Brad and his friends more closely? Why did they believe what was told to them without checking their alibis?
Re-Writing Questions	What does Carl foreshadow in the novel? Explain:
	How does Sarah serve as Lottie to Trent? Describe:
	Why weren't Brad and his friends questioned more thoroughly? Explain:
Don't Ask One Question That Answers Another	Questions from Riggs' *Miss Peregrine's Home for Peculiar Children* (2011)
To Re-Write Questions, Ask One Rather Than Both	Where did Jacob travel to find Miss Peregrine's house?
	Does Jacob leave Wales with his father at the end of the novel?
	Who was Dr. Golan?
	When did you first realize Dr. Golan was a Wight?
Questions Should be Ones the Average Student Can Answer	Describe the physics necessary for Miss Peregrine's children to remain in their era:
	What techniques were used to create the photography illusions in the pictures from the 1800s?
	What anatomy deformities did the children have, and what would their prognosis be if in real time?
Re-Writing Questions	What was most difficult to understand regarding Miss Peregrine's children remaining in the same era and not aging? Explain:
	What techniques do you use when posting photos that are like those from the 1800s pictures? Describe:
	Which character did you find most interesting, and why? (Or frightening, etc.)

Questions From Several Novels
This is another way to build strong critical thinking skills and allow students to broaden their understanding of both novels and characters. Students must comprehend the characters and story very well to answer such questions. Asking about students' personal experiences as compared to the reading is another strong way to improve skill and understanding.

Questions from *The Rag and Bone Shop* and Thrash's *Honor Girl: A Graphic Memoir* (2015).
Describe Alicia's stay if at Maggie's summer camp—what would be her worst/best experiences, and why?
Would Jason be able to make friends at summer camp, or would he still be a loner? Why or why not?
Would Jason's parents be relieved once he was away at camp? Why?
Who would make a better camp counselor, Sarah, or Trent? Why?
Even if you have never been to summer camp what in the story most resembled an experience from your own life? Why/how?

CONVERSATIONS AND SCENARIOS REGARDING NOVEL CHARACTERS

Conversations Among Characters From the Same Novel

If desiring students to discuss, use critical thinking skills, truly understand and remember what has been read, then material must be continually referenced, rather than studied for a unit and forgotten afterward.

One method for accomplishing this is having students reply to questions among and between characters from the same, and different, novels. This can be through discussion or writing, individually or in groups, and students can answer the questions, or create them. Below are examples of conversations among characters from the *same* novel, Thrash's *Honor Girl: A Graphic Memoir* (2015), with many possible creations.

- Erin and Tammy are sitting together at lunch. What would Tammy say to Erin about her friendship with Maggie?
- If Erin had returned for Maggie at the novel's end, what would they have said to one another?
- If Maggie's father had asked her why she didn't win the Spirit of the Rifle award, how would Maggie have responded?

Conversations Among Characters in Different Novels

It is equally valuable to create conversations among and between characters from *different* novels. However, for this to work well, novels with characters sharing interests/problems/issues must be selected for questions that can address similarities. These allow the formation of the above skills, and tie elements of novels and characters together, showing students commonalities among and between them. Below are examples of conversations among characters from Riggs' *Miss Peregrine's Home for Peculiar Children* (2011) and Weeks' *Pie* (2011), among many.

- Aunt Polly's children are her pies, with Miss Peregrine caring for misfit children. How would each describe their "children" to one another?
- Alice continues Polly's legacy and becomes a pie maker, with Jacob staying in Wales. How would they defend their decisions to one another?
- Which of Miss Peregrine's children would Jacob select as likely to be best friends with Alice, and how would he introduce them?

Student Responses to Multiple Character Scenarios

Another valuable activity is creating scenarios using characters from one or more novels for students to consider reactions and responses. As above, novels with characters sharing interests/problems/issues should be selected. The activity allows the formation of the above skills and injects individual student opinions and responses regarding novel and character elements by having them address the question as themselves, rather than the characters. Below are examples from Cormier's *The Rag and Bone Shop* (2001), Gantos's *Dead End in Norvelt* (2011), and Riggs's *Miss Peregrine's Home for Peculiar Children* (2011), with many other possibilities:

- If Miss Volker could visit with Jacob before he leaves for Wales, what advice would she give him?
- Does Jason belong with Miss Peregrine's children more than Jacob? Explain.
- Describe a scenario where Trent [from Cormier] is interrogating Jacob's grandfather, Miss Peregrine, or Mr. Spizz. What would he ask each, and why?

An enjoyable way to practice the skills above students' considering characters in a party or prom setting; while deceptively simple, characters must be well understood and known for responses. Middle level students might be more familiar with a school dance and high school a prom, but either one is acceptable, with other scenarios.

These are best in a table/grid format, may be used with any YAL novel, and completed in multiple ways (individually, with partners, in groups), but students should decide selections and compare responses. Below is a sample using a prom setting:

- Which character would _____ and why?
- Wear matching outfits *and be* voted best and worst dressed?
- Be voted prom king and queen, *and* complain about not winning prom king/queen and demand a recount?
- Most likely to bring a freshman *and* a college student as dates, and they are . . . ? *plus* Attend with brother/sister as date?
- Be stood up by date, *and* have date leave prom with another?
- Fight with date and break up, *and* fight with another, about . . . ?
- Arrive when prom is half over, *and/or* leave after 20 minutes?
- Spike the punch, *or* spend most of the time in the restroom, hiding?
- Have parents chaperone, *and* dance with a teacher, *and* have a great prom?

Thematic Multiple Character Categorizations

For this activity, select one emotion/situation/issue that multiple novel characters share in some way, and have students categorize and provide a rationale. Again, student knowledge of characters (and the novel) must be thoroughly understood. This may be completed in different ways (individually, with partners, in groups) but students should compare responses with perhaps the whole class deciding upon selections.

Below is a sample, to be used with any YAL novel and a variety of terms. This is an example, not a complete list for all characters, and from Cormier's *The Rag and Bone Shop* (2001), and Thrash's *Honor Girl: A Graphic Memoir* (2015), with the Connecting Term *Shame*. Shame is experienced by these characters or should have been. Indicate how (while characters have several examples, only one is listed), with responses best placed in a table or similar format:

- *The Rag and Bone Shop* illustrates shame by Trent's continued questioning of Jason after realizing his innocence, Jason's mother allowing him to be questioned by the police alone, Brad killing his sister, Brad's parents bringing Trent to blame another, and the Police Chief's shoddy investigation.
- Shame is seen in *Honor Girl: A Graphic Memoir* through Erin's failing to return to say goodbye to Maggie on the camp's final day, Maggie's mother constantly criticizing her and obliviousness to who she is, Tammy's arrangement for Maggie's receiving Honor Girl for silence of

being LGBTQ+, and Maggie's brother knowing she's deeply depressed, but failing to help.

Main Story Points Activity

It can be difficult for students to determine among a novel's *most important* events and all others. They may view all as equally important or unable to determine key situations from those lesser (fantasy and science fiction are particularly difficult). If students list their most important novel events, they may have anywhere from five to 50, but by providing a *number*, they must carefully review the plot to determine its truly significant occurrences. Numbers should be from eight to ten, depending upon the novel's length/complexity.

Aside from the above skills, this activity also requires thorough novel understanding, careful attention to plotline, and challenges students to determine the events they feel are key to the story. This is also open to interpretation, as different occurrences will be selected for the same novels and allows the activity's completion in multiple ways (individually, with partners, in groups). Students should compare responses and perhaps decide upon a final selection for the novel used.

For the assignment, students list the novel's eight pivotal plot points in order of occurrence, (providing rationales if desired). Points may be illustrated, written, or both. An example from Cormier's *The Rag and Bone Shop* (2001) is below:

- At last, Jason's summer vacation!
- He reluctantly goes to Brad's and witnesses their tense moments.
- Alicia is found dead, unmolested, and laid down with tenderness.
- Jason volunteers for questioning at the police station.
- Trent interrogates him relentlessly.
- Jason says what Trent needed to hear.
- Trent learns Jason is innocent from Sarah.
- Jason takes a butcher knife from the drawer, thinking of Bobo.

REFERENCES

ABC News. (2020, November 3). *South Dakota 2020 election results.* https://abcnews.go.com/Politics/south-dakota-2020-election-results/story?id=73573016\

American Hospital Association. (2019, February). *Rural report: Challenges facing rural communities and the roadmap to ensure local access to high-quality, affordable care.* https://www.aha.org/system/files/2019-02/rural-report-2019.pdf

Ballotpedia. (n.d.a). *North Dakota Abortion Procedure Ban (2012).* https://ballotpedia.org/North_Dakota_Abortion_Procedure_Ban_(2012)
Ballotpedia. (n.d.b). *South Dakota Abortion Ban, Referendum 6 (2006).* https://ballotpedia.org/South_Dakota_Abortion_Ban,_Referendum_6_(2006)
Ballotpedia. (n.d.c). *South Dakota 2008 ballot measures.* https://ballotpedia.org/2008_ballot_measures#South_Dakota
Best Places. (n.d.). *Most secure U.S. places.* https://www.bestplaces.net/docs/studies/secure.aspx
Carter, C. (2015, October 1). Montana interstate speed limit raised to 80 mph—mostly. *Bozeman Daily Chronicle.* https://www.bozemandailychronicle.com/news/montana-interstate-speed-limit-raised-to-80-mph-mostly/article_7dee866c-c7ca-5002-aee3-72c6335fd1be.html
Cormier, R. (2001). *The rag and bone shop.* Dell Laurel Leaf/Random House.
Countryahh.com. (2022). List of all counties in Minnesota. https://www.countryaah.com/alphabetical-list-of-all-counties-in-minnesota/
High Speed Internet.com (2017, Feb. 9). *Most popular dating site by state (MAP).* https://www.highspeedinternet.com/resources/popular-dating-app-state
Insurance Institute for Highway Safety (2022). *Maximum posted speed limits by state.* https://www.iihs.org/topics/speed/speed-limit-laws
Jenkins, C., & Trotta, D. (2017, March 30). *Seeking end to boycott, North Carolina rescinds transgender bathroom law.* Reuters. https://www.reuters.com/article/us-north-carolina-lgbt/seeking-end-to-boycott-north-carolina-rescinds-transgender-bathroom-law-idUSKBN1711V4
Keifer, K. (2017, July 31). *Who really owns American farmland?* The Counter. https://thecounter.org/who-really-owns-american-farmland/
National Center for Educational Statistics. (2022). *School local locations.* https://nces.ed.gov/surveys/ruraled/definitions.asp
National Endowment for the Arts. (2017a). *U.S. trends in arts attendance and literary reading: 2002–2017.* https://www.arts.gov/sites/default/files/2017-sppapreviewREV-sept2018.pdf
National Endowment for the Arts. (2017b). *Rural arts, design, and innovation in America.* https://www.arts.gov/sites/default/files/Rural%20Arts%2011-17.pdf
National Geographic Society. (2017, May 31). *What cities have the most unpredictable weather in the U.S.?* https://blog.education.nationalgeographic.org/2017/05/31/what-cities-have-the-most-unpredictable-weather-in-the-u-s/
Native-Americans.com. (2014, Feb. 25). *South Dakota Indian reservations.* https://native-americans.com/south-dakota-indian-reservations/
O'Bryan, M. (2020, Nov. 4). *Recreational and medical marijuana passed in South Dakota, so what's next?* Kota TV Territory. https://www.kotatv.com/2020/11/05/recreational-and-medical-marijuana-passed-in-south-dakota-so-whats-next/
Pew Research Center. (2018, May 22). *What unites and divides urban, suburban, and rural communities.* https://www.pewsocialtrends.org/2018/05/22/demographic-and-economic-trends-in-urban-suburban-and-rural-communities/
Pew Research Center. (2019, October 17). *In U.S., decline of Christianity continues at a rapid pace.* https://www.pewforum.org/2019/10/17/in-u-s-decline-of-christianity-continues-at-rapid-pace/

Ratcliffe, M., Burd, C., Holder, K, & Fields, A. (2016/2021, Dec. 8). Defining rural at the U.S. Census Bureau. USCB. https://www.census.gov/library/publications/2016/acs/acsgeo-1.html#:~:text=The%20U.S.%20Census%20Bureau%20defines%20rural%20as%20what,researchers%20may%20use%20a%20different%20definition%20of%20rural

Rho, H. J., Brown, H., & Fremstad, S. (2020, April 7). *A basic demographic profile of workers in frontline industries.* Center for Economic and Policy Research. https://cepr.net/a-basic-demographic-profile-of-workers-in-frontline-industries/

Riggs, R. (2011). *Miss Peregrine's home for peculiar children.* Quirk Books.

Rosenblatt, L. (1995). *Literature as exploration.* MLA. (Original work published 1938).

Thrash, M. (2015). *Honor girl: A graphic memoir.* Candlewick.

Union of Concerned Scientists. (2019, June 19). *Global Warming in the Midwest.* https://www.ucsusa.org/resources/global-warming-midwest

U.S. Census Bureau (2018a). *American community survey 1-year estimates. Census reporter profile page for Midwest Region.* http://censusreporter.org/profiles/02000US2-midwest-region/

U.S. Census Bureau (2018b). *United States quick facts.* https://www.census.gov/quickfacts/fact/table/US

U.S. Department of Agriculture. (2020, May 28). Rural education. https://www.ers.usda.gov/topics/rural-economy-population/employment-education/rural-education

Wilger, S. (2016). *Definition of frontier* [Policy brief]. National Rural Health Association Policy Brief. https://www.ruralhealthweb.org/getattachment/Advocate/Policy-Documents/NRHAFrontierDefPolicyPaperFeb2016.pdf.aspx

World Population Review. (2020a). *State demographics.* https://worldpopulationreview.com/states/

Chapter 2

Consideration of Canonical Adult Classics vs. Young Adult Literature

Canonical adult classics are secondary ELAs' chosen literature but frequently unsuited to many students, and as often accompanied by desultory teaching methods, comprehension is not necessarily attained. However, young adult literature (YAL), is written specifically for those in grades 6 to 12, allowing for all adolescents to read novels mirroring their own lives and of lives different from their own.

ADULT CANONICAL LITERATURE IN SECONDARY ELA CLASSROOMS

Most secondary (i.e., grades 7–12) ELA educators, especially those in grades 9 to 12, primarily teach adult classics (aka *the classics*, *the canon*, *canonical literature*). They are described, as commonly by the ELA community, as those titles of high literary quality meriting critique and study with their themes, situations, and issues universal to human nature. Their elements (plots, stories/events, characters, and settings) are vivid and influential, speak to readers over the years, and are reread (Hipple, 2000).

Applebee et al.'s (2003) groundbreaking review of works taught in ELA classrooms showed classics as predominant, with additional field experts (Blasingame, 2007; Gibbons et al., 2006; Santoli & Wagner, 2004; Tatum, 2008; and Tomlinson & Lynch-Brown, 2010) as also determining adult canonical literature reigning.

Further, various online booklists continually show canonical titles as ubiquitous; two examples are Grossberg's (2020) list of thirteen books most frequently taught in high schools having all adult classics but *The Giver* (Lowry,

1993), and Goodread's (2020b) larger survey of most-used titles containing 63 YAL titles from 747 novels.

Reasons for adult classics' public-school cementation are numerous, with continuity surely being the strongest; titles are unchanging and continually present in anthologies and classroom novel sets. ELA educators doubtlessly read them in high school, with post-secondary English courses further studying them. Similarly, parents also read them and expect their continued use, as they are seen as necessary for quality ELA education.

Equally formidable are national and state mandates, high-stakes testing, standards and accompanying requirements, and exams required for students preparing for post-secondary education, all heavily influenced by classic literature. Incorporating more, or any, YAL requires upending venerable curricula for titles presumably largely unfamiliar and its genre perceived as lesser quality.

Challenges From Adult Canonical Literature in ELA Classrooms

Perhaps more accurate depictions of classics are Mark Twain's famous titles, "A classic is something that everybody wants to have read and nobody wants to read," and "'Classic'—a book which people praise and don't read" (Goodreads, 2020a). These novels doubtlessly contribute to the continually decreasing rates of adolescents' overall reading and reading for pleasure.

Few students are readers; less than 20% of U.S. teens reported reading books for pleasure, with Natanson (2018) also stating one in three high school seniors had not read a book for pleasure during the past year. Similarly, the National Endowment for the Arts' (NEA) 2018 study found only 52.7% of adults had read at least one book for pleasure during the past year (including those beginning, but not completing, one).

However, the American Psychological Association (APA; 2018), found over 80% of teens and adults used social media every day, with Rideout (2016) noting teens (ages 13–18) averaged nine hours of daily technological use; subtracting time spent for academics left six and a half of those hours used for social media/entertainment. Likewise, tweens' (ages 8–12) daily average was six hours, four and a half claimed by leisure, both showing reading's lesser influence.

English language arts educator researchers have continually expressed consternation with students' graduating without desiring to read for pleasure (Bond, 2011; Christenbury & Lindblom, 2016; Cole, 2009; Hayn et al., 2017; Knickerbocker & Rycik, 2020; Nilsen et al., 2013; Short et al., 2014).

Although individuals are allowed unprecedented access to literature through the continually expanding Internet alone, if teens and adults reading consists of only one novel a year, this questions ELA educators' literature selections and teaching methodologies. Further, as adults surveyed are parents or otherwise role models, they also presumably negatively affecting contemporary students' reading.

These educator researchers above, and those earlier (Bushman & Haas, 2006; Herz & Gallo, 2005; Hipple, 2000; Lesesne, 2010), have also long expressed concerns regarding classics' domination and teaching methodologies. Because such works were intended for then-contemporary adults with corresponding writing styles, many adults and adolescents find them difficult to read and comprehend today. Students can understand and enjoy canonical classics, of course, but titles chosen must best complement their age and reading level, with those not used later or retired. Providing appropriate literature, including the classics, and teaching it well is vital for student comprehension, learning, and preparation for subsequent grade levels.

Unfortunately, quality teaching does not necessarily occur; educators are increasingly over-burdened with classics requiring arduous preparation, students are participating less in class and more with social media regardless of school rules, and long-held teaching practices are uninteresting to them, failing to produce authentic learning.

Presumably, the most common teaching of all literature, including classics, is using the school's curriculum guides and materials, plus ELA textbook supplements. These additions include complete unit and lesson plans with teaching instructions and corresponding materials as author information, discussion questions, vocabulary, activities, quizzes, writing activities, exams, and more. Their goals and objectives match those of professional ELA organizations and current national set, with reading and grade levels coordinated (i.e., an eighth-grade text's readability matches the average eighth-grade student), and ready for use.

All such information is welcome and helpful; these items naturally vary in quality but are meant to be adapted and provide an array of materials, rather than used exclusively. Still, using supplements lessen heavy workloads with content matching literature. Students thus complete textbook packets containing assignments and assessments covering the entire novel. Works are often read aloud with plays read by selected students by scene.

Discussions are generally teacher-directed and short, focusing on literal information (e.g., state the theme; name the protagonist and antagonist; etc.) reexamining basic elements, and confirming understanding, with such single answers prohibiting further talk.

Unfortunately, these materials do not guarantee students are reading the taught classic; downloading various Internet summaries, explanations, and interpretations of them are routine, used for classroom assignment completion, and substituted for reading the text.

Other methods of teaching too-sophisticated classics include graphic novels. Their retelling of classic literature through easy-to-read abridged texts is a burgeoning market, and used in place, or in tandem, with the original. Likewise, another long-held practice is pairing YAL and classics with similar themes, such as *Night* (Wiesel, 1972/2006) with *Never Fall Down* (McCormick, 2012), or *The Scarlett Letter* (Hawthorne, 1850/2020) with *Speak* (Anderson, 1999/2011). While it's productive if both titles are equally emphasized, the YAL novel is likely referenced to interpret the classic or used instead by those unable to read the original work.

Such novel pairing implies YALs central purpose is *supporting* or *abridging* canonical literature as a comprehension tool. Worse, it insinuates that YAL is not a complete, separate genre, consisting instead of novels with simplified content and writing style, intended *to assist better novels* rather than read on their own merit and considered appropriate for only lower-level or younger students.

This practice causes YAL viewed as of lesser quality and prestige by many, especially those assuming canonical works superior. Ironically, this denigrates a literature group that is far better suited to the average student than many of the adult classics for which supplemented.

Unfortunately, these methodologies serve to teach students *about* the material rather than learning *from* it; surface knowledge of the text is acquired rather than true comprehension of its content. While appearing that student understanding has been achieved by correct worksheet and package completion—as information necessary for assignments is also teacher-summarized, available online, or completed by or with peers—high scores can be easily attained regardless of actual knowledge.

Most definitive, however, is simply turning to a literature section and asking, "What does this (passage) *mean*?" Student responses lacking comprehension should raise the more important question of why works so difficult for average students' reading and understanding are taught at all. It should also clearly indicate that the common teaching activities and strategies used have produced little learning and will not without textual understanding. A quick appraisal before using any work is if multiple supplements and interpretations are necessary for student understanding rather than reading and discussing the work itself, genuine comprehension is unlikely.

Teaching must allow interaction with literature, its discussion among peers and educators, and challenging, interesting assignments requiring command of the work for completion. It should produce students' enhanced knowledge plus the ability to imagine, predict, and consider different and varying scenarios for events and characters, including future occurrences and circumstances.

Above all, selected classics, their teaching, and assignments should *matter*; desultory teaching of works with their reading and understanding unnecessary for passing grades will be unsuccessful regardless of title taught. As current works and practices are continually repeated, main achievements are seemingly producing and reinforcing students' reading antipathy.

Definition of Literature for Adolescents

The literature written for students in the secondary grades (6–12) has a myriad of titles, including *adolescent literature, young adult literature, contemporary teen/adolescent literature, juvenile novels/fiction/literature, junior novels/fiction/literature, teen novels, teenage literature*, among other combinations. *Young adult literature*, and its accompanying abbreviation YAL, are used here, chosen by personal preference for its ostensible inclusivity and contemporary resonance. However, its title is of lesser importance than those novels within it.

Young Adult Literature Titles

Just as there are multiple titles designating the YAL genre, there are also conflicting views as to which novels are considered contemporary young adult. Definitions include novel protagonists being teens, titles popular among adolescents, novels read by teens, and any novel written for them, and more. The definition here is *those novels written specifically for contemporary adolescents aged 11–18* (i.e., grades 6–12), which separates authentic YAL from other works and focuses upon title currency, although older titles should be used as applicable.

Of course, adolescents should be able to read and enjoy a wide variety of novels, but access and variety do not negate the importance of understanding YAL; if educators are to use it, they must be able to define, identify and defend their selected titles for teaching or recommendation.

Importance of Young Adult Literature

If educators aspire students developing an appreciation of literature and desiring to read for pleasure, then works taught must match current cognitive levels with accompanying teaching methodologies requiring student engagement, something not necessarily occurring through canonical classics' predominance.

Developmental theorists (Carlson, 1980; Erikson, 1968; Havighurst, 1972; Piaget & Inhelder, 1969; Rosenblatt, 1938; Vygotsky, 1978) concur, and support YAL as most appropriate for adolescents' maturity and cognitive development as do those YAL/ELA researchers cited above. Further, Cart's (2008) position paper promoting YAL was adopted by the Young Adult Library

Services Association (YALSA); his central point being all adolescents should be able to read contemporary novels that realistically and honestly depict themselves and their daily lives.

Adolescence is a tumultuous time for most; many feel alone, unsure, or anxious by their unfamiliar physical, cognitive, emotional, and social changes, with various home or other negative situations additional burdens. Reading YAL allows teens seeing role models and others like them, introducing them to a community of peers sharing the same experiences and difficulties, and displaying others coping, surviving, and thriving.

Likewise, the YAL/ELA researcher educators above (and novels themselves) continually demonstrate that YAL offers the same literary quality as adult classics through clearly defined, thoughtful, sophisticated plots and structures with consistent viewpoints, significant settings, moods, and tones. Characters are dynamic, speaking authentic and compelling dialogue, with traditional literary elements and distinctive vocabulary throughout. However, YAL is written in styles fitting and engaging to contemporary adolescents, an important difference.

Teaching YAL also allows meaningful connections to students' lives in ways difficult to achieve with adult classics. Although those texts' themes, situations, and issues are universal, they were experienced by adults from the distant past, not contemporary adolescents. Further, students can genuinely discuss these works rather than abridged interpretations or Internet summaries.

YAL also enables students' recognition and understanding of literary elements, forming opinions, reconsidering, and challenging others,' pondering alternatives by imagining characters behaving differently, determining likely endings if open to interpretation, relating events, issues, and characters to other novels and society, critiquing writing styles, predicting future character situations, and more, certainly confirming YALs significance and substance.

The Importance of Young Adult Literature Featuring Diversity

Of course, it is equally, if not more, important for all adolescents and specifically those rural, to read of others *unlike* them. Literature representing society's many diversities, especially underrepresented groups, as confident, intelligent, and pro-active role models in realistic, contemporary settings must be read and taught in classrooms to assist in creating awareness, openness, and acceptance toward others among all students, a long-held position by YAL/ELA researcher educators (Andrews, 1998; Bushman & Haas, 2006; Christenbury & Lindblom, 2016; Cole, 2009; Daniels, 2002; Knickerbocker & Rycik, 2020; Nilsen et al., 2013; Tiedt & Tiedt, 2005).

In tandem, Cart (2003) also stated that while aware of non-majority students, schools are generally unsure how to oversee them. Those identifying as lesbian, gay, bisexual transgender, or questioning (LGBTQ+), non-Christian, homeless, migrant, or having a disability are not always accepted socially, with continued antipathy at school making lives doubly difficult. Such students are also in rural areas and treated similarly, but they and potential resources are naturally fewer, also seriously problematic.

Schools have incorporated various policies and procedures (plus plastering walls with posters promoting acceptance), but without following them common. Generally, minority students remain ignored, patronized, bullied, or otherwise stigmatized by classmates, with educators and parents often equally unwelcoming.

Cart insisted, "Kids need to learn empathy. They need to learn how the *other* can become *us*" (p. x), so it appears crucial that majority adolescents understand the sometimes-tremendous differences or difficulties that characterize peers' everyday lives. Such differences should not be viewed negatively, with students learning to treat all peers respectfully. Cart's recommendation for achieving this is, "through reading fiction that captures—artfully, authentically, and unsparingly—the circumstances of kids" (p. xiii) in underrepresented groups, that is, YAL.

Rural Adolescents and the Importance of Young Adult Literature Featuring Diversity

Rural adolescents are essentially like others elsewhere other than individual lifestyles and are no more or less prejudiced than any other teen, but most are white in the UM, with nearly all having no, or very little, personal experience with those of different races or ethnicities. Additionally, rural residents are also an underrepresented group, stigmatized by those non-rural. These teens must learn to view diversities through a dual lens, realizing that by considering or treating other groups negatively, they themselves are likewise regarded by others.

Non-white rural adolescents and those from other underrepresented groups are few in the UM, and frequently separated, segregated, or otherwise not fully integrated into their schools and communities, sometimes by choice, others not. Regardless, they need assurance of others resembling them in general as well as in their often-unenviable situation as the, or one of few, minorities where living.

Reading YAL featuring characters like them and seeing them having and managing the same struggles, issues, and situations seems imperative for rural teens seldom represented or valued and of course all adolescents, regardless of where living. These novels are more than valuable; they can be vital, perhaps life-changing, for those many rural adolescents with few or no peers with whom to share their lives, or certain parts of them, and likewise assist others in their better understanding, tolerance, and acceptance.

DISCUSSION QUESTIONS AND SUGGESTED ACTIVITIES

Discussion Questions	Suggested Activities; Students Will . . .	Key Diversity Points
1. What YAL novels have been assigned in your ELA classes? Both students and educators may respond to these questions.	Students' list assigned YAL novels; educators could list, then state why assigned. How many YAL novels were assigned, vs. classics, and what does this imply?	How balanced is one's curriculum regarding diverse characters/authors, whether YAL or classics? If unbalanced, how does one proceed toward correction?
2. Which canonical classics have been taught in your ELA classes? This could be an extension of the above.	Students' list assigned classics; educators' list and state why assigned. Are these truly the best titles for contemporary students? Which ones are better than others?	Classics should be honestly evaluated regarding their value to contemporary students. How balanced are they regarding diverse characters/authors? For changes, how to begin using different titles?
3. Were these classic novels understood by students via regular instruction, or were Internet summaries and other extensive assistance necessary?	Discussion can focus upon how much extra instruction was necessary for various titles, and what is considered too much? If online materials were needed, did this result in learning *about* the novel, but not *from* it?	For those needing additional assistance for understanding, what methods were used, for whom, and do they create an unwelcome diversity among students?
4. If there were difficulties understanding the classics taught, was a main problem that the title may be inappropriate to student age, or its teaching methods?	Discussion can consider which classics are unwisely assigned, with many unable to comprehend. Common teaching methods may also be explored; are they largely solitary, or dynamic, and do they encourage using supplements rather than reading the text?	Which students are having the most difficulties, and why? How could this groups' understanding be improved?

5. If many classics are not understood by students nor their teaching best practices, how is their continual teaching justified?	Discussion can ponder the issue of appropriateness; classics are not *taught* if not understood. Why such titles are repeatedly used is also considered.	Understanding is often unequal among students, but is there an assumption of certain students not comprehending some texts regardless, so their use is continued for those who can? Does this practice create a sharp classroom division?
6. Which canonical classics are essential reading for ELA students, and why?	Answers will doubtless vary widely, but repeated titles and rationales for teaching should be noted. How are these books best chosen with so few agreeing which to use?	Individual diversities regarding selections will be shown, but who determines novels classics, and does this process preclude educators, thus creating their minority status?
7. What currently defines "canonical classic," and what are the newest titles on the list?	Comparisons of those titles continually used could be discussed, and what does their use imply? Which newer selections could be considered in lieu of those less appropriate?	Selecting newer titles may meet the needs of more students, including those diverse.
8. Which canonical classics have you not read, and why?	Discussion focuses upon why certain novels were unread, and commonalities among titles. For titles frequently taught but unread, what messages are sent?	Which students are not reading, or not having read, various classics, and how are they viewed and/or treated in the classroom? Where are divisions among students?
9. Are any curricular canonical classics denigrating or otherwise offensive to students?	Novels as Twain's *Adventures of Huckleberry Finn* (1885/2019) are considered venerable, but deeply offensive to Black students. Discussion can consider whether this title and others likewise inappropriate are taught, and why. What does continued teaching imply?	Why are novels denigrating any group continually taught?
10. Of the canonical classics currently taught to students, how much diversity is within them?	Such titles with diverse characters or authors used can be listed and discussed. Further, a focus should be whether their diverse/minority aspects are particularly stressed when teaching?	Are diverse/minority characters or authors overlooked in novels, as are some minority students? What messages are sent if diversities are present in titles, but given little attention?

REFERENCES

American Psychological Association. (August 20, 2018). *Teens today spend more time on digital media, less time reading.* https://www.apa.org/news/press/releases/2018/08/teenagers-read-book.

Anderson, L. H. (1999/2011). *Speak.* Square Fish Publishing.

Andrews, S. (1998). Inclusion literature: A resource listing. *The ALAN Review, 25,* 28–30.

Applebee, A., Langer, J., Nystrand, M., & Gamoran, A. (2003). Discussion-based approaches to developing understanding: Classroom instruction and student performance in middle and high school English. *American Educational Research Journal, 40*(3), 685–730. http://www.jstor.org/stable/3699449

Blasingame, J. (2007). *Books that don't bore 'em.* Scholastic.

Bond, E. (2011). *Literature and the young adult reader.* Pearson.

Bushman, J., & Haas, K. P. (2006). *Using young adult literature in the English classroom* (4th ed.). Pearson Merrill Prentice Hall.

Carlson, R. (1980). *Books and the teen-age reader.* Harper & Row.

Cart, M. (2003). *Necessary noise: Stories about our families as they really are* (pp. x, xiii). HarperCollins.

Cart, M. (2008). *The value of young adult literature* [Policy brief]. Young Adult Library Services Association. http://www.ala.org/yalsa/guidelines/whitepapers/yalit

Christenbury, L., & Lindblom, K. (2016). *Making the journey: Being and becoming a teacher of English language arts* (4th ed.). Heinemann.

Cole, P. (2009). *Young adult literature in the 21st century.* McGraw-Hill.

Daniels, H. (2002). *Literature circles: Voice and choice in book clubs and reading groups.* Stenhouse Publishers.

Erikson, E. H. (1968). *Identity: Youth and crisis.* Norton.

Gibbons, L. C., Dail, J. S., & Stallworth, B. J. (2006). Young adult literature in the English curriculum today: Classroom teachers speak out. *The ALAN Review 33*(3), 53–61.

Goodreads. (2020a). *Mark Twain quotes.* https://www.goodreads.com/quotes/1035168-a-classic-is-something-that-everybody-wants-to-have-read

Goodreads. (2020b). *Required reading in high school.* https://www.goodreads.com/list/show/478.Required_Reading_in_High_School?page=8

Grossberg, B. (August 26, 2020). *The most commonly read books in high school.* Thought.com. https://www.thoughtco.com/most-commonly-read-books-private-schools.2774330

Havighurst, R. (1972). *Developmental tasks and education.* David McKay.

Hawthorne, N. (1850/2020). *The scarlett letter.* Pure Snow Publishing.

Hayn, J. A., Kaplan, J. S., & Clemmons, K. R. (2017). *Teaching young adult literature today* (2nd ed.). Rowman & Littlefield.

Herz, S. K., & Gallo, D. R. (2005). *From Hinton to Hamlet: Building bridges between young adult literature and the classics.* Greenwood Press.

Hipple, T. (2000). With themes for all: The universality of the young adult novel. In V. Monseau & G. Salvner (eds.), *Reading their world: The young adult novel in the classroom* (pp. 1–14). Heinemann.

Knickerbocker, J. L., & Rycik, J. A. (2020). *Literature for young adults: Books (and more) for contemporary readers* (2nd ed.). Routledge.

Lesesne, T. S. (2010). *Reading ladders: Leading students from where they are to where we'd like them to be.* Heinemann.

Lowry, L. (1993). *The giver.* Houghton Mifflin.

McCormick, P. (2012). *Never fall down.* Balzer + Bray/HarperCollins.

Natanson, H. (August 20, 2018). *Yes, teens are texting and using social media instead of reading books, researchers say.* Washingtonpost.com

National Endowment for the Arts (2018). *U.S. trends in arts attendance and literary reading: 2002–2017.* https://www.arts.gov/sites/default/files/2017-sppapreviewREV-sept2018.pdf

Nilsen, A. P., Blasingame, J., Donelson, K. L., & Nilsen, D. L. F. (2013). *Literature for today's young adults.* (9th ed.). Pearson.

Piaget, J., & Inhelder, B. (1969). *The psychology of the child.* Basic Books.

Rideout, V. (2016). *The common sense census: Media use by tweens and teens.* Common Sense Media, Inc. https://www.commonsense media.org/sites/default/files/uploads/research/census_executivesummary.pdf

Rosenblatt, L. (1938). *Literature as exploration.* Appleton Century.

Santoli, S., & Wagner, M. (2004). Promoting young adult literature: The other "real" literature. *American Secondary Education 1*(33), 65.

Short, K., Tomlinson, C., Lynch-Brown, C., & Johnson, H. (2014). *Essentials of young adult Literature* (3rd ed.). Pearson.

Tatum, A. (2008). Overserved or underserved? A focus on adolescents and texts. *English Journal, 98*(2), 82–85.

Tiedt, P. L., & Tiedt, I. M. (2005). *Multicultural teaching* (7th ed.). Pearson Education, Inc.

Tomlinson, C. M., & Lynch-Brown, C. M. (2010). *Essentials of young adult literature* (2nd ed.). Pearson.

Vygotsky, L. S. (1978). *Mind in society: The development of higher psychological processes.* Harvard University Press.

Wiesel, E. (1972/2006). *Night.* Farrar, Straus and Giroux.

Chapter 3

Importance of Young Adult Literature With Upper Midwestern Settings, and Locating Titles

It is difficult to locate young adult literature (YAL) set in the Midwest or the Upper Midwest (UM), as there are far fewer titles representing this group, with many historical fiction rather than contemporary. Determining existing novels' locations is also surprisingly challenging, with titles featuring the UM, their importance to these teens, and location assistance emphasized.

RURAL ADOLESCENTS AND YOUNG ADULT LITERATURE

While presumably most adolescents, regardless of where living, enjoy and progress from reading YAL novels of various genres and particularly those featuring contemporary teens, their issues and situations, UM teens benefit least. Locating YAL featuring UM characters and settings is difficult with many of the best novels regarding quality/appeal either older (10+ years) or historical fiction, neither portraying today's rural teens. Further, while adults involved with YAL espouse adolescents read of those like and unlike them (and rightly so), a presumption made is these novels equally represent them.

However, the average adolescent reader seems to be categorized as White, middle-class, from suburban or otherwise comfortable households, with those diverse frequently largely undistinguishable from White peers. Minority protagonists are often found in grittier YAL, with their situation (non-White, homeless, non-documented, migrant worker) the primary plot/problem and setting often southwestern locales or inner cities. Southern rural teens have a larger portrayal, but often stereotyped as fundamentalist, backward, or poor.

Midwestern and UM teens have lesser portrayal, and these settings having minority protagonists are rarer still; overall, these adolescents are largely overlooked in YAL.

Lack of Rural-Themed YAL

The majority of YAL contemporary fiction regardless of location or genre (e.g., fantasy, mystery/suspense) seldom portrays UM characters. Rural teens are generally better represented by Southern and Upper-Northeastern settings, but such portrayals may also be as unlike UM adolescents' lifestyle as those featuring suburban or urban locales.

Trends in YAL (e.g., blank/free verse, teens with magical powers, werewolves/vampires, dystopian settings, Blacks facing prejudice) are common after a significant title appears, such as Collins's *Hunger Games* (2008) or Thomas's *The Hate U Give* (2017). Few, if any, such titles have been set in the UM with scores of similar-themed novels quickly appearing. Neither is there a demand for YAL set in the UM, and as its population is far smaller than other areas it is doubtful publishers would be eager to begin a new series or other promotions with an already limited audience.

For rural teens to fully benefit from YAL, then they must also have wide selections and varieties of genre titles in which they can read about themselves, the same as peers elsewhere. If UM teens have less opportunity to read about themselves and peers elsewhere are not provided their stories, then they will remain largely invisible. Likewise, this group's lesser inclusion in contemporary YAL, regardless of genre or category, sends a message of their lesser value, surely recognized by UM readers.

Carger (2003) spoke of minorities reading about themselves in literature, stating what is common for mainstream students—connecting with characters having similar appearances, names, and life experiences—is especially gratifying and welcome to those rarely seeing themselves in classroom novels. Boyd (2002), DeLeón (2002), Aronson (2001), Lo (2001), and Chew (1997) all stated minority teens reading YAL featuring like characters helps them shape and explore the many facets of their own identity, vital to how they will perceive themselves and others. Also found was connection and understanding between and among those similar through familiar themes and situations, better socialization, and desire for change.

It must be remembered rural UM teens are also a minority, but not represented as such within YAL, another overlooked title opportunity. Further, as stated in Chapters 1 and 2, the least represented of all groups are UM minorities; likewise, they are nearly invisible in YAL. Many such minority teens may have no like peers at all their age, a significant disadvantage as they are neither able to share specific events, issues, and difficulties of their situation with others nor read of them in YAL, both essentially unknown to majority adolescents.

Moreover, rural majority UM teens doubtless have a lesser understanding of their few minority peers, and those with none have little opportunity to learn. It seems such YAL titles would be crucial to these teens, and naturally valuable to others elsewhere if wishing to move from diversity (being present) to inclusion (playing a small role) and finally belonging, that is, an equal.

Importance of Place in YAL

Like all other teens, those in the UM should read of others living similarly, and better, their state. Who doesn't enjoy reading of familiar places in YAL? Positive depictions enhance one's sense of belonging, ownership, and pride in what is portrayed, with equally strong reactions evoked from those negative.

Adolescents can enjoy discussing an attraction described with friends, exclaim with others that the park discussed is larger and tidier, complain that a business used does not exist, or confirm the protagonist's diner is also a local favorite, with many having eaten there last week. Students may also act as a sort of tour guide for various novel places or what occurred there in the past, contributing additional information, such as sharing a great-great-grandparent managed the hotel shown or a grandmother created the gardening club depicted.

These connections bring additional pride, enjoyment, or defense of one's town/state chosen for a novel's setting, essentially proclaiming these teens' home and lifestyle as important and matter. Knowing others are also reading these novels assists rural teens in gaining a stronger sense of recognition, connection, and equality among adolescents living elsewhere.

Place does matter, and for UM teens, particularly those in the smallest towns having increased negative lifestyle changes, such reading and associated involvements can be life-changing, with Getting Smart's study of Place-Based Education (2017), Donovan (2016), Gruenwald (2003), and Maguth and Hilburn (2011) having designated specific benefits for adolescents reading YAL set in their states:

- Realization that every place and person is important, including their hometown and themselves, learning to appreciate what one has, and understanding that one's town also builds who we become.

- Development of a sense of belonging, pride, and ownership with their hometown, and later extending this understanding to how their town and state connect to regions, the nation, and the world.
- Comprehending individuals throughout the world have more in common than not.
- Understanding, creating, and maintaining positive relationships with others and learning to make responsible decisions.
- Acquiring and successfully applying the knowledge, attitudes and skills needed to understand, control, and increase social/emotional learning.
- Development of the ability to feel and demonstrate empathy for others that is not based upon individual views (i.e., personally like/dislike, approve/disapprove).
- Individual growth, becoming less naïve, and development of the ability to consider and challenge the validity of previous assumptions or beliefs.
- Gaining, developing, and successfully collaborating with others, applying problem-solving skills, and recognizing individual ability regarding being positive change-agents and leaders.
- Becoming invested in their schools and communities; working with others to improve them.
- Understanding that improving/strengthening/promoting education and employment can increase population and economic growth, assist in reducing poverty, and lessen feelings of alienation or apathy among individuals.

Of course, these benefits are best derived from quality titles, with YAL featuring rural/small towns ranging from lower quality to stellar, the same as all other genres. Recommendations for evaluating YAL with rural/small town settings are below.

Common Plotlines for Contemporary Rural-Themed YAL

These titles, as other genres, also have common plotlines, features, and overarching elements; for example, fantasy includes magical powers, mythical creatures, good vs. evil battles and so on, and quest motif regardless of storyline. Naturally, works with rural/small town locations have multi-faceted plots, subplots, and blended genres (e.g., adventure/suspense) but commonly feature protagonists eager to leave their hometown, or conversely, finding it their salvation. Categorization and explanation of rural/small town plotlines are below.

Locating Rural-Themed YAL

Evaluating quality of rural-themed YAL novels is easy; identifying their state locations can only be described as nightmarish, often requiring extensive time and effort, with states not always named.

Those working extensively with YAL, particularly librarians or post-secondary ELA/reading educators, rely heavily on novel reviews for purchases, teaching, recommendations, and so on, as no one has access to or can read all the thousands of titles already available and newly published. Reviews are in multiple places, both professional (e.g., *The ALAN Review*, Kirkus Reviews, Booklist), and commercial (e.g., Amazon or Barnes & Noble online bookstores).

Multiple online sites (e.g., BookBub, GoodReads, Bookpage, or Reedsy) feature professional and individual reviews, all covering every genre, and specialized organization sites, (e.g., Science Fiction and Fantasy Writers of America, Mystery Writers of America) focusing on specific titles. Publishing houses (e.g., Scholastic, SoHo Press, Sterling) and individual author websites provide additional materials (e.g., author interviews, discussion guides, etc.), and reviews can also be found by simply entering its title in a browser, likely linking to the above sites or others similar.

However, book covers, reviews, initial novel chapters from online bookstores, reading/discussion guides, publishers' promotional materials, or author sites failed to identify state settings for approximately 40% of the titles used here. If not within a review or initial online chapters, state locations can sometimes be found (if named) but searching requires approximately 45 minutes for *each* title.

Such hunts are surely far beyond the time or patience of anyone but the most desperate or bored, with reviews meant to assist in determining whether to read/purchase the title. A better use of time would be reading the book, unrealistic regarding expenses and defeating the purpose of deciding its reading or use, and hardly helpful to those seeking titles set in a particular state.

This is also limiting, as when needing titles most will select from those with identified states, not necessarily of best quality or interest, and novels from under-represented areas may be missed, giving adolescents even fewer choices of YAL featuring their area and situation. However, guides assisting title setting searches are below but again, these take an extensive amount of time with approximately an additional 25% success rate at best.

DISCUSSION QUESTIONS AND SUGGESTED ACTIVITIES

Discussion Questions	Suggested Activities Students Will . . .	Key Diversity Point
1. Do you feel it is important to know the novel's location/setting?	This fits a classroom debate, with students stating afterwards whether their original opinion changed, and why.	Place is part of identity; ignoring denies stronger reader engagement with the novel.
2. Why would an author not identify their novel's setting, and what message might this send?	Reasons could be brainstormed and then narrowed to those most likely with rational discussion.	Unidentified place can imply invisibility, unimportance, and/or without differences. The rationales for the question below will likely be addressed as both imply similar conclusions.
3. When rural settings are unidentified, reviewers commonly use phrases as a *small town where everyone knows everyone else* or *a typical small town*. Are such descriptions problematic?	Responses and rationales could be discussed and recorded, with those strongest discussed further.	This stereotypical description removes identity and portrays all by one negative definition.
4. What attributes must a title contain to be considered a *rural/small-town* novel?	Students may need guidance regarding the setting's prominence; but all responses lend to discussion and eventually a listing of essential elements.	As before, students understand rural communities are diverse, regardless of size.
5. Why are there so few YAL titles set in the UM/rural areas published?	Librarians or others working with YAL professionally can assist with responses, further considered by students.	This could mirror the UM; fewer authors from these states, lower populations equal fewer titles, or locations deemed of lesser importance and interest.
6. Should all students, regardless of location read YAL set in UM/rural areas?	This opinion question could be used for discussion or debate.	Students should read of all areas and lifestyles.

7. Is it preferable having novels portraying the UM/rural areas unrealistically over not being published?	This question is basically asking which action is the most damaging and why, with student responses being considered and discussed.	How does either choice harm those living in rural locations, and specifically those diverse?
8. How many YAL titles set in the UM/rural areas won Newbery or Newbery Honor awards, and what are the implications of these numbers?	What conclusions can be made from yearly award lists (Caldecott Medals can also be reviewed)? Other national (or any) awards for these novels may be pursued.	Do rural teens have less representation in awards and novels taught in schools?
9. Do YAL novels have any role regarding societal negative or stereotypical views of UM/rural areas?	This could be debated, focusing on rurality negative representation and which aspects are essentially correct, exaggerated, or incorrect.	Are other areas continually presented stereotypically, and how does this compare to the UM? What does this mean for UM teens?
10. What do you feel is most needed regarding YAL set in UM/rural areas?	Individual choices will vary, and further narrowed to listing three items deemed essential with rationale.	How would minority students or those otherwise diverse respond to this question?

EVALUATING RURAL/SMALL TOWN PORTRAYAL IN YOUNG ADULT LITERATURE

Features of Quality Portrayal	Features of Poor-Quality Portrayal
The town's setting is integral to the plot and appears continually.	The story's events are essentially independent from its setting; the town appears infrequently. A story begins in a small town, but characters soon relocate to a larger city with this setting predominant.
The town, era, characters, and rural lifestyles are portrayed authentically.	The town, era, characters, and rural lifestyles are not always authentically portrayed.
Readers identify with the multifaceted characters, believable as small-town residents.	Some characters are unbelievable to readers or as small-town residents. Stereotyping, biases, or tropes of rurality appears.
Necessary definitions or explanations regarding issues/elements specific to small-town living are adequately and correctly provided.	Necessary definitions or explanations regarding issues/elements specific to small town living are missing, incorrect, or inadequate for understanding.
The author has a thorough understanding of small towns and includes numerous details portraying the town's individuality.	The author's portrayal of small towns is missing descriptive aspects that would better depict its uniqueness.
References regarding national/international societal events and persons of the era are included as applicable, indicating those in small towns are as aware and knowledgeable of contemporary events as any other.	Necessary references regarding national/international societal events and persons during the story's timeframe are misinterpreted or dismissed, hinting residents are insulated, less intelligent, or uninterested in occurrences unless directly affected.
Readers have a realistic and balanced view of the positives and negatives of rural lifestyles from the story.	Readers have learned little of the realities of small towns and their residents from the story, perhaps viewing as all positive or negative.
Readers can compare the featured story's town, characters, and storyline with their situation and home.	Readers see little comparison among the town, characters, and story to their own situation and home.
Readers grasp that although lifestyles may be somewhat different, teens share similar situations, concerns, and emotions, and are more alike than different.	Story characters and situations are weakly presented, with readers unable to make personal connections or otherwise view themselves as like those in the novel.

COMMON PLOTLINES FOR RURAL/SMALL TOWN PORTRAYAL IN YOUNG ADULT NOVELS

Beginning Situation	Unexpected Event	End Situation
Teen desperate to leave town for college or other plans.	The opportunity disappears unexpectedly; teen bitter and depressed.	Negative behaviors and nursing wounds commence, with teen beginning work and discovering a talent and interest. Residents are rediscovered along with newcomers; friendships and romance occur. Teen enjoys new success and happiness, choosing to remain with a bright future.
Coastal resort towns during summer. (Generally, three situations, often related/combined)	Local teen disliking given summer employment.	Teen's job becomes more interesting with town newly appreciated and a romance appearing.
	Teen visitor grieving a sibling's death or serious accident that occurred the previous summer; returns to discover accident's truth.	Teen faces dangerous situations while moving closer to truth, but overcomes to discover facts, usually shocking, and begins healing.
	A local teen or visitor unexpectedly becomes embroiled in an eerie, mysterious situation.	Teen begins sleuthing with unexpected danger and multiple surprises, but ultimately solves mystery.
Teen is so troubled he/she is arrested or parents unable to effect change.	Angry teen is sent to rural relatives or work situation in lieu of jail.	Teen's anger and misbehavior ignored, and he/she eventually grudgingly participates in chores and other duties. Over the summer he/she learns coping skills, realizes misconceptions of others, and bonds with relatives or new friends made; often plans to return next year.
Teen and/or family not accepted by their town due to diversity (e.g., sexuality, race) or teen fighting for unpopular social cause.	Teen and family harassed or otherwise victimized by peers and town adults with situation becoming dangerous.	Teen receives assistance from unexpected sources, with ending showing various successes and compromises.

Beginning Situation	Unexpected Event	End Situation
Teen's family living in a city, but not necessarily securely. Magical realism is often featured here.	A crisis or employment opportunity requires moving to small town.	If secure family moving, the teen initially despises town but eventually gains friends, romance, and enjoys new surroundings. If insecure family, problems are eventually faced, and resolution begins. New friends assist, and delightful or unexplained events may occur, helping teen in problem-solving.
Teen's family is solitary and isolated, due to extreme dysfunction (e.g., cult or other abusive situation) or attempting to hide status (e.g., family undocumented or wanted by authorities).	Teen either begins to understand lifestyle restrictions and wants to escape, or unaware of status until documentation needed (e.g., car license). Discovery and its changes are risky and dangerous.	If family is dysfunctional, loyalties and love for family members waver with initial escape attempts thwarted. Assistance leads to success with teen beginning healing. If family is undocumented with some legal, other assistance is generally received but compromises often necessary with endings possibly bittersweet. If hiding from authorities, the crime (often surprising) is resolved with teen's lifestyle perhaps changed, but with promise. It should be noted such plots usually do not solve these complicated situations, but endings are hopeful.
Athletics and Championship Games (Sport situations are also frequently combined)	Two long-time best friends are considered for single sports scholarship. Both desperately want to leave town but cannot without offer. Remaining home means losing dreams and succeeding father in dead-end job.	Scholarship battles bring bitterness and divides between friends. Generally, others assist the teen without the offer, but endings may be happily unexpected or bittersweet.

Category	Description	Outcome
	A team's star player suffers a concussion or other injury but keeps it secret, intending to play in championship game, risking injury/death. Sibling or best friend must find the courage to inform others of injury and face town's wrath.	The sibling or friend informs coach/parent, bringing frustrations and resentments. Parents and others assist all in gaining better perspective of game vs. future life events with positive, often surprising, endings.
Town and families' facing hardships but living generally satisfying lives.	Town suffers sudden and severe economic downturn, with families losing jobs and unable to provide for themselves.	Teens work to discover a way to save town, with situation's gravity portrayed. Incidents saving town may be contrived, feature various legal loopholes, or otherwise outwit authorities. The realities of many readers are depicted, perhaps providing hope regarding personal situations.
Teens enjoy their rural lifestyles and hometown.	A likeable, often irrepressible, teen's enjoyable daily life is portrayed.	The teen is involved in humorous and challenging situations, all resolved or learning coping skills. Stories are full of hectic fun and have promising endings.
Historical Fiction	A small town is featured in depicting important events of various eras. The protagonist may be a famous historical figure or ordinary teen involved in events of the time.	Readers learn of events and people from the past (perhaps their area or state), their lives and situations during the time shown.

LOCATING SETTINGS IN YAL USING GENERAL ONLINE SEARCHES AND PUBLISHER/AUTHOR/ REVIEW SITES AND SUPPLEMENTS

Steps	Location	Instructions/Information
1	In the browser, enter "setting of (title)."	This *may* identify the setting. If not, its related sites below *might*, but beginning such a search is usually a time waster, with multiple, identical sites and none listing the state. If two or three related sites do not provide the place, stop searching.
2	Student projects/WIKI's, other novel content	These frequently appear with the above search, and while perhaps incomplete or of lesser quality, some include the novel's state.
3	Commercial review sites, such as *GoodReads*	A location *may* be stated in a review, but "a small town" is more likely. Although there may be hundreds of reviews, if the first few (1–10) don't identify the state, others likely won't either.
4	Publisher websites	This information is the same as those from online bookstores.
5	Author website, interviews	Novel information is the same as that of online bookstores and publisher sites. However, author interviews *may* reveal the novel's setting.
6	Authorized supplemental material	Authorized supplements, i.e., from publishing houses or the author, are usually reading and discussion guides. Unfortunately, most do not include the state, using "a small town" instead. These are also located separately online, but opening will reroute to a publisher/author site.
7	Unauthorized supplemental material	Unauthorized supplements, i.e., those from anyone posting online, may contain the state setting, but more likely use the familiar "a small town."

LOCATING SETTINGS IN YAL USING PROFESSIONAL ORGANIZATIONS, PROFESSIONALS, JOURNALS, AND COLLEAGUES

Steps	Location	Instruction/Information
1	Professional organizations and journals	NCTE's *The ALAN review, Study & Scrutiny: Research on Young Adult Literature*, and ILA's YALSA are devoted to YAL and publish novel reviews with approximately 60% naming the state setting. *Voice of Youth Advocates* (VOYA), formerly the premier journal for reviews, and ILA's *SIGNAL* have recently ceased publication with the latter's back issues archived.
2	Professional ELA/reading journals	Professional journals from NCTE (*English Journal*), ILA (*Journal of Adolescent and Adult Literacy*) and others will feature longer YAL reviews, but one to three titles per issue. Again, the state is revealed some 60% of the time.
3	Publishing houses	This is a long shot for the daring but calling publishers and requesting speaking with a teen/youth section representative may result in learning a novel's setting.
4	Professional national conventions/conferences	National professional conferences/conventions have multiple offerings devoted to YAL, such as NCTE's two-day (YAL) ALAN Workshop. Obviously, these are hardly convenient resources, but if attending while seeking titles, publishing representatives should be knowledgeable regarding settings, among others.
5	State affiliates and conferences	NCTE and ILA state affiliates have yearly conferences and numerous resources and assistances, all tailored to educators within their state. Those YAL titles having state or region settings are generally highlighted.
6	Regional authors and conferences	Authors publishing regionally or statewide often use their state in novels. Likewise, they frequently speak at affiliate conferences, or their novels represented. There are fewer regional ELA conferences, but these also feature novelists with YAL settings within the region represented.
7	Local/university/state librarians and professors	All librarians and professors working with YAL are recommended for contacts and resources. Librarians are more likely to have information regarding settings; however, unless experts regarding small-town YAL, both they and the professors are generally using the same resources already available.
	Colleagues/administrators and school personnel	Remember to ask colleagues of all subjects and positions about specific title settings, as these are often excellent but overlooked resources.

LOCATING SETTINGS IN YAL USING PARTIAL LOCATION INDICATORS

Steps	Location	Instructions/Information
1	Another distinctive city named	Novels may use a state's larger city for identification, such as *Our town is about half an hour from Las Vegas* or *It's an hour's drive to Dallas*. However, do not rely on these unless obvious (Los Angeles, Denver), as many are shared by states; The World Atlas (2018) reported *Springfield* as name to over 40 U.S. cities/towns, and *Greenville* thirty-plus, among numerous others.
2	Specific landmarks, geographical elements, or historical sites	Geographical and historical landmarks will name a location's state, such as *We live near Mt. Rushmore*, *Most of my family works at Pike's Peak during the summer*, or *Our town's claim to fame is that it's near where William Faulkner lived*. Landmarks such as the Grand Canyon, the Liberty Bell, Plymouth Rock, Niagara Falls, etc. will also identify the state, although some may be in two places (e.g., Niagara Falls is in both the United States and Canada).
3	Nonspecific landmarks, geographical elements, employment	Novels can frequently be narrowed to region, although more difficult (e.g., stating an ocean or coast is near covers multiple places). Still, one can usually identify a novel's region by descriptors and/or employment common to an area such as covered bridges, fall foliage, seafood/fishing/docks, steel/coal, Revolutionary War or Civil War landmarks, prairies, farms/ranches, crops, deep snow, tornadoes, orange or lemon crops, cactus, strawberry or lettuce fields, heat, earthquakes, drought, mountains, wildfires, forests, apple orchards, rain, etc.
4	Southern states	Southern locations are usually easily identified, as settings frequently feature often-used character names (e.g., Miss Lillian, Bobby Ray, Billie Jo, JuneEllen, Earl, etc.) who speak with southern accents, weather, and scenery indicative of the region. Other familiar elements are hanging moss, wisteria, lethargy from the heat and humidity, Civil War sites and statues, cemeteries with elaborate monuments, swamps, or former plantations, crocodiles/alligators. Foods are also descriptive, as sweet potato pie, grits, hush puppies, key lime pie, sweet tea, etc.

REFERENCES

Aronson, M. (2001). *Exploding the myths: The truth about teenagers and reading.* Scarecrow.

Boyd, F. B. (2002). Conditions, concessions, and the many tender mercies of learning through multicultural literature. *Reading Research and Instruction, 42*(1), 58–92.

Carger, C. L. (2003). A pool of reflections: The Américas award. *Book Links, 12*(3), 34–39.

Chew, K. (1997). What does e pluribus unum mean? Reading the classics and multicultural literature together. *The Classical Journal, 93*(1), 55–78.

Collins, S. (2008). *Hunger games.* Scholastic.

DeLeón, L. (2002). Multicultural literature: Reading to develop self-worth. *Multicultural Education, 10*(2), 49–51.

Donovan, E. (2016). Learning the language of home: Using place-based writing practice to help rural students connect to their communities. *Rural Educator, 37*(2), 1–12.

Getting Smart. (February 9, 2017). What is place-based education and why does it matter? https://www.gettingsmart.com/2017/02/what-is-place-based-education/

Gruenewald, D. A. (2003). The best of both worlds: A critical pedagogy of place. *Educational Researcher, 32*(4), 3–12.

Lo, D. E. (2001). Borrowed voices: Using literature to teach global perspectives to middle school students. *The Clearing House, 75*(2), 84–87.

Maguth, B. M., & Hilburn, J. (2011). The community as a learning laboratory: Using place-based education to foster global perspectives. *The Ohio Social Studies Review, 45*(28), 27–34.

Thomas, A. (2017). *The hate u give.* Balzer + Bray.

Chapter 4

Rural Public Education and Diversity Issues

Although curricula and methodology are the same in rural schools as elsewhere, all else is markedly different. They are the community's social hub and main employer and serve as an extended family for its students and personnel. Educators and students are predominantly White, and the smaller the town, the fewer students, with most having three, two, or one school building(s).

RURAL EDUCATOR CHARACTERISTICS

As Whites are predominant in the United States (USCB, 2018) and more so in the UM, the same is true of its educators. National averages showed 80% of teachers as White, then dropping sharply to 7% and 9% for Blacks and Hispanics, respectfully, with Asians 2%, American Indian/Alaskan Natives 1%, Pacific Islanders fewer than 1%, and 2% claiming two or more races. Female educators outnumber males (76%/24%), with the female/male ratio being its highest in elementary schools (89%/11%), and 64%/36% in secondary (NCES, 2021a, 2021b).

While data stating the percentage of rural educators also from this background are not reported, as elsewhere, most have middle-class backgrounds (NCES, 2021a, 2021b). A frequent educator adage is that those taking these positions either specifically sought them or were sole offers and accepted with the intention of leaving as soon as possible. Regardless, all educators graduating from accredited post-secondary institutions have had similar program requirements and coursework; rural educators are created by teaching in rural schools.

RURAL STUDENT CHARACTERISTICS

As stated in Chapter 1, there are far fewer non-Whites in the UM with minority populations widely dispersed. These states had a total of 3,536 incorporated cities/towns (Countryahh.com, 2022a, 2022b), and the 10 most populated were examined, with 12 having all four groups (Asians, Blacks, Hispanics, Native Americans), and 27 with three (Hispanics, Blacks, and Asians). Both Iowa and Minnesota had too few Native Americans in these cities to register (Kolmar, 2020).

The largest minority population for all states is Hispanics, then Blacks, Asians, and Native Americans, although population rankings can be misleading; cities claim three or four minority groups but show percentages of 1% or fewer for several. The UM has 48 Native American reservations with most of these students attending tribal K-12 schools and colleges (Native-Americans.com, n.d.).

GENERAL AND RURAL EDUCATOR SALARIES

Educator salaries vary widely as determined by individual states and depend upon years of service, post-secondary education, and particular district, but the 2020 national average is $64,000, lower in the UM. Teachers in South Dakota average $49,000 yearly, North Dakota and Montana $52,000, Nebraska $55,000, Minnesota $58,000, and Wyoming and Iowa $59,000, ranging from $5,000 to $15,000 less (NCES, 2021c).

However, these numbers are inflated due to also including higher administrator and superintendent salaries. An example is Wyoming's average 2021 salary of $59,000; removing administrator and superintendent pay shows classroom teachers earning from $50,000 to $55,000 yearly, with differences commensurate in all states (Salary.Com, 2021a, 2021b, 2021c).

GENERAL AND RURAL EDUCATOR RETENTION

Educators are exiting, with approximately 16% departing annually, with half leaving the profession and half moving to different schools. Reasons for moving are varied with 2020–2021s COVID-19 pandemic effects still to be seen, but teachers have stated high-stakes testing/assessment, inadequate administrative support, lack of career advancement, and poor facilities before salaries as determiners regarding moving. Those in lower-paying states place more importance on finances (Wang, 2019), but Carver-Thomas (2018),

Carver-Thomas and Darling-Hammond (2017), and Latterman and Steffes (2017) reported rural educators' retention is higher than those urban or suburban, urban highest.

CHARACTERISTICS OF RURAL SCHOOLS

Schools portrayed in the media and YAL are usually suburban or urban, seldom rural, but these adolescents' culture, lifestyle, and social structure are strikingly different and presumably unfamiliar to those non-rural. Urban and suburban districts have multiple schools per grade level (elementary, middle, high), but found only the largest UM cities.

Communities over 50,000 feature more than one school per grade and alternative or other specialized schools, but other than Minnesota and Iowa, these states have one city of 100+, with the next most populated significantly lower. Wyoming has the smallest cities; its largest, Cheyenne, has 65,000, then Casper at 58,000, and then Laramie at 32,000 (World Population Review, 2021a, 2021b, 2021c, 2021d).

Most UM cities have populations far lower than above, with school districts totaling 300 or fewer students. Of these, the largest feature one separate building per grade level, then moving to two buildings (elementary/middle or middle/high school) and usually next to one another, and the smallest one building for all.

Rural schools' social structures and participations are different from urban/suburban ones, and while teens are essentially the same everywhere, schools are not with distinct differences among them, as discussed above. Of course, advantages and disadvantages are determined individually.

Consolidation and Building Concerns

Although many smaller districts are already combined, others still worry of its occurrence once student populations decrease. Naturally, schools need students to remain open and offer quality courses and extracurriculars; a graduating class of three isn't feasible. Merging creates a stronger school, but still devastating to towns.

Even if populations are reasonable, these schools' older, poorer, and smaller communities bring districts less funding, causing ever-present financial concerns, and the smallest towns are often not of interest to legislatures. However, politicians are becoming more attentive to smaller districts, pushing consolidation to lessen costs further (Secondo, 2020). Usually, a new school is constructed near the two towns, or perhaps the larger, better equipped building is remodeled.

Consolidating is unpopular, as students from two schools/towns (often long-time rivals) must now attend one school as a single student body, both losing respective identities and traditions, unwelcome changes from that long familiar. These communities' residents also dislike consolidation, often more than students, having attended the now-disappearing schools. The new school will have a different name, mascot, traditions, and multiple other changes, with resident acceptances tinged with regret.

A crucial concern is continuing employment for both schools' personnel, usually unavailable for all, with the best retained regardless of seniority, bringing resentments and hardships. Those terminated likely face no comparable positions within reasonable commutes, with choices being limited to locations requiring extensive travel or alternative employment, both challenging and stressful with additional expenses on already-lean salaries.

Unsurprisingly, Secondo (2020) and Chavis (2019) found that consolidation does not always improve finances as expected and causes serious losses to both towns. The two most common problems are state governments failing to reallocate additional funds to these districts, thus continuing or creating financial difficulties, and not providing promised long-term support.

Another way to retain rural schools or raise additional funds after consolidation is outsourcing the building, with typical practices housing other educational services (e.g., Head Start, daycare), combining the library and physical education facilities with the town's, serving seniors' meals, and auditoriums for both school and community use. These allow more to utilize the school and contribute to expenses through various fees/rents (Edwards and Longo, 2013; Lambert 2005).

However, such merges necessitate remodeling, additional parking, personnel for managing services, and other numerous and expensive essentials and agreements. Security is paramount with the public inside the building and while daytime access and entrances to classrooms and student areas are restricted, boundaries can be broken. Nighttime activities leave the building vulnerable, but serious difficulties are rare and overall, these are popular and revitalizing.

Rural Educators' Favorable and Unfavorable Aspects of Rural Schools

Rural educators' listing of their worst difficulties faced yearly were summarized (Morton, 2021; Nicosia, 2017; Public Schools First NC, 2021; Showalter et al., 2019; Wang, 2019) with salaries, school finances, facilities, supplies, and professional resources and opportunities continually appearing. Supplies were of strong concern, and although rural educators spend essentially the same amount of their personal income (averaging app. $480.00

yearly) for classroom materials as urban/suburban teachers (Spiegelman, 2018), their lower salaries heighten this total. The below concerns were also identified by the researchers above:

- Multiple preparations/extracurriculars: preparations take equal time regardless of class size, and supervising extracurriculars requires extensive after-hours time with renumeration low.
- Fewer course offerings: basic courses (e.g., 11th English) are taught instead of specialized/advanced ones (e.g., Shakespeare's Plays or American Literature II), and new course development is unlikely with already full student schedules.
- Facilities: rural buildings are generally either modern and reasonably well equipped, or older and poorer with fewer resources and not constructed for contemporary needs. Distant locations have varying technological reception quality, although the COVID-19 2020–2021 pandemic should effect change regarding technological issues in all schools.
- Professional development opportunities: substantial grants and other competitive offerings often require larger populations or other conditions, disqualifying rural educators. Districts far from post-secondary schools are unlikely to supervise pre-service students or otherwise establish ELA partnerships, losing currency exposure. Additionally, aside from Minneapolis, MN, national professional conventions do not meet in the UM due to lacking facilities for 7,000+, hindering attendance.
- Housing: apartments are few and those available are basic with low turnover, rental houses are usually older and expensive overall. Beginning single educators unable or unready for home purchase are at a disadvantage regarding lodging.
- Alternative schooling: charter, home, and online schooling are growing (the effect of 2020–2021's COVID-19 pandemic and virtual classrooms is yet undetermined). Non-public school students make significant dents in smaller populations, notably lowering funding received. Lawsuits regarding their public-school athletic participation are contentious with states' passage varying (Richard, 2021). Other extracurriculars (e.g., orchestra, band) and services are also contested, all causing community strife.
- Poverty: rural areas usually have many underserved students and families, their situations hindering educational progress and opportunities. While assistance is attempted by lunch/breakfast programs, coat/clothing/supply drives, or food pantries, needs reman substantial.
- Medical care: there are fewer medical professionals (i.e., having terminal degrees) meaning drives for other than routine care. Generally, only the largest cities offer specialists (e.g., neurologists, oncologists),

although some service small towns through scheduled outreach. Serious conditions require ambulance/air transports, with alternative medicine and like services usually only in largest cities.

Naturally, these, and more, all directly affect the hiring and retention of quality educators and their later satisfaction. Populations must rise for resources, but towns of 1,000 will not gain the thousands needed for expanded services; unfortunately, the difficulties cited above are essentially without feasible solutions and must be accepted as part of the rural lifestyle.

Of course, the benefits of teaching in a rural school are also significant, and as with the negatives, those below are repeated throughout research and rural educator commentary (Forbes, 2015; Hamblin, 2018; Lawrence-Turner, 2015; The Miles Foundation, 2016; Showalter et al., 2019):

- Community: schools are the town's social center, with residents enthusiastically participating in and attending events/activities.
- Demographics: rural teachers are underrepresented at national professional conferences and other activities; those writing presentation proposals, for example, should receive acceptance. Likewise, students are least represented in Ivy League institutions (Ivy Coach, 2020), with admittance, often with financial aid, highly likely.
- Educator support and students: classes are small; teaching is professional, yet friendly. Students are proud of their school, desire to excel, and usually have multiple responsibilities and strong work ethics. Management issues are typically mild with parents valuing and supporting educators.
- Networking: if needing assistance or information, multiple people are eager to help; as above, colleagues find housing for most new educators. News travels quickly with teachers informed immediately regarding that affecting the school (e.g., a parent's debilitating accident). Teachers also strive to correct various misinformation regarding such occurrences.
- Safety: rural areas have little to no violent crime, but none are immune; residents are not naïve and take reasonable precautions. Those of all ages assist one another, as several will offer one walking a ride, or someone struggling to load purchases in their car soon noticed. All watch children and teens; parents of a child truant or otherwise inappropriately engaged will receive calls.

All the above may be negatives, positives, or yet undecided by beginning educators, but one must experience the rural lifestyle before such decisions are changed or made.

DIVERSITY EDUCATION

Authentic diversity education begins with students learning about others unlike them and is more than simply incorporating texts by and about people of color, various cultural identities, or other minorities. Whatever we wish *learned* must be *taught*, with knowledge and understanding emerging by subsequent, continual discussion of the issues and concerns of those presented and their application/connection to community, U.S. society, and past and current world events.

Rural Educators and ELA/Diversity Education

Rural ELA educators have the same, or equivalent, qualifications, follow necessary accreditation requirements and national mandates, and have the same responsibilities as those elsewhere. Likewise, their ELA textbooks, lessons, units, and teaching materials doubtless mirror those from any other classroom regardless of location.

These educators are also understanding of diversity issues and their importance, knowing if desiring students to graduate as caring citizens able to function in contemporary society, learning of and interacting with others dissimilar is necessary. They also realize students are as aware of diversity issues as others elsewhere, but unlike others, their state's majority population (including the largest cities) are White.

Further, their students are supported by homogenous family, peers, and community with personal extended experiences and friendships with minorities, racial or otherwise, virtually nonexistent. Aside from those with exceptionalities and in special education (EXCP) or out LGBTQ+ (lesbian, gay, bisexual, transgender, queer/questioning, etc.) students, most have never personally experienced others' antipathy, hatred, or violence toward them for being different, and as minorities are largely absent from their lives, they also haven't witnessed such hostility.

These students don't know what it's like to be different because they aren't, and as true understanding of diversity cannot occur without such experiences, educators must find different methods for meaningful instruction. While minorities may be absent from these activities, they can be effective and provide the strong foundation needed for knowledgeable, accommodating adults.

Educator and Community Bias Regarding Diversity

Rural educators are no more or less biased than those elsewhere; Starck et al. (2020) compared teachers' explicit and implicit biases with those of other American adults and found no statistical difference. However, Steckelberg (1999) studied rural UM educators and socioeconomic biases, finding, although stating all students were treated the same, biases existed. Essentially, teachers assisted middle-class students most under the general presumption they would need the most support, financial and otherwise, to attend post-secondary schools.

Those having an upper and lower socioeconomic status were given less attention; upper by believing finances ample for needs and lower from deeming incomes inadequate for more education or family history of additional education uncommon.

Regarding communities, the Pew Research Center national study (2018) reported most Americans primarily interacted with those sharing their same race, social class, or political party. However, those stating living among others racially or ethnically diverse as particularly important was 22% (rural 17%, suburban 22%, and urban 30%).

Likewise, respondents reporting being with those having different religious views as high importance was lower, 11% agreeing (rural 13%, suburban 9%, and urban 12%), and lowest was strong value of relationships with others of varying political views at 8% (rural 6%, suburban 8%, and urban 10%). Essentially, people want the same kinds of communities regardless of location, which may or may not be considered biased, but does indicate living among diversities is itself a minority desire.

Rural White Students and Diversity
Education's Importance

However, knowing the importance of such education doesn't necessarily mean implementation, successful or otherwise; not all rural educators, administrators, or parents may see the value of stronger classroom diversity focus when there are no minorities in the community or school. Moreover, worry of embarrassment or awkwardness regarding discussion when having only a few scattered minorities within a school also invites neglecting diversity issues.

Of course, doing so impedes students' knowledge, attitudes, and practices, both immediately and future, along with making inaccurate assumptions regarding school populations. Exemption fails to account for students relocating before or after graduation, neglects consideration for eventual living and working in areas with multiple diversities or neglects the reality of those returning to hometowns with minority partners, spouses, or blended families.

Another omitted reality is demographics change, sometimes occurring quickly or unexpectedly. Some UM cities are drawing or recruiting those racially or culturally different for various employments (e.g., North Dakota's pipeline, meatpacking plants in multiple states, etc.) with residents needing preparation for newcomers.

Additional situations doubtless overlooked are area individuals, especially students, embarking on vacations, church missions, exchange programs, semesters abroad, internships, and other travels elsewhere. Teens living in locations featuring minority residents or visitors usually have some experience or awareness of those different, but these are few. If they are not providing all students with knowledge of others, then they can only compare another group solely to their own (of course, rural lifestyles are also minority ones), causing erroneous, and often negative, views.

Such information will assist in determining if experiences with others will be enjoyable and enriching or resulting in greater intolerance from incorrect presumptions, pre-existing stereotypes, and other misinformation.

Regardless of where UM adolescents travel or live, interaction with those different seems inevitable; what is not so assured is whether individuals possess the awareness and skills for successful experiences, including being a positive representative of their hometown or state. While one cannot prepare students for every lifestyle difference, general unawareness seems unlikely to produce positive encounters.

Technology and Diversity Education

Technology, especially computers, smartphones, the Internet, and various forms of social media, have made diversity and its issues available to all adolescents. It is also an increasingly valuable equalizer for rural teens in allowing them opportunities for various interactions with those different from them, otherwise inaccessible in small towns.

Of course, believing rural teens having commensurate awareness, knowledge, and/or appreciation of diversity issues as those elsewhere from technology/media is naïve. Further, it can be presumed that any teen, including those rural, is not using such devices to educate themselves regarding diversity although time spent on the subject will contribute to knowledge.

Technology is *a*, not *the*, source for view/belief formations regarding diversity and all other issues, and its massive information offerings cannot all be considered of quality. Teens could just as easily be viewing negative, inaccurate, biased, stereotyped, and/or unrealistic portrayals as those positive and accurate, or nothing related to diversity at all.

Regardless, knowledge of diversity issues from numerous sources including technology and media is helpful, but *combining viewing with classroom instruction is vital* if without direct access to minorities. Teens everywhere need assistance understanding the myriad of information and experiences, and its many facets (biases, opinions, facts) acquired for them to recognize, and later access, accurate information, and most importantly, direction in developing knowledge and a healthy respect regarding those different from themselves.

Societal Controversies Regarding Diversity

Diversities and their many elements and issues (e.g., #Black Lives Matter, Critical Race Theory, Cancel Culture, White Privilege, Immigration, Women's Rights, LGBTQ+, and especially Transgender discrimination, etc.) are moving from simmering to boiling across the country. Shocking portrayals of violence, brutality, and hatred continually appear on phones, televisions, cinema, video games, and more personally in communities, schools, and homes.

Written materials, campaign platforms and speeches, state bills, legislation, proclamations, individual stands and more, abound. Some are stated euphemistically, others baldly asserting justice, individual rights, or protection, yet likely thwarting others' rights and opportunities. These are also seeming ever-present, creating individuals' deeper confusion, enmity, and divisions.

Responsibilities Regarding Diversity Education

The responsibility to protect all children in our lives, not just our own or those like ours, belongs to every adult in the community, and as educators we are responsible for discussing diversity issues with teens and modeling tolerance and dignity toward those different. Diversity education, for students and adults, is vital in the UM, as it houses so few racial minorities, even in its largest cities.

Students must learn about and from those different, for understanding, tolerance, and acceptance, but without minorities in their communities and classrooms, profitable conversations are difficult. However, context can be reasonably substituted by using YAL with like issues and considering character situations and actions during classroom discussions.

Adults should model kindness and empathy, protecting and defending students from harassment and discriminatory actions. Unfortunately, both adults and students often treat diverse teens cruelly in and out of school, with home not always offering comfort if parents are also wary of the community, themselves victimized, or fearing being targeted. Reading and discussing such situations (see suggested YAL titles in Appendix D) allows relief of recognizing another's similar life, or uncomfortably noting privilege.

Although many students are denigrated for appearance (e.g., weight, height, glasses, braces), these are shorter-term issues; braces are removed, or contacts replace glasses. This taunting does not lessen the pain of being targeted for race/ethnicity, both permanent, with novel characters' learning to solve or ease the problems, providing hope and advice.

We must talk with students and share the times diversity has been an issue; the things we do not understand; issues that anger us or of which we are unsure; our worries, frustrations, fears, and biases; situations where we should have acted but did not; issues where our opinions have changed; and events of which we are long ashamed and similarly ask the same of them. Such personal admissions are difficult for anyone, but characters voicing similar concerns creates commonality and invites honesty.

Students must experience adults' persistence in encouraging them to tell their stories and validating when shared. They need to fathom that failing to express themselves allows others speaking for them and its repercussions, illustrated far more disturbingly in novels than discussion. We must honestly and accurately discuss that, while sometimes difficult to recognize, discrimination lurks everywhere, and it is everyone's job to recognize its presence and fight against it each day, also demonstrated by novel characters.

Adults and students must acknowledge racism is entrenched in laws and institutions, and treatments toward others may be different from race, religion, age, gender, sexuality, wealth, appearance, and more rather than actions or behaviors. Teens should already contribute personal instances here, with far more experienced by characters like them. We cannot continue hiding who we are from fearing repercussions and demonstrate that treating others respectfully is not sharing or condoning their views, actions, beliefs, or lifestyle, only kindness, also widely shown in YAL.

Adults and students must also realize and reflect upon how history cannot be altered but moving forward is possible and dependent upon recognizing and admitting past and present injustices without repeating them. Further, it needs to be stressed that trust must exist on both sides in conversations, with productive beginnings considering the small but significant things anyone can do to narrow gaps between themselves and others.

This is hardly simple; multiple discussions will be needed over time, and they will be uncomfortable, painful, hurtful, embarrassing, and challenging before purposeful or rewarding. Still, there are multiple like instances in YAL, showing productive conversations and easing fears of beginning them.

We must speak and act in ways that are respectful, fair, and dignified toward ourselves and others, and understand we may be vilified, lose friendships, anger family, or no be longer welcome in places or events long frequented by doing so. Students should be challenged to become unpopular for what is right and ponder the value of esteem from those discriminating; this too, is repeatedly featured in YAL.

Talking must continue even if frustration and disagreements have built seemingly unbreakable barriers, because if something can be formed it can also be dismantled, rearranged, or otherwise changed with desire and effort and persistence. We can no longer afford to contend race being separate provenances of only those Black, Latinx, Asian, among others; it is about humanity. In tandem, YAL depicts the distinct issues of all minorities, and the power resulting from unification in demanding change.

In tandem, Snow's commitment reminder (2019) stated trends are defined by distinct, generally short, time periods, in which items/issues have predominance until waning. To become a successful movement, issues cannot be one group's sole responsibility. Instead, its members (and we as adults) must maintain continual leadership and support along with sustained validation/involvement from all others for continued success.

Although YAL features rural schools, most are generic portrayals without many of the specific topics (e.g., salaries, educator dislikes) above. Diversity issues, however, permeate novels, unlike classrooms. Some UM educators would benefit from reconsidering the issues and values of incorporating more diversity instruction, such as using one of the myriad examples for determining one's level of White privilege from the Internet and adapting to rural adults.

Educators could then discuss of ideas/practices helpful to themselves and adult residents wishing to create a more inclusive community is also included. These should be modeled by educators and slowly integrating into the community in ways most helpful to individual towns.

YAL LITERATURE PORTRAYING ATHLETICS AND SMALL-TOWN LIFESTYLES

Athletic-themed YAL is especially prominent, with three plots often depicted: winning a university/college scholarship to escape a hometown, a championship game win necessary to bolster the town's dying economy, or a star player committed to playing in an important game with hidden injuries, usually a concussion.

As with all novels, more than one plotline exists, but novels involving athletics/sports all corresponding to Discussion Question 4, Athletics and Pride (not continually repeated below; see Table 4.1). Others represented are extensions of Questions 1 and 2, determining whether to remain in town or leave as quickly as possible after graduation, and 3, 5, 7–8, Economy/Financial Issues, nearly always lacking in smaller areas. Minority Issues are seen by Questions 6 and 9, with Question 10 considering the ample Resident/Community Support, all central to such areas and individual towns' specific challenges.

Female athletes on male teams are seen (Questions 3, 5–10 for these three titles) more frequently as Michigan in Allen's (2019) *Michigan vs. the Boys*.

After her school cuts her female hockey team, she tries out for the males' team, winning a spot. This is not to everyone's liking, regardless of her skill, and Michigan must decide if dealing with various derisions and comments are worth remaining on the team.

Holland's situation is similar, as seen in Biren's (2019) *Cold Day in the Sun*. She's already on the male team and a star player. When their team is selected for an important televised game, the media attention naturally goes to her, the sole female, to her discomfort and others' active disagreement, causing prejudices to surface or heighten regarding females on male teams.

Liv is a star softball player, but after a bad decision she loses her scholarship and transfers to another school. Now, she must convince the coach to put her on the team in Henning's (2020) *Throw Like a Girl*, with her future as a college softball player (also Question 1) on the line.

Readers might consider why females are such a threat to male teams and why targeted, or worse, and especially if star players, contributing to wins. Is the view of males on male teams so inherent we cannot accept females, and what does this mean? And may females be on male teams as long as they are largely invisible or essentially mediocre players, becoming unacceptable if outscoring or otherwise more skilled than males?

Must females be second to males in all ways, never equal or better? Why are male accomplishments celebrated, but not a female's? All of these views permeate the school and community; what do they mean or imply, and how may they be changed, with females and non-team members having a clear view of what it's like being a definite minority, allowing consideration of how such second-class status can be changed by both students and educators.

As for Liv, males also make mistakes, and she has paid deeply and learned from her actions. It would be reasonable for any coach to question to behavior and commitment, but her reputation as a star player would also be well known, and coaches like to win. Would a male in her situation have to beg the coach for a team spot? Readers can also evaluate their own school teams regarding its past or present athletes and consider the differences between males and females. Again, what changes are needed? What can students and educators do to effect them?

Females have the dubious last say in the following two novels, also reflecting Questions 6 and 9, first in Allen's (2015) *The Revenge Playbook*, in which a group of females are tired of their school's preferential treatment of the football team, all males. They are equally disgusted with these males' attitude (especially treating females badly) and other boorish actions, but essentially without consequence, unlike any other student doing the same. The girls decide to teach the team a lesson by sneaking into their annual scavenger hunt, secretly playing, and winning the contest.

Abby, in Barry's (2020) *We Ride Upon Sticks*, is captain of her school's field hockey team and descended from an infamous Salem witch accuser. The team is losing and she's desperate to advance to finals, so her team attempts summoning the former witches' dark powers for some wins.

Readers can discuss attitudes, behaviors, and often-veneration of males on teams; what advantages are given to them, and is this right, and how is it helpful? Their corresponding attitude of being above all rules is disturbing, certainly contributing to negative treatment of females and society's current rape culture. Why is this allowed by educators, and is winning so important that all is excused? The glory of wins will fade, but what about attitudes toward women? Females and those not on teams again have a view of being a minority, and how can they and educators assist others?

It should also be noted that females surreptitiously entered the scavenger contest, playing in secret until their surprise win; another example of females having to hide their intelligence and ability. Added consideration is females playing the complete contest without male notice; what does this imply? Further, will this game see any long-lasting changes, or simply an amusement with the next school year exactly the same as before, and what does this mean?

For Abby, the connection between witches and females should be made, frequently an epithet for them (warlocks, or male witches, seemingly absent from most literature), and long-ago women seen as witches ultimately receiving punishment from men, again secondary as well as a discounted minority. How can students and educators, both male and female, effect change, and is it desired? If not, what does this mean?

Still, the novel is a humorous one, not necessarily implying the above, with students also discussing expectations of both male and female teams, both in society and their schools, regarding winning, and the feeling of failing their town if having a losing season or failing in a championship game (Question 10).

Athletes, male and female, can share how they cope with losing streaks and other important losses, and many have rituals before playing; sharing these would be interesting and entertaining, as well as determining effectiveness. They could also be compared to those of famous athletes or former athletes from individual schools. What other rituals do students have, such as before taking an exam, giving a speech, participating in a play or debate, or another high-pressure situation?

Football and other sport injuries, especially concussions, along with steroid and other illegal drug use, also severely damaging, are receiving attention in YAL and society; the novels below corresponding with Questions 1, 3, 5, 7–8, and 10. Hughes's (2005) *Open Ice* is a familiar story, with hockey long Nick's passion. After a massive concussion, he was told continued play could risk his future, even his life, but as he feels he's nothing without hockey, he intends to play, regardless.

Klass and Klass's (2013) *Second Impact* views injuries somewhat differently, as Jerry is his school's quarterback in a football town. Then Carla, a sports reporter for the school paper, recruits him to co-author a blog chronicling the season from each of their perspectives. After Jerry's teammate is hurt, Carla writes questioning whether game injuries are too high a price for high school students, an unwelcome question causing much controversy and negativity.

Herbach's (2019) *Cracking the Bell* portrays Isaiah, a troubled teen whose life was positively changed by football. A scholarship is the only way he can attend college, but after a dangerous concussion he must decide whether to continue risking his life by playing. Similarly, steroids are seen in McKissack's (2009) *Shooting Star*, with Jerry already a talented athlete but taking pills to become an even better player. While his game does improve, his life soon begins spinning out of control.

Potter's (2010) *Exit Strategy* sees best friends Tank and Zach; Zach plays football, while Tank is a wrestler. Tank is taking steroids, pushed by his coach, and Zach must find a way to help him and stop the school's new drug program, risking both himself and his school.

The damages of concussions, other injuries, and steroids can be discussed by students, with likewise considering their occurrence and danger in their own teams. There are multiple factors for consideration, as teens feeling a sense of invincibility, coaches downplaying injuries, and the fact of scholarships the only way to attend college, something desperately wanted.

Scholarships should also be considered, especially through race and class; how athletics, like the military, is the only way to college for many, notably those underserved and of color. Teens receiving athletic scholarships are often overwhelmed by their contracts and perks, unable to satisfactorily manage coursework, injured, or otherwise cut from the team, all lesser advertised, and certainly worth discussion.

Further, coaches may be unaware of teens using steroids or other enhancements, their incorrect use, or even severity of concussions or other injuries. Teen perspectives are more limited than adults,' not necessarily understanding the very real consequences of playing against a doctors' orders, or that injury or death could result.

Still, athletic achievement is definitely prized in small towns, especially among adults, teens, and communities hungry for winning, with teams and individual players carrying the hopes of their community on their shoulders. Many such towns have gone 10, 15, 20, or more years without a championship season; players on winning teams will do anything to avoid not playing or disappointing their town or school.

Considering whether female athletes also face these same issues should be explored (or are they not seen as important as males, even if bringing a championship) and what this implies is also important. The deciding factors regarding these issues, who decides, and whether they are same for all are additional discussion points well worth attention.

Likewise, ethical questions regarding use and additional illegal enhancements of any kind and winning, or being discovered, sometimes years later in professional sports (especially the Olympics) can be considered, all relating to rural teams. These are all difficult conversations, with the added benefit and hindrance of school/community/church, the town's social structure, and what this means and/or implies included in the above questions.

Teens involved in dangerous or illegal situations in the pursuit of winning are also plentiful, and contributing to Questions 1, 3, 5–6, and 7–9, as Eddie from Connelly's (2019) *Brawler*. He's a wrestler with an abusive father and having anger issues himself. His senior year brings an undefeated season, but his temper flames and he attacks a referee and then runs to avoid the consequences. Eddie is now dodging the law and involved in the seamy wrestling underworld, desperately wanting out but unsure how.

Deuker's (2020) *Golden Arm* is related, with Lazarus's baseball team disbanding but he's given the chance to pitch for an exclusive school, aspiring to the major leagues. A definite problem is interference from his drug-dealing brother, ruining his chances (although his name indicates otherwise) and his own stuttering also not a positive attribute.

Similarly, Trace from Weaver's (2009) *Super Stock Rookie* is thrilled to be a paid super stock driver while still in high school, but he dislikes the time spent and not seeing his friends as often. Once becoming immersed, Trace begins seeing signs his sponsor isn't legitimate, but he's too involved to simply leave and unsure of what to do.

Students can consider how easily teens can become entangled in illegal activities or sports and its contributors, as the desire to win, unsophistication, need of money, and lack of parental or educational adult involvement. Outfits as joined by Trace, above, are frequent in small towns, these organizations relying on the above factors and seeking those teens best fitting them.

Scholarship recruiters are similar in some ways, enticing teens with perks and promises, athletes too starry-eyed to consider their chances of playing in the major leagues, the possibility of injury, or whether able to earn a degree. Regardless, once such students realize illegalities, leaving is not always an option. All of the former premises may be discussed by students, and of any such organizations near them (if suitable to the classroom; students can always discuss with educators privately), including their warning signs.

As for Eddie, his family situation is doubtless known, but if not, his temper is. How can students or teammates assist or otherwise intercede before a life-altering situation occurs? Of course, this may be extended to all students, with another speculation regarding how these situations would apply to females, and accounting for differences.

Novels showing athletics to save a sinking town's economy end happily, not so in real life, but are plentiful and hopeful reads, reflecting Questions 1, 3, 5, and 7–8. All games are heavily attended in small towns as other extracurricular activities, and state championships doubly so. Teams advertise and fundraise throughout the season, the entire community involved and businesses providing additional perks for those playing or attending, all meaning a surprising amount of additional funding, regardless of outcome.

While towns can't change a hopelessly negatively economy by a championship season or be involved in once-in-a-lifetime situations, there's always the possibility of them, the extra funding is helpful, and who doesn't like good underdog stories?

Lupica's (2009) *Million Dollar Throw* features Nick, who's troubled by his town's sinking economy. When getting a chance to win a million dollars if he can complete a pass during the halftime of a Patriot's game, he's thrilled. Of course, once becoming reality and realizing what the money could mean for his town, he's paralyzed by the pressure of making the throw.

Kester's (2019) *Gut Check* shows Wyatt, his coastal fishing town's economy and family devastated by Red Tide. His older brother, Brett, is the team's star quarterback, and this year he also made the team. They've gained national attention from their wins and Red Tide, with the upcoming championship a chance for winning some desperately needed prize money.

Wyatt is the only one who knows Brett suffered a serious concussion right before the game and it would be dangerous to play, but he intends to, regardless, as too much at stake. Wyatt must decide whether to tell others about Brett and presumably forfeit the needed funds or allow him to play at a terrible risk.

Here, readers could consider that such wins saving economies occur in books, not real life, unless extraordinary circumstances, and relay any games that might have been somewhat similar. Another topic is why athletics are continually chosen to save towns; what about debate, drama, orchestra, or any extracurricular other than sports? Is our culture and society only interested in male sports teams, and what does this imply?

A major question is the burdens placed on teens for saving their town, and how adults can allow this in good conscience. Further, another question is the preparations that have been made for a loss, as any player would be devastated by one. How does the community handle a last-minute fumble or other action by a player, losing the game? What are the effects of such a loss on the teen, whose bad play was doubtlessly common during the season among many, unfortunately made when tensions are already outstanding? How can the community and others mitigate negative reactions?

Also considered is the emphasis upon winning in general, how students are treated afterwards, win or lose, and why isn't there more emphasis placed upon losing? Aside from these generally mythical games, winning is so often seen as the only acceptable outcome, but what are the attributes of those losing, especially doing so gracefully? What lessons and more are learned by these teams, and are they far more important than those winning? What does it imply that winners are given the praise and positive attention and losers are given the opposite? And, regarding professional teams, how many people remember winning teams from past years?

Family and school problems also frequently accompany athletes, addressing Questions 1 and 10, with Bo from Crutcher's (1995) *Ironman* seeing his intense anger at his father becoming rage and subsequent relegation to Anger Management sessions. Fellow classmates are a diverse group (also Questions 6 and 9) with problems of their own. They spur and support his entering a triathlon, with all progressing throughout the year (this title also features an older mentor).

Chess, rather than football, is seen by brothers Zeke and Randy playing against one another in a tournament while also trying to manage their father's over-the-top, close-to-maniacal competitiveness, previously unknown, in Wallace's (2009) *Perpetual Check*. Shenice has a different problem in Stone's (2021) *Fast Pitch*: she's her softball team's captain and upon uncovering a family mystery during the season must decide how far to investigate if doing so will clear past family wrongs, even if it receives negative community reactions.

Students can discuss family and parental presence or absence at games and reactions, especially as extended family members generally attend small town games, regardless of whether related to players. Noted can be sharing too embarrassing or controlling behaviors, and whether such extreme competitiveness is worse than no family attending at all.

Additional exploration (although sensitive and couched carefully in class) is of class/race issues, as it takes money and time to attend and play; who are those *not* involved in athletics or not attending games, especially during the summer, and why? Not all have the funds necessary for equipment, uniforms, and other necessities, with those working not always able to take time to attend daytime games, or even evening ones. Is there a way to assist those would like to play, but cannot due to financial limitations?

Friendships suffer too during sports, relating to Questions 1, 3, 5, and 7–8, as seen with Ben and Al in Wallace's (1996) *Wrestling Sturbridge*. Ben is stuck in his rust belt town, destined to work in a factory, the same as his father. Worse, he's relegated to the bench, watching his best friend Al's team becoming state champions.

He decides he can't allow the next wrestling season to pass without challenging Al, so he becomes a serious competitor, and when they are both up for the one, and only, scholarship, many challenges appear. Bones, seen in Wallace's (1997) *Shots on Goal*, has a similar problem, as while he reaches his goal of the soccer team winning the league championship, he must now manage his best friend's resentment. This is made worse by his having a crush on his friend's girlfriend.

Readers can consider how friendships survive competitions, especially life-changing ones, as scholarships or other awards, and how does one win or lose graciously, handling either outcome? What suggestions and stories can readers share? What are some past examples from games and like situations from their school's history, and how were they resolved? If not, how could they have been? And is it just as painful to win as it is to lose, and why/how?

Some minority athletes don't always fare well, relating to Questions 6 and 9, as shown in Buford's (2021) *Kneel*, depicting Black football star Russel protesting an unfair arrest and suspension of a friend by taking a knee during the anthem. He instantly becomes the target of fear and hate in both his school and town, more so than his friend, needing support.

Tingle's (2018) *Trust Your Name*, features Bobby, a Choctaw Native American on his White school's basketball team. He faces much discrimination but always plays cleanly. When asked to form an all–Native American summer league, he's suddenly framed for a robbery at an away game, and now facing his most serious challenge.

Padian's (2013) *Out of Nowhere* illustrates Somali refugees joining Tom's community, hardly this town's desire of being suddenly full of African Muslims. However, when several males join the team, their great plays launching a winning season, Tom and others begin to reconsider their divisive actions and opinions.

A basketball team coach is the protagonist in West's (2011) *Blind Your Ponies*, his team in tiny Willow Creek having had ninety-three losses in a row with the school board planning to disband the team. Everything changes when a 6'11" (White) student arrives, giving the team new life and the entire town dreaming of a winning season, or simply a win.

Readers can discuss minority treatment (including Russel's friend's suspension and better treatment when winning); double standards (the White student was exalted, unlike the Somali males); ethics (Did the Somali males meet requirements to play?); and the overall theme of wanting these students elsewhere, until winning, and then not really being accepted by the school or town. White students can also express concerns over feeling their only worth to a school or peers is through their athletic prowess, and how can this be altered? More importantly, why is this view held, and is it accurate?

It should also be noticed no mention is made of academics; granted, these books are about sports, but are minorities only valued to a school if having athletic talent rather than academic? What do these reactions mean, say about us, and how they may be improved or prevented?

Obviously, this may be a delicate discussion if minority students are present, but their voices should be heard, their views presumably somewhat different from White classmates, depending upon individual school and students. All voices must be heard for any kind of change.

Competitions for different prizes than saving the economy are also seen, representing Questions 1 and 10, with David in Hautman's (2017) *Slider* a competitive eater on the amateur level. After a mix-up with his mother's credit card, he finds himself inadvertently entered in a professional eating contest, and now must train for a major competition.

The small town of Carp has an annual tradition in Oliver's (2014) *Panic*, in which each summer graduated seniors play a survival contest with one winner getting the pot. This year the winnings amount to $67,000, and as the money is the only way that most of the seniors will be able to leave town for college or another opportunity, the contests become increasingly more dangerous to players.

Aside from the ethics of each above, readers can also ponder the continual portrayal of sports scholarships as the only way for teens to leave town for college, with most desperate to do so. Is this representation accurate, why, and what does it say about small towns and its residents? What other opportunities exist for students to attend college, and what about academic scholarships?

Are students aware of the many, often quirky, scholarships and grants available, those found through the Internet? These could certainly be discovered, along with scholarships offered through corporations; those in town businesses could see what home offices are offering and discuss with teachers and students.

Further, how can readers assist in making their town more attractive or welcoming, and why do most students wish to leave? These reasons could be explored, along with practicality; it's one thing to state wanting more excitement, restaurants, shows, nightlife, and so on, and it's another to realize attendance for most is rare due to time, expense, and so on. Adults or others who have lived in larger places could describe and discuss different lifestyles with students, who don't yet understand living in one place is much the same as any other, various attributes being special occasions rather than daily events.

Teens surprised by sports and matching Question 1 include Zeb in Monninger's (2017) *Game Change*, who likes his town and working in his uncle's auto repair shop. He's on the football team, but he rarely plays until the star quarterback is injured and he must substitute in the state championship game. He discovers unrecognized talent and after meeting with a college recruiter, realizes he could have a different future than what he had expected.

Derrick plays basketball in Waltman's (2014) *Slump* (also Question 10), and during his sophomore year, he can't seem to play well, with his life also beginning to spiral downward. He eventually discovers there's more to life than basketball, this new attitude adjustment not particularly helpful to his team as they face an upcoming game with their archrivals.

Readers can again discuss sports being the only way for teens to leave town, and whether doing so is the right decision for Zeb, being content and happy where he is. Does the opportunity to leave town mean one must do so, and is it the right decision for most, as portrayed in novels?

The realism of this story and *Slump* can also be challenged and whether Derrick would really let his team down because being an athlete isn't his most important goal. Likewise, so many sports stories show teens as wanting to be professional athletes. How true is this desire among readers? Or, how many want to become college players, and how many would rather focus on another aspect of higher education, leaving sports to intramurals or other casual participation?

And, finally, there are scores of more whimsical athletic titles (*We Ride Upon Sticks* is also here), fitting Questions 1 and 10, with Scaletta's (2009) *Mudville* portraying a town that lost a fateful baseball game against their archrivals and subsequently saw rain for twenty-two years. Now Roy, his friends, and foster brother are determined to create a team that will defeat their rivals and finally break the rain curse.

Weaver's (2008) *Saturday Night Dirt* features (also Questions 6 and 9) one day at the Headwaters Speedway track, during noon, 3:00, 6:00, and 9:00 p.m. Each time period depicts the varied and colorful characters on the dirt-circle track there on that particular day.

Readers could imagine different formulas for stopping rain or living under such circumstances and perhaps past exceptional, strange, or unique teammates and games from their town, or others nearby. They could also imagine a day in any facility like the Speedway, or simply their gym or ballpark: Who was there during different years, and where are they now? Who are those athletes with names on plaques outside the gym? Has anyone even read them? As above, who are they, what were their accomplishments, and where are they now?

Athletic YAL also ties students more closely to their school and classmates, allowing their peering further toward the past and discovering who came before them, also recognizing that they will soon be joining those who came earlier. Regarding athletics, what do they wish to accomplish before leaving? For what do they wish to be remembered? Responses should be compared and contrasted, noting similarities and differences, from whom, and why. How may students be assisted regarding their goals?

YOUNG ADULT LITERATURE PORTRAYING RURAL TEENS' LIFESTYLES

Teens need to read of themselves and their daily lives, and for most novels with a rural setting the same refrain of the town being stultifying, nothing to do in the present and no hope for a future, and/or a place where everyone's favorite pastime is gossiping about others, there is no privacy. It's difficult to promote the positives of being rural when not seen in many novels and protagonists having one foot out the door to a larger place. Still, this isn't true of all, and some novels beginning with teens ready to leave end with their remaining, happier than ever.

Like those novels centering on athletics, above, these also follow the same broad extension of Discussion Questions of 1, remaining/staying in one's hometown; 2, school life; 4, athletics; 3, 5, and 7–8, economics; 6, 9, minority issues; and 10, the community. Further, as all these titles relate to Questions 1, 2, and 10 (as with the athletic novels above representing Question 4), these won't be continually repeated in novel summaries.

Romance is naturally present, with Kate from Albertalli's (2021) *Kate in Waiting* being thrilled to land a lead role in the play next to Matt, the handsome newcomer. She and her best friend both have a crush on him, but she hasn't considered what'll happen to their friendship if he becomes involved with one of them.

A teen with too much romance is Brooks in Bloom's (2016) *The Stand-In*, a senior needing money for college (also Questions 3, 5, 7–8). After doing a favor for a friend by taking his cousin to a party, calls begin pouring in and he becomes a date for girls without one, cutting into his study time. As the calls continue, he's soon making enough money to reconsider leaving for college at all.

Becca and Brett, seen in Light's (2020) *The Upside of Falling*, are both without relationships. Becca is taunted by her former best friend and says she has a boyfriend without naming him. Brett is the football team captain but is more focused on his future than dating. He happens to overhear Becca's conversation and offers to be her mystery guy, taking the heat from him as well. Acting like a couple without knowing one another is difficult, until they realize their fauxmance is real.

Sophie works for the local florist, likes her job, and attends most local weddings and other events while working on art school sketches for highly anticipated college in West's (2019) *Maybe This Time*. After Andrew, son of the new chef, appears, she has no time for him, but as he's at the same functions he and her job become increasingly appealing, with Sophie wondering if art school is still her goal.

Likewise, with Penny from Gibaldi's (2018) *This Tiny Perfect World* loves her life and town (also Questions 3 and 5–10) and having her future planned. Still, after receiving an unexpected prestigious theater camp scholarship, begins reconsidering her plans and whether the future she had imagined is still the best choice.

Readers can discuss which aspects of these novels are realistic, such as Brett being his football team captain but without interest in dating, and why, and compare to their experiences, or others.' The unexpected also appears: With scholarships and handsome, talented newcomers, how likely are these arrivals? What does romance mean now, as opposed to middle school (or in parents' or grandparents' time), and what are some cultural or religious differences? Are there any major aspects that aren't universal?

YAL portrays many teens in competitions (also Question 10), as Ellie from Bauer's (2000) *Squashed*, the first teen entrant in the fair's pumpkin contest. She's working hard for her pumpkin to reach 300+ pounds (and her losing 20) while watching for tricks from the competition, her wily older neighbor, long the champion and with no attention of relinquishing his title.

Similarly, Creech's (2016) *Moo: A Novel* (also Question 10) shows Reena's family moving to a small town, with life becoming good, especially Reena's attachment to an incredibly ornery cow and its similar owner, who teaches her how to train it for showing and life in general (another mentor figure). Reena grows considerably over the summer, culminating by her eventually showing the cow only she can manage at the fair.

Mejia and McLemore's (2020) *Miss Meteor* depicts Lita intending to be the first Hispanic (also Questions 6, 9–10) winner of her town's beauty pageant. Lita reunites with her former best friend, Chicky, who plans to help her win, as there's never been a Hispanic winner before, with Lita making town history. However, while preparing for the pageant, the girls learn Miss Meteor isn't about perfection, it's about liking yourself and sharing who you are with others, a lesson for readers also.

Similarly, Willowdean and her mother continually fight over her larger-girl size in Murphy's (2015) *Dumplin'*, with her determined to enter the town's pageant, even if she's unable to fit into the dress her mother wore when winning the title. Willowdean's mother coordinates the yearly pageant so there's extra pressure and advice, but she enters anyway, inspiring others with her larger size and confidence, also greatly beneficial to readers.

Polly, from Weeks' (2000) *Pie* (also Questions 3, 5, 7–8) bakes champion pies, their renown keeping their town's economy afloat. After Polly dies suddenly, she leaves everything to her cat, Lardo, and Lardo to her niece, Alice. Alice begins baking experimental pies to replicate her aunt's prize-winning recipes, none found in her belongings and Lardo unhelpful, but some townspeople believe she has the recipes and begin attempting to find them.

Harper has fewer choices in Leal's (2009) *Also Known as Harper*, as while desperately wanting to be a poet, her father's abandonment and subsequent eviction means she must work to keep her family together, with little time to spend on either school or poetry, and especially the upcoming poetry contest she wants to enter so badly. Doing so is seemingly impossible without time or money for its fees, but hope is never lost.

Rural teens are involved in various contests, pageants, state fairs, and cooking in general; what are their experiences and stories? How would they explain these to those unfamiliar? Further, how can they accompany, (or help another to enter) those who've never attended these events? Also, are these events as popular as in years past on both the state and local levels, and if not, why?

Mysteries as subplots or otherwise are seen in many YAL novels including those rural (also Question 10); Weeks's novel is full of sleuthing, and Anna from Bauer's (2014) *Tell Me* is sent to live with her grandmother, soon becoming involved in town activities and becoming happier than ever. While prepping for an upcoming festival, she thinks she sees a little girl in trouble. At first, she's not taken seriously, but she persists and soon the entire town is searching for the child.

Like Anna, Gabe and friends (also Question 10) are also first dismissed when saying they've seen mysterious activities in a supposedly vacant house in Hayes's (1996) *Flyers*. Gabe is filming a movie for a school project and begin seeing mysterious activities and lights in a long-vacant house. They begin investigating anyway, with his father stepping in, providing strong support once they discover the details.

Students on their regular school bus have the same route, same riders, year after year, each boarding and pulling out the cell phone. This year, however, a new stop is suddenly added, but no one's there. Why this occurs becomes an irresistible mystery, allowing students' putting phones aside and getting to know one another while solving the puzzling stop. The further they go, the more each student's personal life is revealed (also Questions 6 and 9), and more connections to others are made, often surprisingly, in Cheaney's (2014) *Somebody on This Bus Is Going to Be Famous*.

Students and educators, plus parents, can relay and reminisce over their own past mysteries (including their town's), especially when younger (Who doesn't have a spooky house nearby?), with many sharing the same ones. Any that might be current should also be discussed and possibly solved. Why we love such mysteries can also be considered, plus the fact that our fears often say more about us than what is overwise revealed; these too are universal, with sharing bringing students closer to peers and adults, as many small-town mysteries are known to all.

Beginnings and endings are common to all literature, with Deja, who is Black, and Josiah, White, seasonal best friends, as each year they work in their town's pumpkin patch in Rowell's (2019) *Pumpkinheads*, going their separate ways after the season. Now graduating and their last night working, Josiah wants to reminisce, but Deja convinces him they must have a night to remember, enjoying all the food and prizes from the park, especially including Josiah finally talking to the girl he's loved from afar for three years.

A different kind of ending is experienced by Delia, twelve, in Wiersbitzky's (2014) *What Flowers Remember*, as after Old Red, who's always lived in her town and master gardener, known for his beautiful flowers and gardens, contracts Alzheimer's. Delia collects residents' stories of him and preserves his heirloom seeds, creating a journal of his life so he'll always have his memories, the journal itself speaking of and for him.

We all have beginnings and endings, with seniors especially so; students can discuss theirs, including those of the near future and later, compare, and perhaps provide advice and assistance (Educators and parents can also share). Again, the same ones will be expressed repeatedly, providing more commonalities.

Rural teens are particularly involved with family as many live in the same town or nearby, with Tyson, thirteen, in Gebhart's (2014) *There Will Be Bears* long anticipating his thirteenth birthday, meaning he can go on a hunting trip with his grandpa Gene. Of course, as time passes, both Tyson and Gene have new complications and situations, and once Tyson reaches his milestone birthday, Gene is in a nursing home. His health is too dicey to go hunting and Tyson's too young to care for him, but that's a later worry as they sneak away for their long-anticipated trip.

Olivia wants to help her family leave their trailer park in Ellis's (2017) *You May Already Be a Winner*, entering every sweepstakes she can find in hopes of a big win (also Questions 3, 5–10) her chances about the same as Tyson's worry-free trip. She has thought of everything except taking care of herself, and when trouble appears, she discovers people are surprising, after receiving all sorts of unexpected help.

Holt's (2006) *Part of Me: Stories of a Louisiana Family* traces four generations of one family through their love of reading, beginning in 1939 when young Rose begins driving her town's bookmobile, never imagining it would spread the love of reading to so many.

The inimitable DJ, who loves her family and town, has trials and joys portrayed in Murdock's series beginning with *Dairy Queen* (2006), *The Off Season* (2007), and *Front and Center* (2009). She staggers from caring for her injured brother, her family dairy farm responsibilities, and desire to play football on the male's team. She doesn't always expect the reactions of those surrounding her but manages to persevere with humor.

Readers' families in small towns (or elsewhere) are much the same, with events from novels compared to students,' discussion plentiful as all are typical rural activities. For those unfamiliar, they doubtless have similar ones to share, again finding commonalities as there's little difference concerning family love and situations, whether good or bad.

Teens determined to solve problems are many, often like athletics tied to economics, with Heagerty's (2021) *Martian Ghost Centaur* (also Questions 3, 5, 7–8) seeing Louie and Felix's hometown long famous for a sasquatch sighting. This used to be a tourist draw, but no longer as popular with a local company intending to purchase the depressed town for its headquarters. The boys can't bear their town being sold, so they begin dressing as Bigfoot to scare those wanting to purchase their troubled town and raise the tourist trade.

Vivian, from Mathieu's *Moxie* (2017) (also Question 4), is furious at her school's administration feeling male football team members can do no wrong, and the females having to manage sexist dress codes, harassment in hallways, and other rude comments. She starts a feminist zine and distributes it anonymously to blow off steam, but as more girls respond she realizes she's started a revolution.

Gretchen and Henry are the youngest in their family, both farm kids, teased and tricked by their older brothers and sisters in Heynen's (1997) *Being Youngest* (also Questions 6 and 9). Their freedom and ingenuity from their numerous adventures cause humorous problems with fun, scrapes, and commiseration abounding.

Sophie in Mills's (2019) *Famous in a Small Town* (also Questions 3–10) has a major dilemma; their marching band has a spot in the Rose Bowl but not funding, so she plans for country singer Megan Pleasant, the town's only famous person, to headline a fundraiser. This would work more smoothly had

Megan not earlier vowed never to return to her hometown, with Sophie now determined to discover her reasons and reconcile her problems.

How can readers relate to the problems and situations in these novels, all typical of small towns, and what are they currently facing? What advice can they provide, and how may some work together to solve? Teens and adults are often reluctant to seek help, but if considering how eager one is to help versus asking for assistance, most will discover they are eager to assist others, perhaps allowing for more to admit not everything can be solved individually. Moreover, focusing on problems, not an individual, allows students another chance of viewing similarities to one another.

Novels with fantastical elements, especially magical realism are burgeoning, as ten-year-old Opal from DiCamillo's (2000) *Because of Winn-Dixie* (also Questions 6 and 9–10). Opal is lonely with her busy father, new town, and wants to know more about her mother, who left when she was three. Going to the grocery store and finding an extraordinary stray dog, named Winn-Dixie, helps her make new friends, have a wonderful summer, and finally become closer to her father.

Jack's hilarious adventures are chronicled in Gantos's *Dead End in Norvelt* (2011) and *From Norvelt to Nowhere* (2013), as he spends his summer in the historic town of Norvelt (also Questions 6 and 9–10) and quickly gets grounded for multiple offenses. He's told to help an eccentric elderly neighbor who writes obituaries, but as she shares information about anything and everything, he becomes involved in even more bizarre and zany situations.

Spencer and his mother are the only two people left in their town, the nearest school thirty miles away, a situation doubtless similar or feared by some rural teens, in Jennings's (2009) *Ghost Town* (also Questions 3, 5, and 7–10). Spencer takes photos of the town, his camera inexplicably photographing long-dead residents. After seeing a ghost camera ad in a catalog, he writes to the owner, begins some correspondence, and starts his own business.

Readers won't have the same situations, but doubtless something similar, and who wouldn't want to experience these novels' events? Who has situations like those above, and who yearns for them? Many teens have other fantastical elements, experiences without explanation, which can be shared, along from favorites from novels or movies or their lives. We all dream and imagine, by closing our eyes, where are our differences, and more likely similarities, here?

YAL asks students to consider the protagonist and other characters and their situations, as well as placing themselves in other's lives; how would they do, act, respond, and why? This combination of careful thinking and extension helps prepare readers for life situations as well as seeing former personal situations experienced by characters like them, both beneficial and essential.

DISCUSSION QUESTIONS AND SUGGESTED ACTIVITIES

Discussion Questions	Suggested Activities; Students Will . . .	Key Diversity Points
1. What are the advantages and disadvantages of small schools, and how do these affect or otherwise prepare students for post-secondary education and life after graduation?	Advantages and disadvantages are listed and discussed and then narrowed to what is considered most positive/negative regarding rural education. Also considered is how prepared students feel for post-secondary school/work and how their above choices will affect their confidence and progress.	Rural education is different, neither better nor worse than any other; likewise, its students are equal to peers. If attributes that strengthen or negatively affect minorities are not mentioned, what does this indicate?
2. How did your school building(s) and facilities contribute to the positives/negatives regarding your overall education?	Students can discuss how their school arrangement (i.e., K-12, 2 buildings) contributed to their overall education.	Rural schools' composition is a minority one. How beneficial, or prohibitive, is this to rural minority students, and what might be improvements for them?
3. U.S. educators use their personal funds for supplies and other school materials. What is your opinion of this?	Students are familiar with various funding drives and other activities for raise money for various trips or items. What amount is contributed by teachers, students, parents, and the community, and what does this mean? What are its positives and negatives? Are some not expected to contribute, and why?	Do schools have presumptions regarding finances donated, and is this behavior similar of minority views/treatments? How much of this funding is spent on minorities?
4. Small schools are a large social venue for communities. What are the effects of so much pride and involvement?	Students can individually respond and them form larger discussions. How is such attention comfortable and enjoyable or suffocating and unwelcome?	The community and parents are ever-present during student activities. How does this relate to the attention given to minorities in the school or town?

5. What are your views of school consolidation or incorporating other facilities into the school?	Many smaller schools are already consolidated with community facilities, and students are familiar with them to some extent. Discussed are positives, negatives, and fears, perhaps narrowing to best/worst.	Consolidation automatically creates minority and majority students. Who falls into each group, and why? How are those already racially/culturally/otherwise different affected?
6. Do you consider yourself, and your community, as minorities?	UM students may not have considered rural as a minority. This discussion will identify what the term "rural" as minority and what "minority" means.	How does being considered a minority from rurality relate to other minority students? What attitudes/actions should be changed to benefit of all? What should "minority" mean?
7. What are the effects of those educators in your school leaving for other employment quickly?	Opinions, experiences (negative and positive), and views are discussed, narrowing to most/least beneficial. Students could also consider what might be needed for educator retention.	Students view their community through the eyes of one unable to reside there and relate to the experiences of minority students and families.
8. Why are educator salaries lower in the UM than elsewhere?	Students can discuss reasons, and how lower salaries affect their education. If wanting to teach, would they wish employment in the UM, or elsewhere with higher salaries?	Are those in the UM not as important as elsewhere, with educators similarly viewed? How does this compare to the UM view of area minorities?
9. There are few non-White educators in the UM. How does this affect one's overall education?	Students consider what White and non-White educators could bring to their education, and consider what is most/least needed and important?	Students can consider the many ways those who are different can positively enrich their education, and what it means, living in places without diversity, or little.
10. Small town residents are quick to help others in numerous ways. How is this positive and negative?	Students' personal experiences and opinions are shared, with consideration of who might not be so assisted.	Who is seen as lesser, and why? Are minorities automatically placed here? What does this imply?

REFERENCES

Carver-Thomas, D. (2018). *Diversifying the teaching profession: How to recruit and retain teachers of color.* Learning Policy Institute. https://learningpolicyinstitute.org/product/diversifying-teaching-profession-report

Carver-Thomas, D., & Darling-Hammond, L. (2017). *Teacher turnover: Why it matters and what we can do about it.* Learning Policy Institute. learningpolicyinstitute.org/product/teacher-turnover-report.

Chavis, C. (August 2, 2019). *Commentary: The cost of rural school consolidation.* The Daily Yonder. https://dailyyonder.com/commentary-cost-rural-school-consolidation/2019/08/02/

Countryahh.com. (2022a). *List of all counties in Minnesota.* https://www.countryaah.com/alphabetical-list-of-all-counties-in-minnesota/

Countryahh.com. (2022b). *List of all counties in South Dakota.* https://www.countryaah.com/alphabetical-list-of-all-counties-in-south-dakota/

Edwards, R., & Longo, P. (2013). "Rural Communities and School Consolidation. Introduction to Special Issue." *Great Plains Research: A Journal of Natural and Social Sciences, 23* (Fall), 91–97.

Forbes, P. (April 11, 2015). *The rewards of teaching in a small school.* Bill and Melinda Gates Foundation. https://usprogram.gatesfoundation.org/News-and-Insights/Articles/The-Rewards-of-Teaching-in-a-Rural-School

Hamblin, N. (January 22, 2018). *The rural advantage: A teacher's perspective.* Rural Schools Collaborative. https://ruralschoolscollaborative.org/stories/the-rural-advantage-a-teachers-perspective

Ivy Coach. (2020). 2020 *Ivy League admissions statistics.* https://www.ivycoach.com/2020-ivy-league-admissions-statistics/

Kolmar, C. (December 29, 2020). *The 10 Minnesota cities with the largest Latino population for 2021.* HomeSnacks. https://www.homesnacks.com/most-hispanic-cities-in-minnesota/

Lambert, R. (2005). "How to Know if Your School or District is Threatened with Consolidation—and What to Do About It." *Rural Policy Matters* (Randolph, VT).

Latterman, K., & Steffes, S. (2017). *Tackling teacher and principal shortages in rural areas* (Issue Brief Vol. 25, No. 40). National Conference of State Legislatures. https://www.ncsl.org/research/education/tackling-teacher-and-principal-shortages-in-rural-areas.aspx

Lawrence-Turner, J. (April 19, 2015). *Rural schools provide benefits to students, communities.* The Spokesman Review. https://www.spokesman.com/stories/2015/apr/19/rural-schools-provide-benefits-to-students/

The Miles Foundation. (2016). *Common characteristics of rural education superstars.* https://www.milesfdn.org/archived-blog/2016/01/common-characteristics-of-rural-education-superstars

Morton, N. (April 13, 2021). *Rural schools have a teacher shortage. Why don't people who live there, teach there?* The Hechinger Report/USA Today. https://www.usatoday.com/story/news/education/2021/04/13/covid-could-make-teacher-shortage-even-worse-hard-hit-rural-schools/7189706002/

National Center for Educational Statistics. (2021a). *Characteristics of traditional public, public charter, and private school teachers.* https://nces.ed.gov/programs/coe/indicator/clr

National Center for Educational Statistics. (2021b). *Characteristics of public school teachers.* https://nces.ed.gov/programs/coe/indicator/clr?tid=4

National Center for Educational Statistics. (2021c). *Teacher salaries.* https://nces.ed.gov/programs/digest/d20/tables/dt20_211.60.asp

Native-Americans.com (n.d.). *Reservations by state.* https://native-americans.com/category/indian-reservations-a-z/reservations-by-state/

Nicosia, M. (June 1, 2017). *Solving the rural education pap: Experts weigh in on new report's findings tying gap to prosperity.* The 74. https://www.the74million.org/article/solving-the-rural-education-gap-experts-weigh-in-on-new-reports-findings-tying-gap-to-prosperity/

Pew Research Center. (May 22, 2018). *What unites and divides urban, suburban, and rural communities.* https://www.pewsocialtrends.org/2018/05/22/demographic-and-economic-trends-in-urban-suburban-and-rural-communities/

Public Schools First NC. (January 12, 2021). The facts on rural schools. https://www.publicschoolsfirstnc.org/resources/fact-sheets/the-facts-on-rural-schools

Richard, L. (May 23, 2021). *Texas Senate passes 'Tim Tebow' bill allowing home-schoolers to compete in public school sports.* Washington Examiner. https://www.washingtonexaminer.com/news/texas-senate-passes-tim-tebow-bill-home-schoolers-compete-in-public-school

Salary.Com. (May 27, 2021a). *Public school teacher salary in Wyoming.* https://www.salary.com/research/salary/benchmark/public-school-teacher-**salary/wy**

Salary.Com. (May 27, 2021b). *School administrator salary.* https://www.salary.com/research/salary/recruiting/school-administrator-salary

Salary.Com. (May 27, 2021c). *School superintendent salary in the United States.* https://www.salary.com/research/salary/benchmark/school-superintendent-salary

Secondo, N. (August 25, 2020). *Rural school consolidation is not the answer.* Harvard Politics. https://harvardpolitics.com/ruralconsolidation/

Showalter, D., Hartman, S., Johnson, J., & Klein, B. (November 2019). *Why rural matters 2018–2019: The time is now.* The Rural School and Community Trust. http://www.ruraledu.org/

Snow. J. (2019). Is #WeNeedDiverseBooks a Trend? *VOYA 42*(2), 50–51.

Spiegelman, M. (May 15, 2018). *Public school teacher spending on classroom supplies.* IES/NCES. https://nces.ed.gov/pubsearch/pubsinfo.asp?pubid=2018097rev

Starck, J. G., Riddle, T., Sinclair, S., & Warikoo, N. (April 14, 2020). *Teachers are people too: examining the racial bias of teachers compared to other American adults.* American Educational Research Association. https://www.aera.net/Newsroom/Teachers-Are-People-Too-Examining-the-Racial-Bias-of-Teachers-Compared-to-Other-American-Adults

Steckelberg, M. (1999). *Attitudes of teachers who teach the rural middle grades toward students of various socioeconomic backgrounds.* [Unpublished doctoral dissertation]. University of South Dakota.

U.S. Census Bureau (2018). *USA facts: Race.* https://usafacts.org/state-of-the-union/population/

Wang, K. (July 29, 2019). *Teacher turnover: Why it's problematic and how administrators and address it.* Fast Forward/Carnegie Learning. https://www.scilearn.com/teacher-turnover/#:~:text=Teacher%20turnover%20continues%20to%20concern%20K-12%20educators%20who,will%20lose%203%20out%20of%20every%2020%20teachers

World Population Review. (2021a). *Ten largest cities in Iowa.* https://worldpopulationreview.com/states/cities/iowa

World Population Review. (2021b). *Ten largest cities in Minnesota.* https://worldpopulationreview.com/states/cities/minnesota

World Population Review. (2021c). *Ten largest cities in WY.* https://worldpopulationreview.com/states/cities/wyoming

World Population Review. (2021d). *Sheridan, WY population 2020.* https://worldpopulationreview.com/us-cities/sheridan-wy-population

Chapter 5

Rurality Denigration and Developing Lifestyle Pride

A typical Upper Midwest (UM) White teen's adolescence, unlike others' elsewhere, is homogenous with personal extended experiences and friendships with racial/cultural minorities virtually nonexistent. However, those rural are also minorities and disparaged in the media and by others, and personally through microaggressions. By understanding these and the best responses, teens can experience minority situations and learn to promote rurality and all residents.

RURAL TEENS' ADOLESCENT IDENTITY

White UM students' identification is the same as elsewhere, from family, friends, classmates, school, community, and other groups, as teams or clubs. If within a community, racial minorities are group members, but ties loosen somewhat during the teen years; individuals or families may wish time spent with those more like them, dating and relationships may become complicated, and other differences can seem more pronounced with numbers so few. Communities having two or three minority families are different from those larger with many.

Although all UM adolescents are the same as those elsewhere, they do have a dual existence as although Whites are the dominant majority, rurality is a minority. Such status isn't necessarily grasped by these teens, as they aren't viewed as such in their communities. Likewise, they may have difficulties considering rurality as a separate, distinct group, often negatively perceived, the same as so-called other minorities with whom their family, neighbors, or themselves may find unfamiliar or uncomfortable. White teens have doubtlessly never experienced fellow residents' antipathy, hatred, or violence toward them for being different because most aren't outwardly so (other than having exceptionalities) or are attempting similarity (LGBTQ+); they are homogenous with most never dissimilar from the majority.

Of course, all rural residents are knowledgeable of the many underrepresented groups, diversity issues, situations, and problems through numerous sources, especially technological, also allowing interactions. However, virtual, or other short encounters are not the same, nor reasonable substitutes, for extended personal communication and experience with those different. It also cannot be presumed that teens' technological viewing and use is of quality, that they are engaging with those diverse, or even elsewhere.

Further, rural White teens' overall personal insulation from those diverse can allow being under-prepared, perhaps shockingly so, regarding communication skills and understanding others' cultural and other social differences. Some may have difficulty navigating these common situations, and others, without personal or other experience with those different:

- relocating before high school graduation or after to college in areas with multiple diversities;
- area employment changes or organizational sponsorship of minorities bringing different racially or culturally groups into the current population;
- working at tourist attractions drawing international and national visitors;
- traveling or studying in other parts of the country or overseas with unfamiliar cultural/religious practices and other differences;
- over or underestimating safety precautions (largely unnecessary in small towns) when in other areas of the country or overseas;
- hesitance, awkwardness, or even fear when in situations in which one is a minority (racial, social, religious, socioeconomic, etc.); and
- being a positive, and accurate, representative of their hometown or state to those unfamiliar.

Before understanding others, rural White adolescents must recognize that they are also a minority, something already known to those racially diverse, as regardless of where or how one has grown up and resided, those circumstances are the norm until having extended personal experiences with others different. However, as most of these teens won't have this opportunity unless leaving the UM, this familiarity is extremely limited.

NATIONAL RURALITY DEPICTIONS

Rural minority representation by media and other venues continues as overwhelmingly stereotypical and/or unrealistic, and especially condescendingly, even by the most sophisticated sites and persons. Put bluntly, a central view is that rural individuals are considered incapable of relocating to a place with higher prestige and employment, and if enjoying their location, stupid.

Common descriptions include its states considered "flyover" ones, with media characters predominantly out-of-date farmers, or businesspersons with antiquated equipment and methods, or otherwise inefficient and unused to complex tasks. Adult and adolescent beliefs are strongly politically and religiously conservative, judgmental, prejudiced, and homophobic.

Individuals are intellectually challenged, speak non-standard English, are leery of higher education, and are uninterested or ignorant of sophisticated events and activities. Both male and females are shown as overweight, badly dressed and groomed, and with dated, unflattering hairstyles.

These portrayals occur so frequently, whether a scene, plot, or through recurring characters in television and film that examples are rife, but two more striking ones are first illustrated by the plot of Cox et al.'s (2010–2015) television show *Hot in Cleveland*, featuring three entertainment industry females facing waning employment and inability to establish meaningful relationships in Los Angeles after age 40.

After an emergency plane landing in Cleveland, they remained as residents viewed them as exciting and gorgeous, clearly illustrating the area's lower standards. While the premise was flawed using beautiful, personable, and intelligent actors, the message remained; larger cities hold the best with those considered lesser relegated to smaller places equally unattractive and unsophisticated.

A second example is Levitan and Morton's (2009–2020) television show *Modern Family*, which ironically casually portrayed gay parents (Cam and Mitchell) rearing their adopted Vietnamese daughter, Lily, in California the same as any other mid-thirties couple while skewering Cam's Missouri home.

Seemingly every state reference is denigrating; Lily is partially named after Cam's boyhood pet pig, his father carved their wedding cake topper from soap, Mitchell's family questioned Cam's relatives affording first-class plane tickets, Cam's burly sister mispronounced and was unfamiliar with trendy foods, or hogs sharing their train transportation.

At the series' end, while readying to move to Missouri, Mitchell lamented they would be entering the Old Testament, that is, a state in another century and leaving behind everything contemporary, familiar, and worthwhile.

Gloria, another character, also sees her former Columbian village stereotypically depicted. Her family appears unaware of modern conveniences, her ex-husband is irresponsible and casually disreputable with Gloria's past equally murky, and drug and other negative cultural references abound.

Her thick accent, mispronunciation of common words, and voluptuous figure in tight, suggestive clothing distinctly separate her from the series' other women (suggesting her lower-class); its men (including her son-in-law), constantly ogling. These portrayals overshadow that Gloria, and similarly Cam, are equally and usually more, admirable, intelligent, capable, and witty than fellow characters. As so many in society are striving to promote fairness, respect, and equality among individuals, it is difficult to provide a rationale for rural characters continually depicted stereotypically.

LOCAL RURALITY DEPICTIONS

Rural cities' local media routinely feature frustratingly offensive images when interviewing area residents for newscasts; typically seen include unkempt families in squalid housing, individuals possessing strident, uninformed/offensive opinions, or largely unaware of the issue in question. Thoughtful, well spoken, or otherwise professional persons are seldom shown, unfortunately reinforcing common stereotypes (and doubtless boosting ratings) of the area predominantly populated by those most backward.

Further, if the covered topic is of major significance, such as presidential elections, weather and other disasters, or momentous state laws/events, those interviews will likely be aired or otherwise seen nationwide, again reinforcing stereotypes to larger audiences.

COMMON QUERIES (MICROAGGRESSIONS) ASKED OF RURAL INDIVIDUALS

Those living in the UM, both teens and adults, are frequently the object of curiosity of those living elsewhere (especially non-Whites), and often asked of their general lifestyle. As with stereotypes, the questions themselves are dubious yet so widely and frequently asked it seems apparent individuals living elsewhere readily believe what has been seen/heard and/or have no concept of other states, both disheartening.

These questions appear repeatedly, with a small sample of those most addressed to rural individuals below:

- Do you *have* electricity/technology/indoor plumbing/paved roads?
- How many *days* did it take for you to get here? (when residents travel)
- Are there any *nice* restaurants or stores here?
- How *far* do you have to drive for civilization?
- (If residents are in another state) Oh, I'll give you a 10% discount! You *deserve* it, living *there*!
- Do you have access to medical care with *real* doctors?

- Are your schools in *one-room* buildings?
- Do you have *any* colleges or universities here?
- Is it *always* cold here?
- But what does one *do* here?
- Do you have any *friends*? (Also asked of non-Whites)
- How can you *stand* living here? (Also asked of non-Whites)
- *Why* would your parents live here?
- *Who* do you date? (Also asked of non-Whites)
- Are you considered an *outcast*? (Also asked of non-Whites)
- (If recently accepted employment) Why did you take a job *there*? and how *long* are you planning to *stay*?
- I imagine you're excited to graduate and *leave* (hometown)!
- I've never met anyone from *(state)*!

Effects of Stereotypes and Microaggressions

The above questions, assumptions, and depictions are all *microaggressions*, which are statements subtly discriminating individuals or entire groups. While familiar to rural adults, they are probably not to adolescents, unless having experience working for tourist attractions or other employers attracting those living elsewhere. These teen employees probably have been addressing the above issues, but otherwise microaggressions usually begin appearing during the late teen years, especially when making post–high school decisions or traveling. Still, all UM adolescents are familiar with rural stereotypes and other negative depictions in varying degrees, but being familiar can mean anything, from ignoring to amused to disliking.

Moreover, teens may not necessarily *personally* connect their underlying negativity to themselves as *individuals*. It is vital, however, that stereotypes and microaggressions be discussed, as doing so allows White teens the experience of being a minority, to recognize others' view of them and their location as *lesser* rather than *different*. Further, non-Whites are allowed power of expression equal to Whites.

Microaggressions' effect upon White rural teens is significant, as they are forming a new, mature sense of identity and self. As they age, hearing comments continually portraying themselves negatively or otherwise subjected to ridicule becomes increasingly tiring and disheartening, and surely contributing to their achieving and/or maintaining a high sense of self-esteem or pride.

This is something that non-Whites have always experienced, which Whites must realize and extend to other prejudices. Particularly painful for any teen is relatives or friends living elsewhere expressing microaggressions, worse when continually repeated with assurances that leaving rural areas is key to a satisfying/better/normal life. It must be remembered non-Whites also enjoy living in the UM, although admittedly in its larger cities.

Microaggressions' definition with accompanying discussion regarding its various aspects should occur in classrooms. Once their meaning is understood, adolescents can learn to address them in ways that can effect change.

Classroom Discussion of Microaggressions and Stereotypes

Educators in small schools generally have their own classrooms; it would be beneficial for parts of student activities and commentary to be posted or otherwise available to the class. Of course, master files of discussions and other information from students should be maintained for reference and re-use. See the Activity for Building Rural Pride and Self-Esteem and the Stereotypes and Microaggressions Activity at the end of this chapter, and YAL titles are listed in Appendix A.

YOUNG ADULT LITERATURE CONNECTIONS

Teens must read of those like and unlike them, in a variety of situations. Anyone's life can change suddenly, dramatically, for better, unthinkably worse, or anything in between. We manage such things differently, by sharing, celebrating, grieving, discussing, worrying, silence, or perhaps too afraid to acknowledge at all. Reading of others sharing the same experiences and their responses provides advice while demonstrating we are never alone, regardless of what has occurred.

We also don't always comprehend the impression or effect we have upon others with responses and reactions; seeing differences between negative and positive ones are hard lessons or pleasant affirmations, allowing us to consider current and future behaviors. The YAL titles below depict teens living in small towns, all experiencing difficulties of some kind, the same ones encountered by others regardless of place, with exploring them more closely bringing the realization that we are far more alike than different, beneficial to all.

Many teens are concerned with body issues, including males, as in Aceves's (2020) *The New David Espinoza* with David using steroids and bodybuilding for a better physique after a humiliating video of him being bullied goes viral. While he achieves the physique of his dreams, he adds male body dysmorphia (a rare topic in YAL) to his existing problems, none solved by an outward appearance change.

Raesha from Alene's (2017) *The Sky Between You and Me* is grieving her mother's death and decides to use her saddle in an upcoming rodeo to honor her. As the saddle is a little small, she decides to lose a few pounds, but her diet soon soars to anorexia, next her withdrawal from friends and family, and her badly needing assistance.

Charlie in Maldonado's (2021) *Fat Chance, Charlie Vega*, is the opposite; she's half–Puerto Rican in a lily-white town, and as a larger teen she's adamant about expressing body positivity despite her mother's criticisms regarding her weight. Her best friend, however, stands by her, and once dating a nice guy she's happier than ever.

Still, her contentment evaporates upon learning her boyfriend asked her best friend out first. *Is she a joke, a way to become closer to her friend, or truly liked?* quickly become nagging questions. Teens, both male and female, can discuss weight issues from all sides; photoshopped media images, those in films and television slim with one larger person derided for size, making weight for sports, and more. How are weight/body issues similar among readers, and how can one support peers?

Others are caring for siblings, not always known to others, as ten-year-old Della and Suki's difficult lives in Bradley's (2020) *Fighting Word*s. Suki watches over Della, but after her suicide attempt, Della realizes no one's been caring for *her*. A hard admission, but Della can no longer remain silent regarding their sexual abuse, another rare topic for YAL.

Layla, 14, also cares for her younger brother in Elison's (2020) *Find Layla*, as both live in a dangerously filthy house with their unstable mother. She loves science and keeps her head down, concentrating upon doing well in school. After she films her home's inside for a science project concerning indoor fungi, amazingly covering most home spaces, mushrooms growing in places, the video goes viral. Help follows, but a bold, embarrassing, and shameful admission for anyone to make and especially a teen.

Little, 16, has a similar experience to Layla's in Hoffmeister's (2017) *Too Shattered for Mending*, in which his older brother is arrested and his one adult figure, his grandfather Big, abandons him. Now living alone in their trailer, he's also watching out for his younger cousin, who is having difficulties. Needing food and without funds he shoots a deer out of season, with the Sheriff offering to erase the fine—if informing of Big's whereabouts.

Students could discuss how such teens might be recognized and assisted earlier, without embarrassment within the school, and treated respectfully regardless of their home situation, not of their desire or making. Could students anonymously donate items to those needing them, perhaps forming a network among schools with offerings, such as clothes, sent to different buildings so not recognized by students? What do these students need, and who can provide? Can schools allow showers before school or other like items? Why not barter for some items, as trading a desk for mowing XX yards, shoveling snow, or running errands?

Teens dealing with siblings, parents, or both in the legal system are common as Little, above, and Tracy, 17, a Black teen from Johnson's (2020) *This Is My America*. She's been writing letters weekly for seven years to an innocence project, begging for assistance regarding her innocent father on death row. His execution date is nearing, but after police arrive in the middle of the night to arrest her brother for murder, she must refocus her priorities.

His charges astound her, obviously in error, with investigating leading to a beehive of documents regarding her town's racist history. Releasing the information is dangerous, but could be life-changing to her family, with Tracy having hard decisions ahead.

Students should note the number of Blacks (and other racial minorities) in prison and death row as opposed to Whites and Tracy's brother's arrest, without warning and late at night. Would the son of an influential resident be treated the same way by police? How else are Blacks, and other minorities, treated with bias in society? What is the school's role in bias, and what curricular changes could be made? What are reasons, and what could be done?

A similar situation depicts best friends Luke and Toby, from Bliss's (2018) *We'll Fly Away*. Dreaming of leaving their town, they plan to go together through Luke's wrestling scholarship, but a series of choices sends them on startlingly different journeys. The novel depicts their senior year through letters Luke wrote to Toby later—from death row.

Deet, within Hill's (2007) *Do Not Pass Go* is horrified when his father is imprisoned for drug possession, but upon visiting him in their hometown jail sees other families in the same situation. Deet feared school reactions but instead discovered others had or were in the same, or equally troublesome, circumstances and given understanding and advice. Deet can now reconcile his father's problems, beginning to learn how to support him without following the same path.

Similarly, Brooke's brother in Johnson's (2019) *Even If I Fall* confesses to murdering his best friend, Calvin, but she knows he could not have done so. Something did happen that night, so she stealthily works to solve the crime. The information she needs can only be gathered by speaking to Calvin's brother, expressly forbidden, but she meets with him secretly to they can discover the truth together.

Rural teens and families may be at a disadvantage regarding legalities; some have lesser education and funds, or unable to secure quality representation. Officers may have little experience dealing with severe crimes, others without a background in law enforcement, with various violations dealt with differently. What is the situation in their town, and what does it imply? How does police treatment help or hinder minorities, and how do their actions shape hometowns? How can one assist such families, aside from offering compassion, other than harassment or other school negatives?

Biracial teens also have difficulties in small schools; Trent, seen in Chappell's (2014) *More Than Good Enough*, is half Miccosukee, half White. He leaves his mother's home to live with his father on his reservation but feels out of place with both parents. Attempting to become reacquainted with his father is difficult, neither knowing the other well. He has a likewise hard time in school and further believes he belongs nowhere, but upon seeing a former friend begins working to prove to her, and himself, that he's of substance.

Gansworth's (2020) *Apple (Skin to the Core)* relays his own similar story, as being depicted as an "apple" by his Onondaga peers, that is, one too White to be accepted on the reservation, but too red (Native American) for White society. He shares his life among the two worlds in which he lives and the fight for acceptance as an artist in both communities.

A similar situation but in reverse was experienced by Tess from Jahn's (2019) *The Next to Last Mistake*, whose beloved farm must be sold as her father can no longer meet expenses. Her family's subsequent move to Ft. Bragg, an enormous, diverse school and community nothing like her small community, is a shock she initially finds difficult. Still, its curriculum is much broader, allowing her to read literature by authors of color for the first time and learn of other diverse topics, with her making friendships with diverse classmates, another first. Here, Tess is also teased because of her background, seen as lesser and unsophisticated by from a farm and small town.

Kitty must also straddle two worlds in Noe's (2011) *Something to Hold*, whose father's job causes their continual moving and her attending different reservation schools. She's one of only a few Whites with the others usually adults, and longs for acceptance, but barriers including her being White and moving so frequently.

Allie, 15, is Muslim in Courtney's (2019) *All American Muslim Girl*, and tired of concealing her heritage, although not particularly devout, hearing Islamophobic comments, and witnessing hateful and ignorant actions, including those against her father. As her boyfriend's father is a famous conversative radio shock jock, revealing her religion gives her pause, but she decides to be honest, wanting to learn more of her heritage and what being Muslim means, especially in her small town.

Lira is also frustrated within Deen's (2019) *In the Key of Nira Ghani*, as although living in her small town for two years, she's still the sole, brown-skinned student and ignored by peers. Her parents allow little freedom and expect her to become a physician, but her heart leans toward music. Realizing she must start her own life, she persuades her parents for more choices and spends time with her music, happier, and when attempting to make friends discovers that stereotyping works both ways.

Lira has been angry that others have not accepted her, but upon reflection sees that she did little to approach others. Once she began speaking with peers, she learned that they presumed she wanted to do that with *them*. How many other students have had misconceptions of others, and what does this imply? What are solutions or actions, so peers don't have to wait two years for friendships? Why are we so afraid to approach others when they are little different? How can educators better assist all students?

Mimi's experience is better in Hilton's (2015) *Full Cicada Moon*; it's 1969, she's half-Japanese, wants to be an astronaut, and is tired of new-school classmates continually asking where she's from. Her science teacher takes her dreaming of space travel seriously, and in time she's happy within school by asserting herself along with remaining true to who she is.

Kiko is also half-Japanese, seen in Bowman's (2017) *Starfish*, with social anxieties and a heritage she barely understands. Disliking living in her small town, she has her life planned on leaving upon receiving her expected art school scholarship. Instead, she's stunned by a rejection letter, but after a friend offers a tour of coastal schools she accepts, despite anxieties, and realizes she has many choices.

Daniel Nayeri's (2020) *Everything Sad Is Untrue (A True Story)* is the author's autobiographical of having lived in Iran, now in an OK middle school, and tells his classmates stories of his personal Iranian history. He begins with how his family became refugees, their perilous trek to the United States, and continues with centuries of Iranian history, tales, and folklore, all to uninterested peers who sometimes feels he's anti-American and remain wary.

More dangerous peer and community reactions are seen by Jessie, portrayed in Purcell's (2018) *This Is Not a Love Letter*, who wakes to an ordinary Saturday that becomes something quite different. Her day is quickly altered after learning that Chris, her Black boyfriend, is missing. She knows he's been harassed and the only Black student in her small school, but also popular and star athlete. Searches are futile, and from his disappearance to discovered suicide, Jessie learns that his struggles were far more vicious than thought.

For the teens above, race makes their lives in town and school far more difficult. While Allie wonders what it means to be Muslim, students could consider the same question. What *does* it mean, to have non-Whites and non-Christians in town? Why is it important to live among those racially diverse, and why are such individuals frequently viewed and treated negatively? What does this say about towns and individuals, and why continued? How else may students treat those who are racially different? If these same students were White, how welcome would they be as town newcomers?

Students can also ponder whether the individual, or only their skin color, determines treatment.

As for Daniel and applying to others from outside the United States, why was he treated badly for having lived elsewhere, and why does speaking favorably of one's home in another country often color one as not properly devoted to the United States? Is one expected to undergo some kind of indoctrination, never speaking favorably, or at all, of elsewhere? Must one's home be criticized and renounced before one can be accepted by peers? What does this imply? How many readers would enjoy doing the same regarding their hometown when visiting another state, or the United States if overseas?

Teens face problems with their church, meaning that they are transferred to the school and town, as the population is the same. Mena, from Brande's (2007) *Evolution, Me, and Other Freaks of Nature*, is banned from her church for exposing them, and her parents, to a lawsuit by sending an apology to a teen who'd attempted suicide after repeated efforts to save his soul. Her parents are furious as are congregants and classmates, and once her science lab partner's views lead her toward considering evolution, she quickly becomes even more of a target.

Another negative experience is Hallelujah's in Holmes's (2015) *The Distance Between Lost and Found*, in which her youth group's most popular boy spreads rumors about her chastity and virtue after she was caught in his room after hours during a retreat. None care for hearing her version, so she remains silent, accepting outcast status and hearing others speak cruelly regarding her. Hallelujah's story turns to one of survival when her parents send her to a camp in the woods for structure, becoming lost while hiking. Now stranded and praying for rescue, she considers what happened that fateful night and its cost.

Another outcast is Dill from Zentner's (2016) *The Serpent King*, whose father is his charismatic church's preacher, with handling snakes the norm. His imprisonment for possessing child pornography quickly becomes not an ideal situation for one living in a town named for the KKK's founder. Predictably, Dill's also a bull's eye for denigrations, but his best friends help him manage and get through the year.

Students can consider the value of individual opinions and how one learns, grows, or strengthens beliefs if only allowed to consider one viewpoint, with disturbing, or embarrassing, consequences if diverging. It should also be noted that Hallelujah was blamed, losing her reputation for being in a male's room, but he was the one relaying false details and without confidence. Are a female's words worthless, regardless of truth, and what does this imply? How would males feel if the situation were reversed?

What does this mean regarding faith, church treatment of parishioners, and what would occur if applied to the public schools and learning? Further, what's the difference between having the same thoughts, or believing the same things, but not voicing them? As for Dill, students can discern the difference between a son and father's actions, and discuss why they were treated as one rather than separately..

Many responses to the above are in Smith's (2018) *Hearts Unbroken*, where Louise joins her school's journalism team. The theater director announces its play will be casting Black, Latino, and Native American students for lead roles, infuriating parents. They quickly form a protest, carefully worded as retaining the school's traditional heritage, but soon threatening notes targeting minorities and filled with racist hate and worse start appearing, with the town and school quickly in a nasty uproar. Louise and the paper must decide what and how to print as they are also facing pressure regarding their stance.

Students should notice it's the parents protesting, not students, and as the play was *The Wizard of Oz* featuring a lion, scarecrow, tin man, munchkins, witches, and more, casting diverse students hardly seems disruptive. It's also worth considering how quickly racist hate speech appeared, involving the entire town. Why must only White students appear in these parts, why were parents so threatened, and how likely is this to occur in students' schools? What is so wrong with casting a minority in a White part, and if reversed, would there still be complaints? How can this be prevented?

Another situation pitting a teen against a town is KJ in Chandler's (2010) *Wolves, Boys, & Other Things That Might Kill Me*, working as a Yellowstone Park guide. After wolves were reintroduced to the park, she writes a school paper column approving their return. Local ranchers aren't so accepting, citing danger to livestock and other issues, with a town war between environmentalists and ranchers soon beginning and quickly growing ugly, with KJ, and all those in favor, targets.

Similarly, Kevin from Lyga's (2008) *Hero Type* became a town hero after saving a girl and his story going national. He certainly doesn't admit he was watching her a little too closely, practically stalking her, which is forgotten as he's caught up in the hype and being interviewed for news casts. He was unprepared for a photographer snapping his removing "Save Our Troops" magnets from his car and tossing them in the trash, again going viral and now being considered anti-American and a traitor by the same people who were praising him the week before, both situations unnerving and suffocating.

Kevin's counterpart is Quinn, seen kissing a boy not her boyfriend, Carey, an overseas marine. This information speeds rapidly by residents, and she's branded a traitor/slut/anti-American by her military-minded small town. Of course, residents don't realize their relationship or current situation, simply outraged at what they assume to be her betrayal to the United States, its soldiers, and her boyfriend.

UM teens are likely familiar with disputes among environmentalists and ranchers, but what are abuses on both sides, and how can both improve? What does the environment and economy need to be healthy, and what does it mean that others cannot discuss, only loudly protest with violence?

For Kevin, students can picture how the same person can be praised and vilified for acts not fully understood. What does it imply, that one is unable to remove stickers or magnets from a car lest being branded a traitor? What if removing them for new, or different ones equally patriotic or saying essentially the same thing?

Regarding Quinn, what does one kiss mean, and as her true situation isn't known, why is she immediately vilified? Is Carey faithful to her? And for both, why does one act brand one as a US traitor? Students can discuss different scenarios for both characters, using their own views and experiences, examining how hastily, and dangerously, quick opinions and actions appear.

Situations involving wealth and class include Ash from Day's (2016) *The Possibility of Somewhere*, with the wealthy Ash having nearly a straight-A average his senior year, pleasing his prominent family. His problem is his classmate, Eden, who has a perfect 4.0, and he's angry that a so-called nothing from a trailer park could beat him for valedictorian. Eden's only chance for college is the award and its scholarship, having worked hard for her accomplishments, and resenting Ash's attitude as she feels valedictorian is something he wants, not needs.

Emily, as Eden, has had a hard life, seen in Ozkowski's (2016) *Watching Traffic*; now graduated high school, she's held back by her town, seeing only her past. When three, her mother committed suicide in a motel room, leaving her covered in blood and not discovered right away. She was constantly given nicknames as *suicide baby* and worse during school, and now residents are continually complimenting her how well she turned out, considering. Whenever she begins to consider her next step, it seems someone pulls her back into her past, making it difficult to feel ready to move forward.

Hallie, in Cooney's (1991) *The Party's Over*, is equally relevant today, as she's Queen Bee of her high school, the most popular girl and enjoying her sparkling crowd, including a wealthy boyfriend. She had planned to remain in her small town with her entire crowd leaving for college but wasn't prepared for their soon forgetting her with different lives and attitude of her no longer quite meeting their status. This was how she treated others last year, and only now does she realize many remained home also; she must make amends and forge a new life with different, but equally interesting, friends.

Students may wish to discern whether Ash minded losing valedictorian due to grades, Eden being female, or poorer and living in a trailer. What do these imply, what were similar circumstances, and how handled? Eden too has misconceptions, as she's unaware of the parental pressures put upon Ash, and his presumed medical major being one he dreads. Money solves many problems, but not all.

Students may be acquainted with those resembling Emily, but when and how does one cease from continually referring to one's past, or otherwise allow its interference with the future? Can Emily remain in town, or will she always be considered the bloodied daughter of a suicide? Hallie is every student remaining home while friends leave for college and work elsewhere; readers can discuss how to prepare and perhaps share older siblings' situations. Can these friendships be kept, or are they natural partings? Why is attending college seen as superior to not? Why can't popular students be friends with those less so, and why is so-called popularity so valuable, as its quick disappearance left Hallie without friends and without skills to make new ones?

Moreover, Mena, Hallelujah, Maggie, and Quinn are powerless females, a theme constantly seen in novels with rural settings, with Darcy illustrated in French's (2017) *Grit: A Novel*, in which she's branded and viewed as the town prostitute for engaging in the same promiscuous behaviors as males. Gossip and worse surround her, but her actions stem from a trauma unknown to others, and her being nominated for Festival Princess as a cruel joke soon becomes unmanageable.

Likewise, Beckett has a shocking surprise in Vincent's (2021) *Every Single Lie*, as one minute she was happy and popular, but the next her reputation gone after finding the body of a dead newborn stuffed in her boyfriend's bag in the locker room. Naturally, she's considered the mother, shamed and vilified, her boyfriend the victim.

Riley is raped by Rhett, son of her town's most influential family, also disbelieved and scorned, causing her to flee her small town, raising her child while Rhett finishes school and enters college in Glines's (2017) *After the Game: Field Party, Book 3*. Maggie knows her story well, as in Ostrom's (2019) *Unleaving*, she's raped on her college campus and as the males she accused were popular athletes, students harass her until she leaves, running to her aunt's for sanctuary.

Johnston's (2016) *Exit, Pursued by a Bear* portrays Hermione dosed with Rohypnol, raped, and left at a party; when her emergency contraception fails, she terminates, with the gossip and harassment waiting for her return to school. Similarly, Camille learns she's pregnant, but termination is difficult in her small Texas town. Her best friend Bea is pro-life, but when another friend offers to drive her to a different state, Bea accompanies them to support Camille in Biggs Waller's (2019) *Girls on the Verge*.

These stories abound in YAL, as in society; with plots nearly interchangeable, popular/wealthy/athletic male rapes female, she isn't believed, and subsequently subject to continual harassment and torment. Beckett's situation is different, but she, too, is automatically presumed at fault and targeted. Students should question why rape continues to be a prolific crime, and why it's females who are automatically blamed in these and like situations. No one, regardless of race, religion, or any difference, desires rape.

Why are males treated differently, and should males be reading these female-oriented novels, perhaps equally, or more, telling and important to them than females? There are extremely few YAL titles featuring male rape; is even considering such a terrible, violative crime occurring to them anathema? Regardless of the discussion's direction, all students should pause before showing anything but compassion to those involved and assisting in lessening such crimes.

School shootings are increasing, with Nijkamp's (2016) *This Is Where It Ends* depicting students beginning school, gathered in the auditorium, soon discovering they're locked in with a shooter. Keplinger's (2018) *That's Not What Happened* portrays a different story; three years after a shooting, its most famous victim has been lauded for proclaiming her faith while dying and the only victim portrayed.

Other students have stories to tell, and know that the faith declaration is false, somehow becoming truth in the confused aftermath, but not revealing the truth continues guilt and is wrong; doing so topples an idol and further devastates parents, both thorny choices.

Students are aware of shootings, but the above ethical dilemma and similar ones could be reviewed. Perhaps the best response for educators and students alike is that if it occurs, teachers will know what to do, because they *are* teachers.

Situations with more positive choices are Carson's, in Gansworth's (2018) *Give Me Some Truth*, in which he wants to accomplish something big his senior year, on and off the reservation. He decides to form a band, difficult at first, but eventually making the music of their dreams. Cash, from Zentner's (2021) *In the Wild Light*, loves his small Appalachian town and family, and when receiving a scholarship to an exclusive prep school is thrilled for the opportunity, but pained by leaving home.

Finally, Knowles' (2015) *Read Between the Lines* is a set of 10 interconnected short stories showing a single day of a typical rural high school. Various teens' voices are relayed, their revelations indicating how much more alike than different we are, and how much in common when detailing daily lives. These stories should resonate with contemporary teens, as well as the YAL titles above.

ACTIVITY FOR BUILDING RURAL PRIDE AND SELF-ESTEEM

Establishing Hometown Pride	Activity
All adolescents are familiar with their homes, and usually travel by route to school, work, or elsewhere paying little attention to what is passed between and among destinations. However, if visiting for the first time, multiple items will be noted. This activity, revised from Author (1997) reacquaints UM teens with the unique features and history of their town while reminding them there is much for which to feel pride. Of course, knowledge of one's area must be acquired before pride or appreciation may emerge.	
The project may be completed in multiple ways, dependent upon educator choice. Much of the work is completed out of class, a planning consideration.	
Step One: Discussing Microaggressions	Examples
Students create a list of microaggressions regarding their rural lifestyle. What have they heard or read about rural areas and those living in them, and what has been expressed to them personally? Students should enjoy sharing the most outrageous, typical, questionable comments heard, with the teacher compiling a complete list.	*Are there buffalo here?* *Do Native Americans live in tepees?* *Are there nice restaurants or stores here?* A stronger sense of community will be formed once discovered how many similar microaggressions—and student reactions to them—are cited. These may also be categorized (most common, fantastical, stereotypical). This also allows students to consider the views or questions they may have regarding lifestyles elsewhere; what comments or questions are made or asked about other places? Non-White students' questions may be markedly different and should likewise be explored.

Step Two: Discussing Rural Preferences
Because perception is crucial in determining satisfaction, students next list their individually perceived advantages and disadvantages regarding their lifestyle.

Examples

Advantages Disadvantages
No traffic Long drives
Town traditions Cold winters
Social network Old school buildings
Historic buildings and facilities

Students discuss and compare lists and will doubtless discover one's advantage is another's disadvantage; there are few absolutes. Cold weather, for example, may be disliked by some, with others eager for winter as it brings snowmobiles, ice-fishing, or skiing.

All students can reconsider their tightly held opinions by hearing different views, gain perspective, and perhaps have some negative attitudes altered or changed.

Step Three: Discovering Rural Beauty
Here, students consider and explore the unique features of their town and surrounding area through photographs (presumably using phones).

Examples

Students are given a few days to photograph items felt particularly interesting, lovely, unusual, frightening, humorous, or otherwise noteworthy. Pictures may be categorized (unusual, humorous) and/or a total, such as five to ten specified, requiring students to narrow photos to those most representative of the category or otherwise favorite.

Photos may be presented (slideshow, video, collage, poster) individually or in groupings with explanations for selections. The entire class may also create categories and select those felt most representative. The different photographs—and those identical—will create discussion of the myriad features of even the smallest town. Many students who have never lived elsewhere will see photos of items they had never previously noticed, or perhaps considered differently. Again, discussion of choices will allow a new appreciation of the uniqueness and beauty of their town and area.

Establishing Hometown Pride	
	Activity

Step Four: Hometown History

Many rural adolescents and their families have lived in the same area for decades, with a common complaint of nothing of note ever occurring. Teens may not be as familiar with their hometown as believed, however, and this step has them researching their town's history and people.	Examples Students can form small groups with each given a topic (or several, depending upon class size) and individuals gather information as decided among themselves. Although much can be found on the Internet, students should be encouraged to interview older residents, visit the historical society, newspaper office, courthouse, museum, and similar places. The example below may be used to record information.
The class can determine the information they most want to discover, and those items can be placed into topics; typical ones include town origin/founders, famous/infamous people, history of buildings/landmarks, schools or churches, notorious/tragic events, natural disasters, town notables, or special events/traditions.	*Topic: History of Schools* *Sources for Research* *Retired teachers* *School newspapers and yearbooks* *District records*
The educator decides the minimum number of sources required depending upon topic and availability, but three sources is generally reasonable. Of course, additional sources may be discovered.	*Sources Used* *District records* *Retired teachers*
Once all information has been compiled and organized within groups, it may be shared with the class through a variety of presentation formats. Students may also present to various larger groups, inviting those interviewed, families, or others. A smaller document, such as a bulleted fact sheet, summarizing information gathered should be required plus sources documented.	Information *The largest graduating class was in 1967 with 35 students; the smallest in 1945 with 25.*

Step Five: Hometown History Discussion

Students and others should engage in rich discussion regarding their town and its history, considering its past, present, and future from multiple views.	Of special note is recording one's history, whether a community or individually. What is unrecorded is forever lost; all students should realize the importance and power of being heard and known, now and in the future.

STEREOTYPES AND MICROAGGRESSIONS ACTIVITY

Files and folders should be created for all activities, with educators determining whether discussion or assignment, completed individually or with partners/groups, and time spent. Here, students receive separate reference sheets defining rural microaggressions and stereotypes with examples (cited in chapter). Discussing stereotypes first and then microaggressions works well; students comment on examples seen/heard for each, with those not on the reference sheets added and duplications counted.

Assignments/Discussion for Stereotypes and Microaggressions

Depending upon educator choice and applicability, these may be assignments or various discussions.

Beginning Activity for Stereotypes and Microaggressions	Discussion Questions/Activities for Stereotypes and Microaggressions
The initial reference sheets are each expanded to charts/tables (for ease of reading and recording).	Those stereotypes and microaggressions heard are recorded, and how perceived discussed. Research should be completed as necessary to refute various claims accurately, with students understanding facts are necessary for accurate support, including dispelling rural depictions.
Students record how/when sheet examples (and those new/different) were seen/heard, and rank by most frequently encountered. Students are to continue compiling examples throughout the unit, or longer. This chart may be used, or others created, for the remaining ideas.	Students recount responses made by themselves or family to microaggressions or other stereotypical comments, including the comment, its reaction, and opinion/analysis of situation.
	Students indicate which is encountered more frequently, stereotypes or microaggressions, and provide a rationale for why this might be.
	State and provide a rationale for which students believe more harmful, stereotypes or microaggressions.

Importance of Responses to Stereotypes and Microaggressions Activity

Once the terms are fully understood, next is discussing the importance of responding well. Students should be encouraged to challenge negative rurality depictions, as silence hints of embarrassment or acceptance of being lesser, continuing the rural status quo. Addressing such remarks or depictions personally is affirmative and powerful, allows correction of rural lifestyle biases and misinformation, and reinforces its value.

As most teens sometimes feel insignificant or powerless regardless of location, learning effective methods for challenging negative portrayals assists in developing a strong sense of self and satisfaction, valuable for both adolescence and adulthood (and essential for non-White teens).

By understanding and attempting to lessen their own minority stigmatization based upon stereotypes and unfamiliarity, rural adolescents can also acquire an authentic understanding of the negatives attached to other such groups and a stronger desire to assist in dispelling them. White and non-White peers will discover another common bond in working together.

Expansion to Other Minorities Activity

Educators may wish to separate stereotypes and microaggressions commonly received by, or unique to, non-Whites, if without racial minorities or perhaps only one, emphasizing stereotypes may differ for various groups, but all are detrimental. Otherwise, minority students should participate in these activities as any other.

Discussion Questions/Activities for Understanding the Value of Replying to Stereotypes and Microaggressions

These activities may be added to the compiled charted information, or students can create additional charts/tables for these activities and subsequent discussions:

Select the rural depictions considered most inaccurate and offensive and compose short statements refuting each one. Discuss both, focusing upon why these depictions are made, continued, so disliked by students, and ways in which they do not resemble the stereotype.

As a group, select the one or two negative rural depictions most cited (especially to non-White inhabitants), and discuss using the same format as above. These would be the most important to dispel.

Students create appropriate responses to either all the negative depictions or focus upon those most common. These can be voiced or written, but those that are considered most thoughtful should be recorded and discussed.

Discussion Questions/Activities for Expansion to Other Minorities Activity

Students, including non-White students, chart common depictions of *other* groups considered most inaccurate and offensive, compose short statements refuting each with appropriate research as applicable.

Students share their depictions and statements with the class and select the one or two negative depictions most cited for each group. Similarities to rural statements would be identified and compared, with discussion of how and why dispelling is particularly vital.

Discerning Sincere Questions From Microaggressions and Responses

Next is recognition between a sincere question and microaggression, as meaning is also dependent upon tone and demeanor, not always correctly interpreted. Being asked how one spends time in an area may be another's interest in learning of popular activities and eager to share or compare those from his/her home, rather than denigrative.

As not all seemingly questionable comments are microaggressions, responding to all as if so, is equally stereotypical and undesirable, important for adolescents' comprehension.

Discussion Questions/Activities for Discerning Sincere Questions From Microaggressions and Responses

Educators demonstrate intent by speaking the above microaggressions aloud, using varied tones and demeanors, to model differences between earnest and negative questions. Students identify which is being conveyed and may practice in other groupings.

Next is rehearsing answering genuine questions; while most teens can instantly imagine numerous responses, sharing them aloud and particularly with strangers, can be difficult. Here, they can begin by either composing responses to the above questions and then saying aloud or saying aloud to others and revising until satisfied with comments.

The goal is for students to be comfortable with their responses and be able to *say* them aloud to others in a confident, conversational style without referring to notes, awkward pauses, or moving from the subject.

Next is practice addressing adults and others not known well, or at all, as these are their likely audience. Educators can model different personas (or have other educators assist) with discussion and practice of appropriate responses for each. Distinctly considered is responding to those of different ages, and to others known or unknown to students.

Responding to Microaggressions

As students have practiced determining tones and demeanors, less time should be needed for recognizing microaggressions.

The goal is to learn to speak with other teens and adults and not to enhance or create combative or otherwise negative situations through sarcastic replies or accusations of stereotyping or ignorance. Instead, it is ascertaining the most appropriate response for the appropriate circumstance.

Discussion Questions/Activities for Responding to Microaggressions

As students have already polished responses to friendly questions, may be used for microaggressions. This practice is to assist with replying calmly and saying what was intended instead of wavering or stopping from intimidation or frustration.

This activity can be first completed with the teacher and students, having them practice responses to the above microaggressions with peers, with discussion and suggestions following.

Practice is needed here, and a reminder that change only occurs by effort, with not responding, or doing so ineffectively, assures situations will remain the same, or worsen. The ability of speaking for oneself well is a great motivator, however.

Further, all teens are without adults' perspective and maturity, and those working with tourists whom they will presumably never again encounter may be making wild or otherwise unhelpful replies. These students may have more difficulty with responses, if enjoying the more inappropriate.

Students should also work with other adults, such as various teachers, school personnel, or townspeople, with the assumption of their activity understanding. While more realistic if working with unfamiliar adults, this is unlikely in small towns, but it is their use of authority when questioning that allows students' more serious and thoughtful responses.

Adults ask the same microaggressions as above, with students responding. The response is discussed, with the adult aiding as needed. Students may work with one or several adults, but they help students create replies they are comfortable voicing.

After working with adults, students can share responses with one another and the class. A major point should be the difference between responses for adults and peers.

Microaggressions and Sarcasm/Fantastical Responses

Not all students have difficulty voicing responses to adults, and those regularly encountering tourists in the summer and other jobs already have experience. Days are long with scores passing through asking frustrating or particularly obtuse questions, and if some respond sarcastically/fantastically, it must be noted that it is difficult refraining from flip replies.

Students and adults should share comments heard and said, or those one wanted to say, but afterward the discussion should move toward its main points, of sarcastic/fantastic replies ultimately ineffective.

Discussion Questions/Activities for Microaggressions and Sarcasm/Fantastical Responses

These practices should involve all students, regardless of prior responses, as all should be informed of impressions. Educators should again ask the above questions.

Students share glib responses typically offered (or desired) as *We can turn Old Faithful on and off in the break room; Mt. Rushmore is placed in a garage in the winter* with discussion focusing on why used and feelings afterward.

Next explored is whether such responses were given to avoid more thoughtful ones, and why.

The respondent's reaction to these replies is also discussed, as *What did the person do or say after the comment was made?* Responses will vary, but should be considered and discussed, focusing on effect. Students should explore the point of using sarcasm or the fantastical, and what was achieved.

Further consideration focuses upon how such responses represented the rural lifestyle, provided information regarding the site visited, or what impressions were left upon visitors. It should be noted that these responses doubtless do more to harm others' views of rurality than remaining silent, perhaps not considered.

Next, instead of glib responses, students ponder other, better responses and what might occur. Then they can explore possible reactions when one is informed of the reality (*the Pony Express isn't used anymore*). Responding to thoughts of difficulties exacerbated or similar impressions upon listeners regarding the speaker and area will demonstrate expressed negativity.

From previous discussions, students already have practice supplying more positive answers, all applicable to microaggressions. Practice here would be responding pleasantly and accurately to the posed question.

For particularly mature students, sarcastic/fantastical responses can be effective and perhaps a better choice. However, the format should be offering a flip reply in a friendly tone, then immediately stating facts refuting what was said.

This is effective (albeit difficult) as it retains the sarcasm, but its bite is immediately tempered by the facts that follow, disproving the microaggression by intelligence, humor, and subtly reminding speakers of inappropriate views.

Practice should focus on teens' tone and friendliness, allowing speakers to feel they are part of the humor rather than its target, and the ability to hold the listener's attention for a factual response.

Unexpected Microaggressions

- The last response type practiced is essentially a reminder that more microaggressions than those above will be heard, or responses questioned.
- Questions or remarks cannot be predicted, but continued practice, additions created, and experiences shared will allow preparation for the unexpected, and handling challenges.

Discussion Questions/Activities for Unexpected Microaggressions

- Rural teens' accomplishments, interests, and daily lives are as significant and varied as others' elsewhere, and a necessary understanding is that their responses to may be received with disbelief when lifestyle realities do not meet another's expectations.
- Speakers may laugh at teens or ask for the real response (*You work for the Farmers Market? How can such a small-town support employees? How large is it—two or three rows?*), with such comments denigrating teens' honesty and their lifestyle. Reiterating the same response (smiling and stating what was offered is true, with additional details added if desired) can fluster most, so practice handling such replies is necessary for teens.
- Educators can lead these discussions, and stress not tacitly conceding to inaccurate views for fewer problems. Assurance that the speaker is the one lacking, not the respondent, should be stressed and truthfulness is stronger than inaccurate opinions. The adolescent's power is from the statement, not its reception, an important realization.

Responding to Impersonal Stereotypes and Microaggressions

- Educators may discuss and assist students in responding to media/technological stereotypes and microaggressions first, or last. Doing so first is anonymous and preparation for addressing others; last allows for greater commentary sophistication, leading to higher probability of personal replies.
- Regardless, understanding that addressing points seen or read calls for a formal response requiring time and effort that few are willing to complete is telling.

Discussion Questions/Activities for Responding to Impersonal Stereotypes and Microaggressions

- If adolescents wish to lessen rural stereotypes, then they must begin doing so themselves through thoughtful, appropriate responses. Educators can create separate response templates, such as for a television show or news/radio broadcasts, which can then be filled with information specific to the negative portrayal seen or heard and personalized as to affects upon its writer. Once completed, they may be submitted as requested by the receiver, located beforehand by students.

With practice, students can increasingly personalize templates, but they allow for an ease of response and allowing many to address negatives. Templates can be shared; a news broadcast suddenly receiving twenty complaints will doubtless pay attention. Similarly, responses increase the likelihood of students continuing to address stereotypes and change perhaps occurring.

While responses may not be received, students should realize this is common and not a reason to discontinue complaints. The power is in their sending (and presumably read by someone), rather than responses, which may also be received with additional invitations made.

REFERENCES

Cox, K., Hayes, S., Jones, L. W., Martin, S., Millner, T., & Obst, L. (Executive Producers). (2010–2015). *Hot in Cleveland* [TV series]. Hazy Mills Productions; Samden Productions, TV Land Original Productions.

Levitan, S., & Morton, J. (Executive Producers). (2009–2020). *Modern Family* [TV series]. Twentieth Century Fox Television.

Chapter 6

Lesbian, Gay, Bisexual, Transgender, and Queer/Questioning (LGBTQ+) Students and Rural Communities

Teens who are LGBTQ+ face numerous difficulties regardless of where living. Rural teens' challenges are magnified by smaller populations and while improving overall, locations and individuals differ regarding support and attitude. Unfortunately, many LGBTQ+ teens, regardless of Upper Midwest (UM) location, find acceptance only after relocation.

LGBTQ+ ADOLESCENTS

Approximately 10% of those aged 13 to 17 identify themselves as LGBTQ+ throughout the United States, a significant population (Kosciw et al., 2019; Movement Advancement Project, 2019). Like those considered exceptional, LGBTQ+ teens are also different from their immediate families; however, the former students' issues are recognizable to all encountered with parents and others presumably focusing upon their best interests and proud of achievements.

Those LGBTQ+ also share acceptance or relationship difficulties with other racial minorities, and both are usually harassed for who they are. However, Black or Asian American teens facing school bullying return home to parents and families resembling them and, having likely experienced the same situations, able to provide effective comfort, assistance, or advice. LGBTQ+ teens are unique here in that most probably have non-LGBTQ+ parents and immediate family to assist with acceptance issues. Additionally, others hide their sexuality, fearing condemnation or worse from disapproving parents and friends, again meaning no needed support or affirmation.

And, unlike other teens, those LGBTQ+ express hesitancy in sharing their true feelings, problems, or issues with parents or friends, even if welcoming, as listeners may consider themselves unequipped or unqualified to provide needed assistance. For example, how do still-unsophisticated teens have productive or enjoyable conversations concerning being asexual, polyamorous, or pansexual with those never having heard of the terms, much less their meaning, and those with unwelcoming families cannot share at all (Kosciw et al., 2019; Mahowald et al., 2020; Movement Advancement Project, 2021; The Trevor Project, 2021; True Colors United, 2021; Willingham & Ajilore, 2019)?

Unlike exceptional teens or those of color, many LGBTQ+ teens have good reason to fear revealing their sexuality to parents, as doing so may mean unacceptance and demand for change, secrecy, or literal home banishment. While homelessness among all teens is approximately 7%, it is 40% among those LGBTQ+ with 13% forced to undergo conversion therapy or otherwise forced to hide their sexuality. Naturally, these prospects are unappealing and doubtless contributing to only one of three such teens declaring their home as a completely accepting one (Kosciw et al., 2019; Mahowald et al., 2020; Movement Advancement Project; 2019; Olito, 2021; The Trevor Project, 2021; True Colors United, 2021).

Educational and Other Victimization of LGBTQ+ Adolescents

All adolescents should be safe and accepted at home and school, but many LGBTQ+ are not, leaving unwelcoming families for schools equally uncomfortable, or worse. Most of these teens stated schools as being openly hostile, where facing the most discrimination, and felt forced to hide, change, or deny their true selves for fear of personal safety or other harsh, and likely continuing, reprisals. Additionally, most relayed they avoided school parties, games, concerts, plays, and other events or attended with pretend boy/girlfriends or large friendship groups (Kosciw et al., 2019; Mahowald et al., 2020).

Majority students' school harassment of those unlike them has occurred for decades regardless of laws and policies, but LGBTQ+ teens are doubly victimized as also mistreated by some educators, administrators, or staff. The most common complaints were adults' homophobic comments, their failing to intervene (or not acting quickly) when witnessing abuses from others, and not reporting them.

Censorship of LGBTQ+ Materials

Additionally, the teaching of or otherwise positive representations of LGBTQ+ persons in class appears miniscule, doubtless hindered by disapproving parents and other adults. In tandem, nearly half of these teens reported being unable to locate information about LGBTQ+ issues or people in school libraries, and school computers blocking such searches.

Doyle (2016) examined banned and challenged materials, noting many educators self-censor (especially LGBTQ+ titles) with 82% to 97% of challenges unreported (although nearly all schools have strict censorship policies and procedures with professional organizations also strong resources). Such silence results in no media coverage and effectively allows censorship, but also discovered was individuals' active support regarding title retention resulted in preserving most targeted books. Activism is vital, as more than half of titles that were challenged or banned were either written by authors of color, represented minority groups, or had LGBTQ+ characters/content.

Positive Effects of Gay/Straight Alliance/Gender Sexualities Alliances (GSAs)

Naturally, LGBTQ+ students' hostile treatment in schools, regardless of location, have lasting effects upon their mental health and well-being, often taking years to overcome. Those fortunate, and far fewer, students in more welcoming ones, unsurprisingly report more positive mental health, acceptance, and higher self-esteem, with a central necessary factor Gay/Straight Alliance/Gender Sexualities Alliances (GSAs).

Schools featuring GSAs (approximately 62%) find them extremely helpful, advocating for and assisting LGBTQ+ teens while promoting tolerance/acceptance among peers and educators. Unfortunately, not all schools have GSAs or strong ones, and student attendance rate is relatively low at 38% (Kosciw et al., 2019), although students hiding being LGBTQ+ are doubtless unlikely to attend meetings. Still, GSAs' effects are positive, as shown by Kosciw et al. (2019), Mahowald et al. (2020), and Movement Advancement Project (2019).

With the above difficulties and more, it is hardly surprising that many such teens skip school, have lower grades, and drop out earlier, and are more prone to depression and suicide (Kosciw et al., 2019; Mahowald et al., 2020; Movement Advancement Project, 2021; The Trevor Project, 2021; True Colors United, 2021), all sobering and significant.

Legalities Affecting LGBTQ+ Adolescents

Another formidable challenge to LGBTQ+ teens is legalities; at the time of this writing, bills targeting LGBTQ+ students have been passed by over 12 states (several overriding Governor vetoes) and on dockets of numerous others. HB 1557 (Parental Rights in Education Bill) states that the discussion of sexual orientation or gender identity by school personnel or third parties may not occur in kindergarten through third grade, or in ways deemed age or developmentally inappropriate for students, according to individual state standards.

A bill banning transgender females from participating in girls school sports in all public schools and some private ones, SB 1165 (Save Women's Sports Act), is claimed as necessary to protect cisgender (i.e., those whose personal identity and gender corresponds with their birth sex) female athletes' opportunities by providing them with even levels of competition and athletic scholarship opportunities. However, Jones et al. (2017) reviewed studies about this topic, finding no research stating transgender individuals have athletic advantages over cisgender peers.

Another bill becoming law is SB 1138, which bans gender reassignment surgery for anyone under age 18, even with parental consent. It also promises to hold physicians performing such procedures liable for unprofessional conduct and subject to discipline by their appropriate licensing units or regulatory boards.

All these bills are touted as granting more parental control, fairness, and protection rather than targeted exclusions of LGBTQ+ students. HB 1557 promotes family decisions concerning curricula, intending to eliminate LGBTQ+ topics and information from schools, placing them in the home instead. Its presumption seems that without this law, LGBTQ+ issues and themes permeate schools to the extent of hindering natural development, with early exposure perhaps creating more such students, and indoctrinating them in becoming pro-LGBTQ+.

Equitable playing conditions for cisgender female athletes is promised by SB 1165, with its view that transgender athletes have inequitable strength/size advantages, although undocumented. It also presents a frightening, somewhat robotic, view of transgender individuals as being invincible players, highest-point scorers, and perhaps injuring teammates. Likewise, such higher performance also presumes their winning the most awards and all-important athletic scholarships.

Similarly, shielding those under 18 (this group presumably unable to make responsible health decisions) from physicians offering gender reassignment surgery is specified as SB 1138s purpose. This bill claims protection for those desiring irreversible procedures, an underlying view of being transgender perhaps a phase, fortified by pro-LGBTQ+ media and others with surgery soon regretted. Another ugly purpose seems halting the transgender population, with additional restraints after age 18, when many young adults are no longer covered by parental insurance or otherwise have less financial and other supports available.

These bills/laws have unclear components and monitoring systems and may be reversed or otherwise changed by higher courts, but currently remain and are increasing. Although actively protested by many, it must be remembered voters (or non-voters) placed politicians introducing and supporting these bills and laws into office.

RURAL LGBTQ+ ADOLESCENTS

The above information and data represented all U.S. LGBTQ+ students, including rural, but these students, while experiencing the same situations, find them harsher than those elsewhere, with LGBTQ+ rural students of color all but invisible (Centers for Disease Control and Prevention, 2019; Kosciw et al., 2019; Movement Advancement Project, 2019; The Trevor Project, 2021).

LGBTQ+ students, like all teens, are essentially the same regardless of where living, but their *communities* are different. As rural populations are lower, so are those LGBTQ+, and more visible in smaller places than larger ones. Living among a community but not accepted by it can be unimaginably demoralizing and hardly preparation for satisfying futures, and doubtless reason rural teens hide their sexuality/gender in larger numbers than those suburban/urban.

The sweeping 2019 GLSEN study of the United States (which included rural areas), and the 2019 MAP study focused on rural LGBTQ+ adolescents, including the far fewer minority (racial, cultural) teens from these locations. On average, rural public opinion is less supportive of LGBTQ+ individuals and issues than elsewhere, but as always, locations and support differ upon place and individuals within it. Still, rural schools are the least safe (and having fewest GSAs and other school supports) compared to suburban/urban ones, with these teens most likely to face various serious and ongoing harassments.

Rural LGBTQ+ Adolescents Friendships and Relationships

Like those exceptional and of color, these LGBTQ+ teens may not have peers their age/race/gender for friendships/relationships in the UM and specifically smaller towns. Class sizes of 15 are very different from those of 250; for example, a school's three Black students may be an LGBTQ sophomore male and two elementary females, or the two lesbian females, a sophomore and senior, not attracted to one another. Numerous other combinations and situations exist, but as small schools have fewer students, friendships and relationships are markedly challenging for these teens. Essentially rural adolescents' school environments are more negative than those non-rural in every possible category or situation, including those cited above (Kosciw et al., 2019; Movement Advancement Project, 2019).

Rural Schools/Communities and GSAs

Rural finances are particularly tight, with resources limited and hard decisions made, inadvertently working against any number of students. If choosing between replacing a dangerous roof or creating a fully operational GSA, for example, then LGBTQ+ students must wait. However, others will also, as the football team or Science Olympiad and more also have wants unmet. Overall, rural schools are of quality and provide rich experiences to students, but like most across the country, are lacking in resources and finances and must serve crucial structural needs first.

It is easy to presume GSAs and other supports can still be created outside the school as in larger places, but it is challenging without funding and especially small numbers (smaller, with some hiding their sexual identity), more so if a town is not particularly supportive.

Religious Communities and LGBTQ+ Adolescents

Rural communities and churches are tightly connected and the presumed view of those LGBTQ+ as non-religious is untrue, albeit confusing; although more likely than those in suburban/urban areas to be devout, they are less likely to be active members of a particular church (NPR et. al, 2019). Whether religious leaders and congregations are actively homophobic or not depends upon place, but rural LGBTQ+ teens are more likely to encounter personal hostility, rejection, or conversion attempts than in churches elsewhere (Kosciw et al., 2019; Movement Advancement Project, 2019).

Naturally, hearing condemnation in sermons and largely unwelcome by congregations can be overwhelmingly hurtful and harmful to LGBTQ+ teens, with little recourse available. Here, options include ceasing attendance, attending, and hiding one's sexuality, attending and promoting being LGBTQ+ (presumably difficult for unsophisticated teens and those facing parental disapproval), or traveling to another town with friendly, but unfamiliar congregations, also usually unfeasible.

That is, the next closest town may not have the same denomination and/or a welcoming congregation, meaning driving an hour, probably more, one way makes such attendance unlikely. Even if attempting, being an active member, serving on various committees and appearing at the many social or other functions, would take an enormous amount of time.

Communities and LGBTQ+ Adolescents

It was indicated that these students also have generally negative community experiences (Kosciw et al., 2019; Movement Advancement Project, 2019), as if discriminated and otherwise treated poorly in school or church, this transfers to the community as residents are the same. These adults echo school and church experiences, again denying LGBTQ+ teens additional social connections, opportunities, and feelings of belonging.

That is, church members and spouses also own the local grocery store or restaurants; they may deny after school jobs to LGBTQ+ students or refuse to sponsor a prom or softball team. Community environments are harsher overall for rural teens than those non-rural in all categories or situations (including those cited above) and are without the assists (e.g., LGBTQ+ youth groups). These teens may be essentially welcomed in town businesses, but noticed, harassed, or discouraged from lingering from adults or peers; those supporting them may face equal treatment.

Legislative Issues and Rural Communities

However, perhaps the most threatening situation regarding the rural LGBTQ+ population regardless of age is legislative issues. Rural states are red, conservative ones, with Governors eager to sign bills negative to those LGBTQ+, especially those cited above. The smallest towns are far less likely to have nondiscriminatory policies (and more apt to have discriminatory ones), plus those residents' political power is nearly invisible (Kosciw et al., 2019; Movement Advancement Project, 2019).

For example, a church or other group may object to anything LGBTQ+-related, creating a ubiquitous presence through pamphlet distribution, speaking at town meetings or schools, or having booths during homecoming, fairs, or other community celebrations. While not unlawful, such dominance and stridency deters those pro-LGBTQ+ from acting similarly.

LGBTQ+-themed novels and other materials may be removed from a public or school library without interference; although illegal, the school board may agree with overturning this action requiring a lawsuit that probably won't be filed. Such issues and more are relayed, showing rurality as particularly vulnerable to various legislation and policies with little recourse.

Rural Minority LGBTQ+ Adolescents

Unfortunately, minority LGBTQ+ students have an even lower quality of life (in all categories above, and in most imagined) than White teens, whether LGBTQ+ or not. There are fewer minorities in the UM overall, even in the largest cities, and few to none in the smallest towns, but they do exist and are certainly visible, often negatively. Already apart from the majority and facing difficulties for being non-White, a second divide and additional target, is this groups' gender/sexuality, for those out.

The GLSEN and MAP studies (Kosciw et al., 2019; Movement Advancement Project, 2019) included rural minority LGBTQ+ teens, but data regarding them were absent for many of the above categories as there were so few identifying from this group (or willing to so classify). Additionally, most minority adolescents (other than Native Americans and some Hispanic/Latinx clusters) reside in the UM's largest cities, not necessarily considered rural by some researchers, and like the U.S. Census, towns of populations less than 5,000 are not surveyed by every organization with estimates used instead.

These teens face school, community, and church slights and harassments disproportionate to all other students. Discrimination may also be somewhat unidentified, as negative treatment could be from race/culture, being LGBTQ+, or both, surely contributing to these students feeling permanently unwelcome and heightening the associated corresponding negative effects of lesser feelings of safety, well-being, and belonging lasting far into adulthood.

CHALLENGES FACED BY LGBTQ+ STUDENTS BY REGION

As might be presumed, discriminations faced by all LGBTQ+ adolescents vary by the type of school (urban, suburban, and rural) and U.S. region. Rural schools indicated higher levels of difficulties in all areas for this group, with those in the South and the Midwest having more discriminative practices than the West or the Northeast as indicated in the research above.

Regardless of location, schools and adults have a responsibility to all students; Cart (2003) noted that while schools are aware of non-majority students, their treatment of them is not particularly positive or helpful, continuing their experiences ranging from invisibility to harassment. Such negativity surely seems essential for majority adolescents' understanding of the often-substantial differences of classmates' lives and situations, plus practicing empathy, recognizing differences aren't flaws, and treating all respectfully, rather than actively adversarial toward those unlike them.

LGBTQ+ adolescents are underrepresented in classrooms, especially those rural, as shown by above data; such absence reinforces their silence, isolation, and increasing unhappiness. Although attaining amiability or understanding of this group or any different from the majority can be difficult, using young adult literature (YAL) with LGBTQ+ protagonists and characters is a way to begin building better relationships among students.

LGBTQ+ adolescents can recognize themselves within YAL, certainly vital to those in the UM feeling alone or having few (or few out) peers for friends, relationships, or older role models. Now-burgeoning titles from all genres feature purposeful, confident, and inspiring characters representing all spectrums of LGBTQ+ identities (and race/culture), the same as their markedly younger authors. Online bookstores and other prominent sites have separate sections of the newest and best LGBTQ+ YAL, with publishers (such as Lorimar) exclusively offering these themed novels, all marketed to teens.

It seems equally vital and valuable that teens read of others dissimilar and in different, or unfamiliar, situations from themselves, and engaging in meaningful discussions regarding them. Naturally, using YAL with LGBTQ+ characters is one significant way to raise student awareness and increase sensitivity and tolerance of these peers, lessening the negativity faced from majority teens and often educators. Of course, using these titles does not guarantee more positive educator and/or student outlook and behavior, but avoiding them assures encouraging changes won't occur.

What does it mean to an LGBTQ+ UM English language arts (ELA) education student, assigned Thrash's *Honor Girl: A Graphic Memoir* (2015) for whole class reading and discussion in an Adolescent Literature class? This graphic novel is Thrash's autobiographical account of her realization of being a lesbian at her venerable summer camp with its upper-class Southern girls, and her disastrous first crush, later becoming a ghastly relationship attempt, with a counselor when she's 15. The following comment was included with the student's novel review:

> *Honor Girl* has been the most memorable graphic novel that I have read. I just want to say that in my twenty years of life and as an English major, this is the first text that has been assigned to me portraying LGBTQ+ relationships. Coming to this realization has felt like a slap in the face from every other teacher or professor that I have ever had, but it has also brought me great joy.
>
> Thank you for assigning this book, you may never know what students in your classroom have never seen themselves represented in text before throughout their educational career. I am excited to be a teacher so that I can uphold this representation for my students before they are twenty years old and astonished at the lack of content that they have been able to fully relate to beforehand. This goes not only for LGBTQ+ representation, but for members of all different cultures and communities. (Student, 2021)

Presumably this student spoke for numerous others, and it is chilling to consider those who would have benefitted from these titles, had they been used in their classrooms. Rural educators owe their LGBTQ+ students a great deal, with using like YAL a way to begin improving their school experiences. Even better is using Readers Theater as another way to discuss these titles (the above student's class activity for *Honor Girl*), with instructions and examples included for this strategy in a section below.

YAL novels portraying LGBTQ+ protagonists are burgeoning, and many are set in small towns (although seldom in the UM, true of all genres).

Unfortunately, these settings often follow the standard themes of school and community harassment, parental and religious intolerance, and protagonists' failed attempt to hide sexuality, leading to difficulties above. There are titles showing these teens' acceptance, but fewer.

Still, prejudicial situations persist regardless of location, of course, and are as important as others showing teens living positive and enjoyable lives. The best titles are multifaceted, presenting multiple issues and complex characters rather than one-note stories, as the typical LGBTQ+ teen grappling with school/community/parental/religious harassment until graduating, moving, and beginning a better life.

A wider range of sexuality is also seen, rather than the standard gay male, lesbian female, or bisexual teen, and as with all titles, if one's sexuality isn't represented in a novel with a small-town setting, use one representing the teen rather than location. Unfortunately, regardless of setting, there are few Black male LGBTQ+ protagonists; females, yes, but males remain underrepresented (with the very few LGBTQ+ SPED seen apparently only in nonfiction). A few of these novels are included here, although not rural.

LGBTQ+ novels are a lifeline for like teens, who may not wish to be seen reading them, an area in which ELA educators can assist. All teens should read novels featuring these characters, aside from enjoyable they realistically portray these adolescents' lives. Opening their pages can begin non-LGBTQ+ readers' understanding, tolerance, acceptance, and friendship of those very much like themselves.

As with Chapter 7, many discussion questions are dependent upon individual situations and/or not covered by YAL, such as best titles, new laws and bills suppressing anything LGBTQ+ and especially that transgender, or media representations, among others. Other situations are discussion question topics, and so indicated (see Discussion Questions and Suggested Activities section near the end of this chapter). And, like Chapter 7, it's beneficial for students to categorize titles themselves as most fit several topics and discuss issues within them rather than limited to a single theme.

Since LGBTQ+ portrayal in YAL has drastically changed over the years (Discussion Questions 3, older vs newer titles, and 5, titles most beneficial), it's important for students to know of their evolution, to trace in novels over time, reading and discussing their widening and increasingly realistic and relevant titles. Eric's brother, Pete, in Kerr's (1986) *Night Kites* is one of the first prominent gay characters (even though a secondary one) and as most of the era, has AIDS. Still, he's writing a short story, its full text in the earlier, and first short story anthology, edited by Gallo (1984).

Kerr's later (1995) *Deliver Us From Evie* portrays Parr disgusted with the harassment (also Questions 6, community reaction, and 12, relationships) his lesbian sister, Evie, receives, but she's beginning a romance with Patsy, daughter of an influential banker, his homophobia challenged when learning of her sexuality.

Wittlinger's (2007) *Parrotfish* depicts Angela, outwardly female, but dressing as a male and wanting to be called Grady, an early transgender portrayal with its protagonist harassed and also unaccepted at home. He does find two unexpected allies at school, allowing his confirmation of his sexuality. Still popular, its updated version was published in 2015, with language and other details revised for contemporary readers.

Another early transgender character (also secondary, as is Pete from Kerr's novel), is Sage from Katcher's (2009) *Almost Perfect.* Here, Logan has a bad break up with his girlfriend (also Question 12) and unable to move forward until meeting Sage, but as she's transgender Logan is unsure of his feelings, and that of his town, should be begin a relationship (readers should also note the title's message). Regarding these early novels, how much has changed regarding them and today's societal views?

Contemporary protagonists include Amanda from Russo's (2016) *If I Was Your Girl,* who just wants to survive senior year as her town cannot accept her as a transgender female (Question 6), soon leading to her brutal attack. She moves to her father's town and finds happiness but is again exposed before ready to tell others of her sexuality.

Chris is also transgender and a victim of community hostility in Smith's (2019) *Something Like Gravity.* He's spending his summer in a small town after a previous transphobic assault and meets Maia, recovering from her sister's death. While neither are sure if they are emotionally ready to begin a relationship, their friendship is helpful to both (also Question 12).

Students can consider the enormous changes in one's life, touching every aspect, from being transgender, added to physical ones, and the strength needed for such a transformation with the current political climate another layer of difficulty. Another consideration is various medical needs, not available to all, especially those underserved. Is transgenderism only for those privileged, able to move above politics, and what does this mean?

As above, Black males are underrepresented as LGBTQ+ characters (Questions 4 and 5, recommended titles) and certainly those rural so other titles should be substituted, although few. The three titles below feature Black non-rural males, with the earlier Woodson's (1995) *The Notebooks of Melanin Sun* (also Questions 3 and 12) featuring Melanin, stunned to learn his mother has fallen in love with another woman, further shocked after learning she's White. While LGBTQ+ literature features parents being startled upon learning their son/daughter's sexuality status, teens are also, with other like titles below.

Felix from Callender's (2020) *Felix Ever After* must redefine his relationships with others, and most importantly, himself, after a transphobic attack (also Questions 6 and 12) and Remy in Winters' (2019) *How to Be Remy Cameron* has been assigned far too many labels describing himself (gay, Black, a brother) and must decide how wishing to define himself.

Hudson's (2020) *The Boys of Alabama* does portray a rural Black teen, as Max, new to town, unexpectedly falls for another male and begins questioning his faith. As on the football team, he must be careful regarding his actions, being discovered as LGBTQ+ would hardly be welcome (also Question 6). Why Blacks are so underrepresented in LGBTQ+ YAL should be of consideration to teens, regardless of race.

A frequent situation in rural-themed YAL is the protagonist readying to leave for college, then unable at the last minute from emergencies as a scholarship or internship falling through. Teens entering pageants for funding is a common theme, and representing Questions 6 and 7, parental reaction.

Females of color are not as reticent as males; Johnson's (2020) *You Should See Me in a Crown* offers Liz, a teen whose music scholarship suddenly falls through. If she is able to attend college, then her only hope is entering a prom queen pageant for the scholarship funds, although detesting the spotlight, with further issues arriving after falling for her main competitor (also Question 12).

Likewise, Winnie in Kann's (2019) *If It Makes You Happy* is loving her summer as a large, proud girl of color, working in her grandmother's diner with family, when she becomes the town's Summer Queen. She also despises the spotlight, but her experiences allow her to admit and reconcile her asexuality. Readers should note a female perfectly happy with being larger, her self-confidence and awareness of her many wonderful qualities attracting many, along with asexuality, emerging in LGBTQ+ titles.

More pageants are seen in Murphy's *Pumpkin*, with Waylon eager for graduation to live the life he wants, meeting a hitch when a video of him in drag goes viral (also Question 2, school reaction). Nominated for prom queen as a joke, he gamely decides to run for real. Similarly, J. T. in Self's (2016) *Drag Teen* is also without college funding, his friends convincing him to enter a drag queen pageant in NYC, a bit distant as living in FL, but they tell parents they're leaving for spring break in Daytona while heading north (also Questions 6 and 7).

Like pageants is Grayson from Polonsky's (2014) *Gracefully Grayson*, who's hiding the fact he's female inside, and after summoning the courage to try out for a female role in the school play, discovers how unaccepting many can suddenly become (Questions 2, 6, and 7). For these novels and others like them, students can consider whether these pageants and competitions are outdated tropes, somewhat negative in portraying desperate teens reluctant to participate, or still relevant, and why.

An elaborate plan gone horrendously wrong is Sky's in Couch's (2021) *The Sky Blues*, in which his promposal to long-time crush Ali, an Arab-American male he's unsure is gay, is ruined by a racist and homophobic prank. He and his friends work together in discovering the culprit (Questions 2 and 12), as the novel below.

Friends also support another in Dugan's (2019) *Hot Dog Girl*, showing Lou's love for her hometown amusement park and working there with her best friend, Seeley. She also likes Nick, another worker, and a fake dating plan with Seeley to make Nick jealous causes her realization she's bisexual and must decide to whom she's attracted. Students can discuss ways in which they've helped their own friends in similar dating circumstances, and the likely unexpected outcomes resulting, another similarity to those LGBTQ+ and doubtless experienced by most readers.

Woodson's novel, above, shows Melanin shocked to learn his mother is LGBTQ+, with other novels likewise. Cisco from Belgue's (2006) *Soames on the Range* is bullied (also Questions 2 and 6) when his father divorces his mother to move in with his boyfriend, and Harmon's (2008) *The Last Exit to Normal* has Ben moving to the small town where his father's boyfriend lives, Ben having far more difficulty accepting their relationship than welcoming residents.

Ben's negative reaction vs his town's far friendlier one should be explored by readers, perhaps connecting to novels with distraught parents; while not condoning negative views, seeing teens with the same confusion and anxiety makes such positions more understandable. Although many may suspect another is LGBTQ+, others discover suddenly with first reactions not necessarily reliable. Readers can consider teens' reactions and best ways of easing confusion or negativity, perhaps applying to adults. Regardless, reactions need to be understood, with seeing those of teen characters helping translate adults' views.

Parental and church reactions are often negative (Questions 6 and 7) as Parker from Kenneally's (2012) *Stealing Parker* discovered. After his mother declares she is a lesbian, divorces his ultra-religious father, and moves away he must reconcile that whirlwind of change, bring serious difficulties to his life. Unlike Ben, he's ruthlessly judged and treated by his father's religious community.

Similarly, Alyssa's father discovers she is gay in Peters's (2011) *She Loves You, She Loves You Not*, and sends her far way to live with her mother, a woman she barely knows. As she becomes acquainted with her, she must somehow reconcile her father's views.

Question 6 again appears with community/religious opposition and appalling violence against LGBTQ+ teens within Bick's (2013) *The Sin Eater's*

Confession when Ben's best friend Dell dies, and he helps on the family's farm. Jimmy, Dell's gay younger brother, takes a suggestive prize-winning photo of Ben while asleep, enraging his fundamentalist father (also Question 7) and horrifying Ben, who doesn't want to be seen as gay. Even after Jimmy's atrocious attack, Ben remains silent, worsening the situation.

Although this novel is older, teens can contemplate another not assisting another in a life-threatening situation lest being considered LGBTQ+, and what this implies. How many share similar circumstances, as ignoring a negative situation toward another minority as not wanting to appear affirmative toward that individual or group? How far is one willing to go, and what effects will inaction bring in the future?

Patrick also suffers unspeakable brutality in Myracle's (2011) *Shine*, as while everyone knew he was gay and friends protected him (showing positive reactions), he's found at a gas station unconscious, beaten, and tied to the gas pump with its nozzle in his mouth. Although many assume he was attacked for not selling alcohol to underage teens, a friend believes differently and begins investigating what occurred.

How would readers manage being bullied for a family member's sexuality, or forced to live with a virtual stranger based upon theirs, both from parents espousing faith, and how are these actions beneficial to anyone? Further, is there a reason why students could not be welcoming, as those encountered by Ben, and what does maltreatment contribute to either teen's situation?

Students can see the reality of physical harm, even death, to being LGBTQ+, perhaps realizing for the first time these students must live every day as a target for those they know, and others they don't, with negative situations often unexpected. Can they apply this reality to their own lives, and how can they lessen violence against peers, whether aware of being LGBTQ?

Another teen sent away, although not LGBTQ+, is Liam in the appropriately named author Going's (2009) *King of the Screw-Ups*, as after he messes up yet again, his exasperated father sends him to his uncle, who is gay, for the summer (Question 7). He thoroughly enjoys himself, another positive family representation, but students might note the presumption of Liam and his uncle viewed as inadequate, and best together so his father can forget both for several months. On the flip side, trust and acceptance is shown by Liam's father in his sending him to his uncle without worry.

Naturally, religion and its corresponding parental and community reactions (Questions 6 and 7) play a large role in many novels, unfortunately usually negatively, as Mike from Mittlefehldt's (2016) *It Looks Like This* attempts a secret relationship (also Question 12) amid religious parents and an unwelcoming town. Once his romance is revealed, ugly and dire consequences await, with far worse for bisexual Tanner, portrayed in Lauren's (2017) *Autoboyography*, also keeping his sexuality hidden in his LDS community.

As such secrets are difficult to keep in small towns, once known he's rejected by his family and must decide whether to live as they desire (i.e., as non-LGBTQ+), or build the life he wants elsewhere, away from them.

Readers can speculate the enormity of such a choice; how must it feel to know one's sexuality is so repulsive to parents and family that it must be denied if remaining with them, otherwise, move away with little to no contact? What other minority must make such a decision, and if couched in language as insisting one with cerebral palsy, autism, or blindness remove their exceptionality if wishing to remain in the family, would it cause reconsideration, or not?

Novels also show devout teens struggling to reconcile their sexuality with their church's oppositional stances, as Jude in Reardon's (2013) *The Revelations of Jude Connor* demonstrates. He's also living in a fundamentalist community and wanting to join his church and be baptized. As he's attracted to another boy (also Question 12), he must reconcile his sexuality with his church's views, wondering if he could ever be welcomed within the congregation.

Paul, seen in Sanchez's (2007) *The God Box*, doesn't realize he's gay until Manuel appears (also Question 12) and he feels a strong attraction to him, causing his struggle with his new reality and how it fits with his fundamentalist faith. Similarly, Marley from Self's (2017) *A Very, Very Bad Thing*, is attracted to newcomer Christopher (also Question 12), but Christopher's Christian televangelist father and family don't accept homosexuality. They begin a relationship anyway, but happiness only lasts until discovered.

Libby from Watts's (2018) *Quiver* is from an extremely religious family who separate themselves from the secular world as much as possible. When meeting her new neighbor, Zo, they quickly become fast friends. However, as Zo is genderfluid (another lesser seen sexuality) her parents forbid her from any further contact, but they continue their friendship in secret. Trouble looms for the two after discovered by Libby's younger sister who announces she's informing their parents about them.

There are positive religious examples, including Billie in Stevens's (2017) *Dress Codes for Small Towns*, who's bisexual and enjoying her town and minister father's love and acceptance. Not quite as friendly, actually rather cowardly, is Joanna's minister father in Brown's (2016) *Georgian Peaches and Other Forbidden Fruit*, who supports her sexuality, but asks her to keep it hidden upon him marrying his third wife and moving to a new town. Joanna reluctantly agrees, not anticipating the conflict and worse soon appearing.

Specific faiths need not be targeted in discussions, but students should consider why those LGBTQ+ are renounced by many religions, with the Christian bible also firmly opposed to other situations, as adultery, divorce, and so on, but not so denigrated by society. Is such negativity interpreted incorrectly, or are all biblical sins to be treated equally harshly, rather than selecting one? What would occur if this happened, and how does one reconcile religion with various acts of hate? Can non-LGBTQ students imagine what it would be like to be rejected from their churches due to sexuality? Another consideration is some churches of the same domination welcome those LGBTQ, others don't. What does this mean, and what does it say about the core faith?

Teens are also banished to various facilities as punishment for being LGBTQ+ or to conversion therapy (Question 7), as Eden from Hopkins's (2009) *Tricks*, sent to a religious boot camp as punishment (where starved and molested) for sleeping with her boyfriend, but meets LGBTQ+ teens with similar stories while there. Connor is kidnapped and taken to a conversion camp in Sass's (2020) *Surrender Your Sons* by his mother who cannot accept his being gay. As it's located just outside the United States, it avoids various legislation regarding treatment and can retain those there indefinitely, unknown to Connor, who soon plans to escape and destroy the facility.

Maggie attends a venerable summer camp in Thrash's (2015) *Honor Girl*, where she discovers she's gay when 15. As the facility approves of only WASP females, Maggie is watched and warned of her crush upon a counselor (also Question 12). The last evening she wins their highest award, Honor Girl, by remaining quiet about her sexuality, causing lasting pain and frustration.

Students can discuss the irony of Eden's religious parents sending her to a Christian boot camp to instill values, where she is instead raped and starved. Did this occur because attendees were considered immoral, perhaps evil, and somehow deserved it, or is such treatment seen as a way of achieving desired results? How could her parents have considered this camp's treatment as worthwhile? Likewise, the value of conversion camps can also be considered, or possibly how much can one change, questions for both facilities.

Maggie's treatment was as severe emotionally; she had summered at the camp for years and it was an important part of her life; discovering she was gay while there and immediately watched, cautioned, and criticized and then awarded for her silence was much to reconcile in so little time, all unexpected, with her remote parents essentially sharing camp views.

All teens are hesitant when beginning relationships, with those LGBTQ+ no different (Question 12). Burd's (2009) *The Vast Fields of Ordinary* introduces Dade, his sexuality secret and in a bad relationship, but upon meeting Pablo he discovers what he wants in a partner and finds the courage to tell his parents of his sexuality (also Question 7). Ollie's family moves and he enters a new school in Gonzales's (2020) *Only Mostly Devastated* and sees his last summer's crush there, not as eager to see him, a complicated on and off relationship following.

Ramona is one of only two out lesbians in her small town from Murphy's (2017) *Ramona Blue*, and when her girlfriend moves, begins spending time with Freddie, a childhood friend. As their relationship grows, she becomes confused regarding her sexuality, eventually realizing she's bisexual. Somewhat similar is Mara portrayed in Lunden's (2021) *Like Other Girls*, who's used to being one of the guys, but when trying out for the male's football team must realize and reconcile her closeted sexuality.

Dan, too, is confused in Ryan's (2012) *Way to Go*, his future, career, and sexuality all unclear. His working in his mother's restaurant and meeting new friends, speaking with them, and considering conversations allows his confidence to grow and answers many questions. Surely students can share relationship stories and issues, noting that whether LGBTQ+ or not, they're remarkably the same. How can teens help one another or provide advice?

Teens are also unsure of how to reconcile being LGBTQ+ and how, or whether, to tell parents and friends, along with worrying of their community and church reaction, all connected as small towns have one population, but not various groups. Obviously, this is something those non-LGBTQ+ never consider, but certainly should through discussion and meeting Discussion Questions 2, 6, and 7.

Individuals must find ways most comfortable to them regarding realizing, accepting, and sharing their sexuality, as David from Anonymous (2014) *The Book of David (Anonymous Diaries)* writes in his diary, depicting the difficulty of being gay in a small town. Similarly, James in Logan's (2016) *True Letters from a Fictional Life*, writes letters never intended to be sent to various people in his town saying what he would like to express to them, but can't. He discusses himself and his sexuality, and after the letters find their way to recipients, it's easier for him to live the life he desires.

These teens write to reconcile feelings; how many students do the same, or how else do they deal with various issues and problems in their lives? When does writing become ineffective, discussing with others more effective, and why? James's letters were sent to others, would this have horrified or relieved them, and why?

Many LGBTQ+ teens must keep their sexuality secret from fear (addressed in multiple books and including many above and fitting Questions 2, 6, and 7), hardly a problem for those non-LGBTQ+. These students need to understand how life-changing, frightening, and possibly dangerous such revealing is, especially when done by another.

Bjorkman's (2009) *My Invented Life* depicts Roz, curious of her sister's sexuality, and when not receiving an answer pretends to be a lesbian herself. Her sister doesn't yet wish to reveal her status, but the confusion and entanglements of Roz's games cause ensuing difficulties she hadn't considered, teaching her the value of discretion.

Similarly, Adam is closeted within Kadence's (2013) *On the Right Track* and meets Ru, damaged by being outed by a former boyfriend (also Question

12 as the novel below); they must discuss their pasts before becoming comfortable as a couple. Pan and T.J. act as friends to avoid harassment in Marino's (2009) *Magic and Misery*, but after Pan is discovered and both are derided and harassed, he relocates from fear (also Question 6); T.J. is now forced to reveal his sexuality.

Becca scorns secrecy from Quigley's (2009) *TMI*, not understanding discretion doesn't equal lying, and accidently outs a gay friend, finally grasping the consequences of providing too much information to others. Libby from *Quiver* above, was enjoying a forbidden friendship, now held hostage by her younger sister. How long can Libby appease her, and how is her younger sister practicing their religious tenets?

Students have doubtless had information about themselves, relationships or otherwise, that they'd prefer not revealed. What are some examples, and were they revealed deliberately, or accidently? What happened afterward, and how did they feel, that is, relieved, or otherwise? When is telling another preferred for the individual's sake, and when not? If they could redo the situation, how would it be handled?

Whether LGBTQ+ students or not, all teens can share the multiple emotions felt when life-altering, or any, private information is revealed, and especially giving those non-LGBTQ+ adolescents pause regarding sharing another's sexuality along with its purpose. What is accomplished by doing so?

Naturally, LGBTQ+ teens grieve the loss of a partner, but cannot always do so publicly if hiding sexuality, all relating to Questions 6, 7, and 12. Grieving is discussed in Chapter 8 and in titles above; here, Ivy, from Blake's (2018) *Ivy Aberdeen's Letter to the World*, sees her house destroyed by a tornado, with a notebook in which she'd detailed her secret feelings for another girl missing. She grieves the lost notebook, but also fears it being discovered and read by another.

Daniel, seen in Peck's (2009) *Sprout*, faces a happier ending; after his mother's death he and his father, both deeply grieving, move to a small town across the country. They suffer long, intense grief in individual ways, then both begin new promising relationships, as the novel below.

The death of Griffin's boyfriend in Silvera's (2017) *History Is All You Left Me* worsens his OCD and sends him into a long downward spiral of negative behaviors; he must receive assistance for his long climb back to normality. Non-LGBTQ+ teens are supported by family and friends when a relationship ends, regardless of reason, but those LGBTQ+ are not, if their sexuality is hidden. Students can discuss how sharing and discussing is vital to grieving, and how its absence hurts and hinders.

How can teens assist any who are grieving, helping them as an individual, rather than using as an opportunity to recognize being LGBTQ+? Another discussion point is once again, many LGBTQ+ strive to always keep their sexuality secret; how much more difficult is this during times when feeling extreme sadness and pain?

These, and more, YAL titles are rich with discussion, with emphasis on individuals first, sexuality second; we are all far more alike than different. Differences, as the divide between those LGBTQ+ and not are created, how can we remove them? Readers Theater is a place to start, along with other discussion questions and forms.

READERS THEATER RATIONALE, INSTRUCTIONS, AND SAMPLE SCRIPT

Readers Theater Rationale

When art is integrated into ELA curricula, students use creative processes for knowledge acquisition, improving concentration, higher-order thinking, perception, and creativity (Cho & Vitale, 2019; Eisner, 1994; Oreck, 2004). Using Readers Theater (RT) from LGBTQ+-themed YAL integrates the arts but also primarily allows these students a classroom voice; assists peers in increased understanding, tolerance, and friendship toward them; promotes heightened questioning of stereotypes and negative societal influences; and encourages educators' increasing the use of YAL (de Silva & Villas-Boas, 2006; Levy & Byrd, 2011).

Lesesne (2010) continually promoted reading aloud, as it positively affects students' attitudes toward books, reading, and improves their reading ability. Similarly, Trelease and Giorgis (2019) affirmed those reading most read better, accomplish more, and are more apt to remain in school.

Unlike traditional school-wide plays with their sets, props, costumes, line memorization, and numerous practices, RT's short (three to four pages) scripts and time frames are a more accessible and effective classroom activity for all grade levels.

For RT, students read the script as it was meant it to be heard, using enunciation, voice and facial expressions with gestures and other movements allowing audiences' envisioning its events. Such performances would naturally improve vocabulary, comprehension, and retention skills, as speaking dialogue aloud forces students' close work with the script in interpreting meaning. This expressive reading also doubtless enhances perception and confidence of selected word inflections and other subtleties; further, during small group preparation, students assist one another, sharpening collaboration and other skills.

IMPORTANCE OF READERS THEATER SCRIPTS REGARDING LGBTQ+ FRIENDSHIPS/RELATIONSHIPS

As cited in this chapter, many students identifying as LGBTQ+ face a difficult and challenging adolescence, more so little to no classroom exposure to like-themed YAL or other materials. Educators should note the positives gained by this group when allowing the reading and candid discussion of such YAL.

An often unrecognized, yet significant, need of these teens is advice and assistance regarding friendships and relationships. Those LGBTQ+ teens do not necessarily have the simple luxury of turning to friends for sharing and suggestions; they may be closeted, have fewer friends, and/or find discussing these issues uncomfortable with those who are non-LGBTQ+.

If ELA educators desire safe, supportive, schools welcoming all students, effecting change begins in classrooms. Using RT with YAL LGBTQ+ protagonists navigating friendship/relationship issues appears extremely advantageous for supporting these teens and assisting peers' understanding of their daily lives and struggles. Further, recognizing that relationships are not the area in which these two groups share the least commonalities but instead the most seems a promising beginning toward better inclusion.

Readers Theater Benefits to LGBTQ+ Students

RT scripts from YAL featuring LGBTQ+ protagonists navigating romantic relationships is beneficial to all teens but perhaps life-altering to those who are LGBTQ+. For them, RT will likely be the first time they have had their relationship issues addressed and, further, treated honestly and respectfully in classrooms. Additional benefits of RT (and perhaps equally or more valuable to those non-LGBTQ+) include those below (Johnson & Hazlett, 2021).

- LGBTQ+ characters' words are spoken aloud and may provide the first opportunity for students to *hear* these voices, rather than merely hearing *about* them, a distinct difference and advantage.
- LGBTQ+ characters provide necessary and realistic role models for like teens regarding relationships and reassurance that most situations are not unique, but shared, handled, and overcome by others.
- As all students speak characters' words, friendship/relationship difficulties specific to LGBTQ+ teens are heard, permitting their validation and greater awareness by those non-LGBTQ+. It also assists in better understanding differences, perhaps advancing peer tolerance/acceptance/friendship.

- Students' plan scene readings and perform as a single group, with similar personal situations shared during discussions, another opportunity for connection.
- Students can enjoy themselves and classmates' comments; RT grants everyone the opportunity to simply discuss relationships, usually humorously, revealing their universality and difficulties, with differences more insignificant than divisive.

Performance Preparation and Concluding Discussion

The YAL novel should be read and discussed as usual with all RT information previously discussed. Educators create scripts themselves, depicting key scenes with examples and instructions below. After novel discussion, RT begins.

Students are randomly placed into groups, scripts are provided, and characters are assigned (LGBTQ+ students should not read only like characters, the same as male/females; parts should be mixed to note performance variations and meanings more acutely). The remaining class period, and probably more, are for practice. Separating groups will lessen discussion noise; students may go elsewhere throughout the school for more space, with the ELA educator assisting and monitoring.

Groups are ready to perform when able to voice their character's words so credibly they *are* that person along with entire script familiarity, enabling smooth reading rather than silences from one missing his/her turn or two cohesive speakers and another stumbling.

During RT, students will literally see what was already read, observing nuances unrecognized in previous discussions, with viewing scenes likely bringing reconsideration of initial conclusions and opinions. Particularly important is that reading aloud continually reflects the *character's* situation/view, rather than the *students'* opinion regarding it, a stage unmet without RT.

Instructions for Creating Readers Theater Scripts

Selecting Scenes From Novels

The scene must be critical to the story, have ample dialogue, and a beginning, middle, and end. Skip those with long descriptive passages as they require narration; audiences should hear character voices, not narrator summaries.

Two or more characters should be speaking. If any have only one line, the narrator or another as appropriate may voice.

Creating a Scene:

1. Photocopy/scan and print the scene. While onerous, it is easier and faster to type the entire scene than attempt to maintain one's place in a novel (especially paperbacks) or manipulate scanned/PDF text.
2. Identify/highlight descriptive passages for narrator summarization; assign single lines as applicable.
3. Type the dialogue as written, identifying each line's speaker. Add interpretations, moods, emphases, or gestures, and then bold:
   a. *Kyan: (hits forehead angrily)* "Oh, *no!* I can't *believe* I forgot to meet Janae today!"
4. Substitute nouns for pronouns with unclear antecedents and identify all characters by name:
   a. Instead of *Hannah:* "Look! Isn't *it gorgeous*? use *Hannah*: "Look at the *sunset*! Isn't it *gorgeous*?"
5. After writing the scene, create the entire script.
   a. Title the scene, adding page numbers.
   b. Describe the setting and list any props.
   c. List the characters in order of speaking, with narrator first. Place a short description of each character, such as *protagonist, protagonist's sister*, etc.

Performing the Scene

1. Mimic the scene; if characters are in a car, two could sit in front, two behind. Props are unnecessary unless key to the scene, such as characters arguing over a photo or attempting to solve an equation.
2. The narrator reads character names, then introduces the script using a few sentences. Another narration may occur elsewhere, if necessary.
3. Characters arriving later in the scene should stand aside, entering quietly just before their speaking part.
4. Student readers practice their lines until fully prepared. These are not memorized, only read until familiar with them and those of others in the scene.
5. The narrator begins, and then the first speaker reads their lines, with the script read until completed.
6. Conclude the script with the narrator; using a few sentences, end the scene/script with a hint or question of the protagonist's thoughts or what might occur next.

Sample Scripts: Readers Theater Script One

From Silvera's *History Is All You Left Me* (2017), this script depicts friends Griffin, Theo, and Wade, but Griffin and Theo have begun a relationship and are unable to tell Wade. While browsing in a bookstore, their secret is revealed, and they discuss the new relationship and preserving their friendship (pp. 21–24).

Characters:	
Narrator	
Griffin	
Theo	
Wade	
Narrator	It's routine for Theo, Wade, and Griffin to go to Barnes & Noble after school to do their homework, but classes are almost over, so they browse the shelves instead. Theo was supposed to tell Wade about his dating Griffin last period but couldn't. Griffin is not a fan of secrets as they can turn people into liars, and his lying days are over.
Theo	I want my *own* memoir.
Griffin	Only *one* person can make *that* happen.
Theo	I don't have a title yet.
Wade	*The horror!* I'll probably call mine *Wading through Life*.
Theo (fake yawns)	I can't *wait* for *that* laborious read.
Wade (flips off Theo)	I'm going to go get an iced tea from the café. You guys want?
Griffin	Yeah, actually. My treat though. (He gives Wade a gift card from his birthday)
Wade	You sure? (Griffin nods)
Narrator	Once Wade leaves, Griffin gives Theo the why-didn't-you-tell-Wade-about-us-glare, but he turns away, eyes back on the bookshelves.
Griffin	*How about Theo McIntyre: Zombie Pirate Slayer?*
Theo (smiles, but avoids Griffin's gaze)	But if the zombie-pirate apocalypse doesn't happen, it'll get confused as a fantasy novel. I *refuse* for my existence to be mistaken as fiction, damn it! Maybe I should keep it simple. How about *Theo: A Memoir?*
Griffin (shakes head)	You're my favorite Theo and all, but you're not the *only* one.
Theo (turns to Griffin)	You know *more* Theo's? Give me their addresses so I can put an end to this madness.
Griffin	How about *C-Theo-PO?*
Theo	Nah. Too insignificant. Cool chapter title, maybe. I have *your* title though. *Griffin on the left.*
Griffin	It's *perfect.*

Narrator	Griffin wants to kiss Theo and pulls him by the hand into the next aisle. He doesn't act on the kiss because he doesn't want to rush it or feel as if they are doing it behind Wade's back.
Griffin (whispers)	We *have* to tell Wade, dude. If you want to do it by yourself, that's cool, but if you want to tell him together, that's also cool. But we're *not* leaving this bookstore until we do so.
Theo	Deal. *(Squeezes Griffin's hand)* What time does the store close again? I—
Wade	Whoa.
Narrator	Wade is standing at the end of the aisle, hold a tray of iced teas. Griffin jerks his hand from Theo's.
Wade (shakes head, manages a small smile)	This whole squad business was fun while it lasted.
Griffin (surprised)	What are you talking about?
Wade	How long have you two been dating? I *knew* this was going to happen. You guys doubt my psychic ways, but I called this *last* year. I just didn't tell anyone.
Theo (shocked, voice high-pitched)	You had a vision where Griffin and I were hooking up *and* the world was going to end?
Wade (smirking)	Pretty much.
Theo (shaken)	Your visions are kind of gay. You should get that checked out.
Griffin (trying to get hold of himself)	*Wait.* How did you know Theo and I liked each other? *Don't* say because you're psychic.
Wade	You don't have to be a psychic to have seen *this* coming. Your chemistry was all over my face. *(hesitates).* That came out wrong. Anyway, I'm *not* going to be some third wheel, guys.
Griffin	It's *not* game over for us. Think of it as a *new* game, if anything, with new levels and new worlds.
Wade	New obstacles for *me* if I want to see you guys, and new game modes *exclusive to you two.*
Theo (winks)	You're welcome to join in our *exclusive activities.*
Narrator	Wade lists every example of love gone wrong, mainly from comic books: Green Lantern's girlfriend who was killed and had her corpse stuffed in his fridge; Cyclops and Jean Grey, high school sweethearts who keep losing each other to everything the world throws at them; Ant-Man, who douses the Wasp with bug spray.
Theo (turns to Griffin)	I *promise* to *never* bug-spray you, Griff. Do *you* promise to never bug-spray me?
Griffin	I promise (mouths to Wade so Theo can see and make the situation more normal) *Lying!*
Wade	*Promise me* you guys won't destroy the squad when you break up.
Theo (quietly)	Maybe show some *faith* in us, dude. But sure, I promise we'll be adults if we do break up.
Wade	You're sixteen. You're *not* an adult.
Theo	I'm counting on us being together for a while.
Griffin (takes deep breath)	I also promise I won't destroy the squad if we breakup either. Can we *please* go back to looking at books?

Narrator	Theo gestures for them to come together, and he wraps an arm around both Griffin and Wade.
Theo (fake whispers to Wade)	We have to do a group hug so Griffin doesn't feel left out.
Wade	I hate you both!
Narrator	The boys laugh, and like that it's over and there are no more secrets, and Griffin keeps smiling longer than anyone else because Theo is betting on them being together for a while. This is good, as it will give him enough time to come up with the perfect title for Theo's memoir.

Sample Scripts: Readers Theater Script Two

This script is from Sass's *Surrender Your Sons* (2020), in which protagonist Connor's mother cannot accept his homosexuality. She arranges for Nightlight Conversion Camp to kidnap and transport him to their Costa Rica location. While there, Connor is constantly watched for any indication of homosexuality with an initial review after a week. If failing, his stay extends to three months—or more. He befriends Molly, another camper, and they discuss their situation and possible escape at breakfast (pp. 126–30).

Characters:
Narrator
Connor
Molly
Lacrishia (camp worker)
Darcy (camp worker)

Narrator	Connor and Molly are eating breakfast, discussing the camp, and plotting escape.
Molly	So, Darcy and Lacrishia told me we're here for a weeklong probation and then we get reviewed.
Connor	A *week*? So, what, we just play along, pass the review, and go home?
Molly (shakily)	Uh-huh, that's one plan. But if we don't pass the review, our one-week stay is automatically extended to three months.
Connor (surprised)	*Three months?* Well, we better pass our review then (laughs).
Molly (whispering)	Or . . . or . . . you and I run to the beach. We steal their boat and get the hell out here *right now*.
Connor	*How?*
Molly	We'll *find* the right moment.
Connor	Do you *know* how to drive *that kind* of a boat?
Molly	I've driven speedboats *before*.
Connor (hesitantly)	Listen . . . I can make it through *a week*.
Molly	And *then* what?
Connor	I'll pass their stupid review and then go home.
Molly	What if you *can't*?
Connor	I can fake it.
Molly	*Everyone* thinks that—

Connor (angrily)	I CAN FAKE IT! You don't know what this month has been like for me. The *last* person who gave me advice on coming out and never hiding or fighting back and *blah, blah, blah* was my boyfriend, and *it screwed me over*. As for your *"wing it"* escape plan, an ex-camper I know somehow got an injury that made him nearly quadriplegic, and every staff member here has a mega-charged taser and isn't afraid to stick me with it. *So, I'm sorry, but I'm leaving in a week, and I'm leaving safely.*
Molly	All *right*. But you ought to know my cabinmates sound like they've been waiting a long time for their ship to come in. Ask your boys how successful *they've* been at faking it—
Lacrishia	More coffee, dumplings?
Connor	No, um, thanks, I'm awake.
Molly (holds out cup)	Fill 'er up!
Lacrishia (wincing)	Sorry. *Girls* are only allowed *one* coffee per day.
Narrator	They've stumbled onto another one of Nightlight's arbitrary, hypocritical rules: *Return to nature! But here's some supermarket shower gel. Boys don't belong in the kitchen! But here's a jaunty musical number to start your morning!*
Darcy (reaching for plates)	All done with these? Limiting our coffee intake keeps us calm and agreeable. *Darcy suddenly becomes intense and lowers her head.* You two shouldn't whisper. When you whisper, people lean in to hear. Talk in a normal voice, that's when people tune out. You were whispering and I was right over there. Now I know Molly is planning to run for the boat, like *nobody's ever thought of that*. And Connor is planning to fake it through a week and go home, like *nobody's thought of that, either*. Welcome to our crisis, already in progress.
Molly (challenging)	*So, what are you, on our side?* You weren't talking this bluntly in the cabin this morning.
Darcy	Well, that's cuz there might be snitches in our cabin.
Connor	So, are we supposed to just stay here *forever*?
Darcy (giggling)	Connor! You arrived ready to stir the pot, didn't you? I couldn't *believe* my ears last night when you started mouthing back to the Reverend about *Ricky Hannigan*, of all people.
Narrator	Connor had delivered meals to the elderly Ricky, who had been in a long-ago accident. After his death he left Connor a Broadway Playbill in his will. Inside its pages Ricky had written HELP CONNOR NIGHTLIGHT, which made no sense to Connor at the time.
Connor (astonished)	What do you know about Ricky?
Darcy	You could probably tell me a lot more than I could tell you.
Narrator	Darcy pulls a folded wad of paper from her pocket.
Darcy	Nightlight is just like school, only you're watched more closely. Question is: in school, you ever get into trouble? Like, *if you were passed a note—*
Narrator	Darcy slid a folded paper across the table, her fingers pressed on top.

Darcy	Would you unfold it out in the open for people to see, or would you find a way to read it later, nice and private?
Connor (confidently)	I don't *get* caught.
Narrator	Darcy lifts her fingers from the folded note, and Connor drops Ricky's Playbill on top of it and slides both items back to the safety of his lap. She scoops the piled-high plates into her arms, and she and Connor nod to each other. Molly doesn't know what to make of either of them.
Darcy	Any of this gets back to me, I'll deny it. Church is up next, then a class called Home Life Behavior. We'll talk again, but not until class. Do *not* approach me before I approach you.
Narrator	Darcy vanishes their plates through the saloon doors into the kitchen.
Molly (whispering)	Well, what's it *say*?
Narrator	Connor unfurls Darcy's note and hides it in the middle of the Playbill's pages. If anyone caught Connor with the Playbill, it was in his backpack so they've already seen it and determined it's nothing. Briggs walks past, and Connor's arm trembles with the memory of his taser shock. When Briggs finally leaves, Connor opens the Playbill—deep-breathing until his hands stopped shaking and finds Darcy's secret message.
Connor (Whispering while reading the note)	*When they ask you to be my husband, say yes.*
Narrator	Connor is confused by the note; surely it wasn't meant as literal marriage, but what? Molly isn't interested in helping decipher it and is more determined than before to commandeer an escape boat. Both head toward morning classes, worried and thoughtful about what's ahead for them.

DISCUSSION QUESTIONS AND SUGGESTED ACTIVITIES

Discussion Questions	Suggested Activities; Students Will . . .	Key Diversity Points
1. Is LGBTQ+-themed YAL and other like information interspersed throughout the curriculum or otherwise available.	Students can easily list what is formally, and informally, offered by the school, any pertinent details, and evaluate. How may students assist others?	Are LGBTQ+ students represented and assisted less than all other groups, and why? What other minority groups face similar situations? What does this imply?

Discussion Questions	Suggested Activities; Students Will . . .	Key Diversity Points
2. What school supports are used to prevent or manage harassments of LGBTQ+ students, and where this group turn if there are none and/or condoned?	A difficult discussion but students can easily list various instances and those involved and evaluate. Educators can provide national LGBTQ+ organizations for additional assistance, plus students considering how to help peers.	If educators and schools do not support those who are LGBTQ+, what does this imply?
3. What are differences between older and contemporary LGBTQ+-themed YAL?	Students should be provided a novel list for comparisons. The portrayal of LGBTQ+ characters can be traced through the decades, with discussion and evaluation.	How have LGBTQ+ novels progressed in YAL, and how does this relate to societal views and these teens? Do schools share progressive views?
4. Which groups remain underrepresented in LGBTQ+-themed YAL, and why?	Students should search YAL novels online, noting protagonists and those most/least represented. A running list could be created with titles continually added. For underrepresented protagonists, students may locate other titles featuring them, and consider different connections to those LGBTQ+.	How to these representations compare to rural LGBTQ+ students' school and community standing? What does this imply?
5. Which LGBTQ+-themed YAL titles would be most beneficial for non-LGBTQ+ students to read, and why?	Teachers and students could share titles with another running list created with titles added and rationale. What does it imply if these titles are unfamiliar?	What novel choice differences would be seen among those LGBTQ+, and not? How could this discussion be held if these group members are hiding being LGBTQ? What novels might other groups wish peers would read, and why?
6. How does the community and its churches support (or oppose) those LGBTQ+?	What LGBTQ+ supports are offered by the community and churches, and what are student opinions of them? What improvements are needed?	How does rural LGBTQ+ treatments relate to society in general? What are negative or positive attributes specific to rurality? Is this group the least valued, and what does this mean?

7. What hope is there for LGBTQ+ teens fearing unsupportive parents and hiding sexuality, or for those not accepted by parents or families? How may these teens be otherwise supported?

8. Many bills targeting the LGBTQ+ population are increasingly being passed into law by various states. How are these harmful to all, regardless of sexuality, race, or gender?

This should be discussed objectively rather than through specific student experience. Educators should provide various supports, both local and national, and allow individual students to discuss issues privately.

Students discuss laws and their intentions (and often-misleading wording or premise) and effects upon those LGBTQ+.

The states of the laws passed/pending may be charted, and if pending in their state, how may students engage in activism?

Laws targeting other minorities can be examined, discussed, and related to those above.

If parents and families are unaccepting of their LGBTQ+ teen(s), are there any possible solutions? What does this imply if not?

LGBTQ+ students and adults are frequently vilified, with rights restricted and attempts to remove LGBTQ+ information and materials from schools/classrooms. Why is this necessary?

Other groups may be next, who and why? How can students protect one another?

Students should also understand protesting is different from voting; those introducing these bills were voted into office. Students must plan to vote in all elections.

9. Are negative beliefs regarding those LGBTQ+ often expressed because they are expected or otherwise held by many?

10. Additionally, why do many vilify those from groups in which they know no individual members?

Students can consider how individual beliefs differ from legislators, society, and individuals. Why is it easier to follow majority opinions than express those different?

The ease of forming negative views regarding the abstract, such as disliking all XXXs, may be pondered. How does this change when personally knowing someone from a disliked group?

Must individuals be acquainted with one another for tolerance and acceptance?

What views and actions are negative without true merit, and what does this imply?

What are similar beliefs/legislation directed toward other minority groups?

Discussion Questions	Suggested Activities; Students Will . . .	Key Diversity Points
11. Many dislike entire groups, such as those LGBTQ+, from negative actions of some, perhaps from their community or broadcast in society. How is this amplified and continued by the media and other sources?	Students can consider how negative actions of some minority group members are replayed in the media and other venues.	Negatives by some are quickly applied to all minorities. No single group is defined by the negative conduct of one, or few. Why is this not true of majority individuals committing similar acts?
12. Many feel those LGBTQ+ are different from non-LGBTQ teens, but how? What are commonalities regarding friendships, dating, and relationships shared with all adolescents regardless of sexuality?	Students can share, laugh, and commiserate with others' experiences, with all stories heard and welcomed.	We are far more alike than we are different, with the same behaviors practiced by most.

REFERENCES

Centers for Disease Control and Prevention. (2019, November 12). *Parents' influence on the health of lesbian, gay, and bisexual teens: What parents and families should know*. https://www.cdc.gov/healthyyouth/protective/factsheets/parents_influence_lgb.htm

Cho, C., & Vitale, J. (2019). Using the arts to develop a pedagogy of creativity, innovation, and risk-taking (CIRT). *Journal for Learning through the Arts, 15*(1). DOI: 0.21977/D915130132.

de Silva, J., & Villas-Boas, M. (2006). Research note: Promoting intercultural education through art education. *Intercultural Education, 17*(10), 95–103.

Eisner, E. (1994). *The Educational Imagination: On the Design and Evaluation of School Programs*. MacMillan College Publishing Company.

Doyle, R. P. (2016). *Field report 2016: Banned and challenged books*. ALA Office for Intellectual Freedom. Retrieved from https://www.ila.org/content/documents/2016_banned_short_list.pdf

Johnson, A. M., & Hazlett, L. A. (2021). Interrogating boundaries through readers theater: Young adult literature text: *Honor girl: A graphic memoir by Maggie Thrash*. In Maldonado, B. (Ed.), *Arts integration and young adult literature* (pp. 137–46). Rowman & Littlefield.

Jones, B. A., Bouman, A. J., & Haycraft, E. (2017). Sport and transgender people: A systematic review of the literature relating to sport participation and competitive sport policies. *Sports Medicine. 47*(4), 701–716. https://pubmed.ncbi.nlm.nih.gov/27699698/

Kosciw, J. G., Clark, C. M., Truong, N. L., & Zongrone, A. D. (2019). *The 2019 national school climate survey: The experiences of lesbian, gay, bisexual, transgender, and queer youth in our nation's schools.* GLSEN. https://www.glsen.org/research/2019-national-school-climate-survey

Lesesne, T. S. (2010). *Reading ladders.* Heinemann.

Levy, D., & Byrd, D. (2011). Why can't we be friends? Using music to teach social justice. *Journal of the Scholarship of Teaching and Learning, 11*(2), 64–75.

Mahowald, L., Gruberg, S., & Halpin, J. (October 2020). *The state of the LGBTQ community in 2020.* Center for American Progress. https://www.americanprogress.org/issues/lgbtq-rights/reports/2020/10/06/491052/state-lgbtq-community-2020/

Movement Advancement Project. (2021). *Advancing acceptance.* https://www.lgbtmap.org/advancing-acceptance

Movement Advancement Project. (2019). *Where we call home: LGBT people in rural America.* https://www.lgbtmap.org/rural-lgbt

NPR, Robert Wood Johnson Foundation, & the Harvard T.H. Chan School of Public Health. (2019). *Life in rural America, Part II.* https://www.rwjf.org/en/library/research/2019/05/life-in-rural-america--part-ii.html

Olito, F. (June 2, 2021). *15 surprising facts about today's LGBTQ people.* Insider. https://www.insider.com/surprising-statistics-about-lgbtq-people-2021-5

Oreck, B. (2004). The artistic and professional development of teachers: A study of teachers' attitudes toward and use of the arts in teaching. *Journal of Teacher Education, 55*(1), 55–67.

Sass, A. (2020). *Surrender your sons.* Flux.

Silvera, A. (2017). *History is all you left me.* SoHo Teen.

Student, Anonymous (personal communication, November 15, 2021).

The Trevor Project. (2021). *The Trevor national survey on LGBTQ youth mental health 2021.* https://www.thetrevorproject.org/survey-2021/

Thrash, M. (2015). *Honor girl: A graphic memoir.* Candlewick Press.

Trelease, J., & Giorgis, C. (2019). *Jim Trelease's read-aloud handbook* (8th ed.). Penguin/Random House.

True Colors United. (2021). LGBTQ youth are 120% more likely to experience homelessness. https://truecolorsunited.org/our-issue/

Willingham, C. Z., & Ajilore, O. (2019, July 2019). *Redefining rural America.* Center for American Progress. https://cdn.americanprogress.org/content/uploads/2019/07/27080905/redefining-rural-america-brief.pdf?_ga=2.214591646.828330074.1634233040-1392242997.1634233040

Chapter 7

Exceptional, Undocumented, and Homeless Students in Rural Schools and Communities

Exceptional students (EXCP) and those who are LGBTQ+ are in all Upper Midwest (UM) schools and communities, regardless of size, but racial minorities are not. Its largest cities have varying minority populations, some groups less than 2%, and most small towns have few, if any. These students share multiple similarities perhaps not considered, but useful in understanding situations and building better connections among them and peers.

POPULATION COMPARISONS

While numbers of all individuals within the United States are known, residence locations are by choice with cities and states showing varying percentages of minorities. For example, Billings, Montana's Black population shows 0.8%; Fargo, North Dakota's is 6%; Minneapolis, Minnesota, reports 18%; with Omaha, Nebraska, reporting 12% (U.S. Census Bureau [USCB], 2018). Such numbers indicate many smaller UM having few to no Black individuals, the same for all other minorities.

However, statistics for two, EXCP and those identifying as LGBTQ+, show the same percentages throughout the nation, meaning these groups are found in all schools and communities, regardless of location. Currently, EXCP students equal 14% of the adolescent population (Council for Exceptional Children [CEC], 2021), with those LGBTQ+ 10% (Kosciw et al., 2019). UM communities may not house some minority groups, but they will have these teens.

Membership Distinction

Minorities are as welcomed and valued in the UM, or not, as elsewhere; people are essentially the same regardless of location. Society is filled with groups and those within them, but there is a difference between membership and belonging. The distinction determining between true and surface membership is the level of involvement offered by majority members.

Many individuals are accorded friendships, interactions, various participations, invitations, and feel welcomed and accepted by peers. However, it is not until denials, whether tacit or blatant, occur, that it is realized one's status is somewhat lesser. These distinctions occur everywhere, but most blatant in the UMs smaller towns.

Biological Family Comparisons

Conversely, only EXCP and LGBTQ+ teens have immediate families unlike them; presumably these biological parents are of neither group, the same for most. All other minority teens usually have parents and siblings resembling them (i.e., Hispanic students have like parents). Moreover, EXCP and LGBTQ+ (if out) families are aware of these teens' situations and daily life issues, but have not *personally experienced* them, unlike other minority families. Being the one different family member, regardless of how loved, can be lonely and isolating.

Negative Family Comparisons

Not all LGBTQ+ teens are out to families, some know they will literally be forced to live elsewhere; others fear facing contempt, pressure to change or behave as non-LGBTQ+ teens, ignored by various members, friends, and more. Leading secret lives is surely miserable; teens are more transparent than they believe with sexuality already known or suspected; regardless, many teens do not have fully accepting families, making their already-difficult adolescence harsher.

Likewise, EXCP teens also face family difficulties; unfortunately, media and other portrayals are of those highest functioning, but real capabilities differ. Care for many of those with low ability is all-consuming or requiring outside assistance, exhausting parents, over-burdening siblings, and associated expenses draining finances and future opportunities. This group is largely unseen in schools, remaining in their classroom without placement in those non-EXCP. Further, once older, most have transitioned to regional cohorts/care facilities, away from public schools (S. Sweeney, personal communication, April 25, 2022)

EXCP teens' experiences, regardless of ability, resemble those LGBTQ+ by both facing disdain, being ignored by some family members, their disability/sexuality creating shame, stigmas, others' avoidance, or parents' concealment attempts. Others may be continually pitied, overprotected, or treated with cheerfulness or amused condescension, and some may become the family focus, with everyone's, and especially siblings,' needs and attention secondary, with these and the above problematic, lonely, and painful.

Unfortunately, it is virtually impossible to discover percentages of LGBTQ+ adolescents with disabilities or in EXCP programs; numbers are available for one or the other, not both. LGBTQ+ adults report disabilities at 30% for males, females 36%, approximately twice as high as those non-LGBTQ+ (Disabled World, 2022). However, these include all illnesses and conditions (arthritis, heart disease, depression) with cognitive and other physical (deaf, blind, prosthetics) exceptionalities largely absent, and as many problems are contracted later in life, not applicable to teens. Still, EXCP LGBTQ+ adolescents exist and surely recognizable to adults in their lives.

Communication Comparisons

As in Chapter 6, UM LGBTQ+ adolescents are often without those to discuss concerns and issues particular to their lives (especially if not out), as are EXCP teens. Family and peers haven't had their experiences, and while other students are LGBTQ+ and EXCP they may be of too disparate ages (3rd and 9th grades) or sort (lesbian, transgender; Down syndrome, cerebral palsy) for support.

Racial minorities situations are similar; teens must talk and be with others like them, and being the only, or one of few, Black, Asian, or Hispanic students (or having none the same age/gender) is limiting and frustrating. While these teens may be in a community group, a gender sexuality alliance (GSA), or regional EXCP cohort, these differ from immediate, and many, conversations among friends/family. Unfortunately, many such teens must wait for interactions with peers resembling them, leaving much unaddressed.

Whites, Racial Minorities, and LGBTQ+ Friends/ Relationship Comparisons

Finding friends specifically like them is harder for all UM minorities, although they engage in friendships and relationships as elsewhere. Unfortunately, those LGBTQ+ seeking romantic relationships and EXCP teens finding non-EXCP peer friendships or deeper relationships is more difficult. Some parents may approve of various friendships, but not romances (an involvement level), and those unaccepting of LGBTQ+ may object to interactions to discourage a son/daughter's sexuality. EXCP teens have like friends, but while other peers are friendly, true friends are rarer.

EXCP Students' Friends/Relationship Comparisons

Unfortunately, as above, EXCP teens face harsh realities early, and unlike all other groups, social situations are unlikely to change. Some are further burdened by cognitive and other maturational situations and abilities not matching any peers,' and it is doubtful non-EXCP students would invite EXCP teens for a date, to the prom, shopping, to parties at other's homes, and so on. EXCP classroom or other cohort peers are this group's social set, with few, if any, deep friendships among those non-EXCP.

Further, many UM activities require more sophisticated or other skills to participate and require close adult supervision; for example, hunting, snowmobiling, ice fishing, camping, or sailing, even with family, are inappropriate for some EXCP teens, again limiting. If engaging in these or others, they are presumably with parents and family and perhaps a EXCP classroom peer if of like ability/interest, not necessarily common.

Romantic pairings are also difficult; non-EXCP teens are unlikely to begin such relationships with EXCP students. These would be among EXCP peers, but as above, their many differences often preclude pairings. Parents may express strong disapproval, wary of ability for responsible relationships and of those eager to take advantage of these less sophisticated students.

Still, adults working with EXCP students pay attention to social skill development and friendships, arranging for various activities and events outside school, all assisting and providing opportunities for closeness, a sense of belonging, and simply having fun with others (S. Sweeney, personal communication, April 25, 2022; C. McMurry-Kozak, personal communication, November 30, 2021)

Educational Comparisons

All students, including majority ones, face varying harassments at school regardless of location, and UM districts, as elsewhere, feature anti-bullying and similar programs and policies for awareness and tolerance. Of course, their success is dependent upon how well they are emphasized and followed at school and home.

As in Chapter 6, LGBTQ students have numerous school difficulties, worse for those of color, with curricula for and about them largely absent. Rural adult minorities of color (teen percentages vary greatly, due to reluctance to identify as LGBTQ+) reported harassments or other prejudicial actions directed toward them, with Latinx/Hispanics the most at 44% (the next largest were liberals, at 37%), Blacks, 36%, and recent immigrants/LGBTQ+ 30%. However, in stating their own prejudices or those seen from others toward these groups, rural Whites' percentages were significantly lower (NRA, 2018).

These numbers were averages, with negative actions and frequencies varying, but presumably of similar occurrence in rural schools by both adults and students regardless of size. Similar negative behaviors toward those LGBTQ+ (as explained in Chapter 6) are likely encountered by other minorities, (all acceptance levels) with most common additional situations or teaching methodologies below:

- misunderstanding Native American culture; penalizing students for various practices or misusing sacred symbols in classrooms as decorations;
- asking any minority student to serve as spokesperson for his/her entire group;
- providing minority students with reading materials only about their specific group;
- studying authors and others of note from specific groups only during certain months, or rarely;
- focusing upon negative actions of noted minorities rather than balanced portrayals, discriminatory teaching;
- having lower expectations for minorities and parents, providing lesser assistances, or more frequent/harsher management penalties;
- not providing enrichments for gifted/talented students;
- celebrating only Christian holidays (e.g., Christmas, Easter); even without students of color, not all religions observe the same, and all should be aware of different events and practices;
- promoting and assisting only Christian prayer groups and other causes (e.g., while legal for all groups to meet in public schools, adults may be unwilling to serve as advisors);
- only Christian prayers offered at school ceremonies;
- not noting surface acceptance and assisting (i.e., a student may be a valued athlete, but not otherwise included by peers); or
- expecting various student modifications to fit school culture, rather than individual allowances (W. Sweeney, S. Sweeney personal communication, November 15, 2021; C. McMurry-Kozak, personal communication, November 30, 2021).

EXCP students are generally protected and cared for in UM public schools (especially those smaller), as siblings tend to supervise or otherwise intervene when in larger groups (assemblies, cafeteria). However, their non-EXCP classroom treatment can be equally negative as other minorities,' with the following particularly common (and again, levels of acceptance) and serving to essentially isolate them further from peers:

- reactions and communication toward them sympathy, disdain, over-attentiveness, or patronizing
- educators failing to call upon them in class or invite their discussion participation
- failing to be placed in groups or pairings for projects, instead working alone or with the classroom teacher
- educators spending far more attention/assistance to EXCP students than others
- regardless of the assignment, they are sent to the EXCP classroom for its completion, or expected to work with EXCP personnel rather than classroom educator
- subjected to more frequent management penalties with desks frequently placed in hallways or otherwise away from peers
- if behavioral issues triggered by classroom routine changes, their absence is requested if guest speakers, films, or various presentations planned
- receiving higher grades than deserved in lieu of additional assistance necessary for satisfactory completion
- as with other minority peers, surface acceptances are seen in school, but not afterwards or with those non-EXCP (W. Sweeney, personal communication, November 15, 2021; C. McMurry-Kozak, personal communication, November 30, 2021)

In larger UM schools with greater EXCP populations, some have successfully lobbied and achieved desired educational changes, particularly creating a smaller EXCP school within the larger one. That is, they take a non-EXCP content course, such as math or English, but do so with other EXCP peers rather than joining a non-EXCP one, with EXCP-only parties, proms, and other activities included (W. Sweeney, personal communication, November 15, 2021).

Further, unlike other minorities, EXCP students have separation from peers by cognitive or physical inability to participate (further accentuating differences) in many extracurricular activities (e.g., games, plays, concerts, debates) or otherwise contribute by decorating lockers, assisting athletic and other teams, working with necessary play or concert tasks, etc. Attending these events, generally with EXCP peers or family, is hardly the same as interacting or invitations to join non-EXCP peers in audiences.

Still, these teens are largely without satisfying friendships and extensive interactions with those non-EXCP, other than family members and associated friends. Such circumstances have seemingly always been inherent within all

US schools and communities, with EXCP adolescents the sole minority group having virtually no opportunity to fully belong to either their school or town.

Community and Social Comparisons

As always, minority receptions depend upon individual situations with negatives and positives occurring in all places, but UM lower populations magnify negatives with fewer like teens or adults available for support or commiseration.

EXCP teens from smaller towns usually have the greatest support, as most are already well known to the community. They are also continually with others, not necessarily afforded to other minorities, as siblings or other family accompany them in town, watching for difficulties and assisting as needed. Merchants, too, will assist, perhaps suggesting items or helping with purchasing; likewise, so will customers, all engaging in friendly conversation.

Still, EXCP teens and adults, as racial and LGBTQ+ minorities, see treatment variations depending upon those with them; pleasant if with others not from their group, less so if only with individuals like them. For example, most towns have a designated bus used for EXCP cohort transport with a supervisor, such as Thursday or Monday afternoons in a grocery or discount store, Tuesday evenings the theater, and all times well known.

Here, they enter, remain, and leave as a group, behavior closely monitored. A cohort with a supervisor serving as spokesperson is more formidable than a teen with family, simultaneously advertising and separating those EXCP from others.

Racial minorities and LGBTQ+ teens (if out) doubtless fail to receive the above supports or protection regardless of those accompanying them, but worse if only with their group. Frequently, community negativity toward those EXCP garners greater social stigma than that to other minorities, yet another reality regarding community distance and stigma.

These two groups are not always welcomed in community businesses; students of color may be watched closely under the presumption of shoplifting or similar offenses, and not encouraged to browse (or at all), unlike others. Both they and those LGBTQ+ will likely hear pejorative commentary, albeit said casually, such remarks were intentional, with EXCP teens experiencing exaggerated helpfulness, directed rather than asked, or addressed loudly, slowly, and as much younger.

Other inequalities are mostly reserved for racial minority and LGBTQ+ teens, as longer restaurant waits, food ordered suddenly unavailable, meals poorly prepared or served, and so on, again proclaiming those welcome and not. Additionally, these teens may not receive employment although better qualified than other applicants or hired for the worst assignments and shifts.

They (especially teens of color) may also be first accused or blamed for any negatives, such as damaged inventory or customer complaints, and unable to respond.

EXCP teens with cognitive disabilities doubtless have no like adult community role models; such difficulties naturally preclude owning businesses or serving as physicians, attorneys, educators, or other professionals, a particular hindrance. In tandem, many UM towns, especially those smaller, have fewer adults of color and those LGBTQ+ in similar positions, or with community leadership presence from local governance, club, and organization memberships.

However, EXCP teens especially, and presumably those of color and LGBTQ+ engage in other scheduled and supported activities for their particular group, both enjoyable and anticipated, and while separate from the community, teens must also engage with those like them.

Of course, these illustrate the worst treatments and situations, seen in all locations, and not all teens and adults remain silent regarding them. Still, many prefer to go elsewhere or assume resigned acceptance, neither effecting change but certainly announcing unwelcome differences and additionally isolating, upsetting, and hurtful.

Religious Comparisons

Larger UM cities feature multiple denominations and places of worship, meeting the needs of its population, including adherents of, for the area, lesser-followed sects (Buddhism, Hinduism). Attendance for all UM religious services differ little from elsewhere in the United States; likewise, individuals create a welcoming, or not, atmosphere.

In smaller UM towns, the church and school serve as main social hubs, typically featuring two or three Christian churches, attended by both Whites and minorities. Non-Christian groups, such as Native Americans, have separate places of worship, sharing town facilities at times. Those without a denomination must either travel or view services from television or the Internet, a significant inconvenience and additional community separation.

Regardless, with small populations, one's social status and treatment in town and school likely mirrors that of congregations, but as elsewhere, individuals, whether few or many, determine attitude and treatment toward attendees.

Those LGBTQ+ teens are welcome or not in Christian churches, and for those not, countless anecdotal stories (and YAL) depict active discrimination against them, their allies, and essentially anyone not homophobic, a central message eternal damnation if unwilling to change. Sermons and activities are regularly directed toward this group and individuals, making it a hostile environment.

Families and teens will attempt to hide LGBTQ+ status if not out, if so, they will likely receive various personal pressures for change. Parents disapproving of those LGBTQ+ are presumably already echoing this stance at home, creating equally hostile and frightening surroundings.

A particularly excruciating situation is devout LGBTQ+ teens and families, whether out or not, as attempting to reconcile sexuality with selected scripture declaring it an abomination. Counseling and other discussion is needed—and not necessarily available—leaving this group with the above negatives and additional turmoil regarding their faith and its meaning regarding them (T. Utesch, personal communication, October 7, 2021; M. B. Davis, personal communication, October 25, 2020; P. Wardlow, personal communication, March 6, 2019).

Although the above portrayals are entirely negative, such situations exist in everywhere; however, it must be remembered allies are also present, with much achieved by intolerance addressed.

Those EXCP are also largely (implicitly) unwelcome in churches; although reasons are different, affects are similar. As above, teens with cognitive deficiencies are customarily portrayed as exceptionally high functioning; those lesser, unseen. Parents of those prone to various distracting behaviors may not be asked to leave teens home or place in the church's nursery, but glares, motioning for quiet, disapproving comments, or individuals sitting far from the teen and family will implicitly send a stronger request than words.

Naturally, such reactions and choices are painful to teens and families, negatively emphasizing their condition, and especially the frequent presumption of behavior by choice, as those LGBTQ+. The nursery is for children, not teens, and decisions about care if remaining home bring more complications and separate the family.

Although such situations must be addressed, a seemingly better solution would be to consult the pastor and congregation, the same as those LGBTQ+, as addressing an issue is easier and less complicated than individuals. Such discussions could continue and if not changing views, bring different, more thoughtful, behaviors.

EXCP adults likely receive equally unpleasant church treatment and receptions, and unfortunately a sober reminder of some teen's futures. If adults belong to a cohort as described above, they arrive well in advance of services with their supervisor(s) assisting their seating in a designated section (further highlighting and separating), usually the rear near a door.

The group is carefully monitored, and any creating disturbances is quickly removed. They leave together during the final hymn or blessing, well before the congregation prepares to exit, and do not attend the usual social gathering afterwards. Such robotic procedures assure they will largely be unnoticed (although the opposite occurs, with all cognizant of them), immediately banished if a disturbance is sensed, sometimes before occurring, and no visiting with others.

Additionally, due to abilities, they would not participate or attend the many church meetings, committees, programs, service rituals/duties, or social events (although if appearing for services, presumably other activities are possible), as would other congregants.

Of course, this EXCP example portrays persons with the lowest cognitive abilities, but it must be remembered communities have those of varying capabilities (likewise, majorities tend to view this group and all other minorities as the *same* instead of *individually*). It is also a question of appropriateness, as if these individuals are largely unable to understand the sermon, kept quiet and focused during by silent activities (coloring, drawing), without allowing any communication with the congregation, is this a dignified and meaningful experience?

Further, while this procedure rather baldly demonstrates the congregation's (and larger societal) view of those disabled, it can be extended to include any other minority or those otherwise different from the majority. Their presence is allowed and tolerated, even welcomed, but only to a certain point; deeper personal interactions and admittance to events/situations in which their voices would be heard and influential regarding various procedures or changes is not necessarily fully welcomed or even permitted. Likewise, as above, such control, whether blatant or implicit, affords neither meaning nor dignity to minority individuals in their many situations with majority populations.

As above, the greatest divide among individuals is seemingly between those non-EXCP and EXCP with significant changes not soon indicated. There is room and possibility for change regarding all minorities and majority populations; educators must establish more frequent communication/discussion with all in classrooms, assure increased participation with others, expect classroom responsibilities and behaviors of all as appropriate, and otherwise treat as valued classroom members.

If there were any groups desperately needing validation, to see themselves, others like them, and adult role models successfully living their daily lives, then reading YAL with similar protagonists and characters will be a lifeline to rural EXCP teens, and especially the most neglected of all, such EXCP teens of color, LGBTQ+, or both. Of course, all minorities, and again those teens feeling most isolated and alone, will benefit from reading novels portraying those similar, and perhaps more importantly, majority students must also read their stories for understanding of often overlooked or discounted peers.

Such YAL titles may or may not transfer to the formation of closer communications and friendships, but it is presumably long overdue and perhaps the basis for better relationships among these admittedly very different individuals.

YOUNG ADULT LITERATURE CONNECTIONS WITH EXCEPTIONAL TEENS

There are scores of YAL featuring every kind of exceptionality, although as with all titles, those rural are harder to locate. Ironically, many depict families living or moving to a small town for its community, caring residents, and sense of protection and safety absent in larger areas; others show characters ignored, taunted, or harassed *because* being noticeably such places. Many things can be hidden, but exceptionalities, like race, cannot.

Exceptional teens comfortable in their towns include Paul from Bloor's (1997) *Tangerine*. His family's move to a smaller town was the first time he was able to make friends and play on a team. His vision is extremely poor with thick glasses, but he thrives. Peers taunted his glasses, a reminder of needless cruelty, and a note of class differences; those with appropriate finances can afford thinner lenses, others not.

The unfortunately named Timminy, an extremely short boy in Plourde's (2016) *Maxi's Secrets*, moves to a small town and makes friends for the first time, as Paul, including others exceptional, while enjoying his beautiful new dog Maxi (Maxi dies, but all dogs on book covers do, and allows his caring for another) and life in general. And, as Terra below, friends help extinguish his self-centeredness.

Like Paul and Timminy, Mariah is a school pariah from her anxiety and panic attacks, as depicted in Amateau's (2009) *A Certain Strain of Peculiar*, but also finds better acceptance once moving to a smaller town. Readers should note she's so used to being harassed that she sometimes resorts to violence in kind, all needless from other's cruelty, with new friends again helping.

Timminy's self-centeredness is echoed by Emma from DeWoskin's (2014) *Blind*, who lived a charmed life until blinded in an accident, unable to accept herself until realizing she isn't the only person with an exceptionality. Friends treating her as before and disliking petulance are necessary, indicating those with new exceptionalities need to be seen as before, mindful of changes but also resuming previous activities or discovering new ways to engage.

Opposite of Timminy is Baxter from Walker's (2011) *Unforgettable*, as his superior memory and intelligence cause him to view those not the same negatively, but likewise must accept a seemingly positive exceptionality as also having negatives.

Morgan within Parker's (2019) *Who Put This Record On?*, is the only Black teen in her school and dealing with anxiety attacks, both difficult, but with assistance from therapy and friends greatly comforting. Constantly criticized for her actions and told how she should act are unhelpful, and readers seeing behaving with compassion and understanding to another when distressed certainly is preferable than negativity.

Cheyenne from Henry's (2010) *Girl, Stolen* and the accompanying 2017 sequel, *Count All Her Bones*, is a highly capable blind teen, her adaptations allowing an exciting and fulfilling life, and her blindness simply being another part of her. Similarly, Buck from Wroblewski's (2008) *The Story of Edgar Sawtelle*, is capably raising and training dogs for his family's business, his mutism handled by sign language or other communication forms.

Bowling's (2017) *Insignificant Events in the Life of a Cactus* and its 2019 sequel, *Momentous Events in the Life of a Cactus*, feature Aven, a middle-grade girl born without arms but managing just fine on her family's western theme park, her friendship with Connor, having Tourette's, enjoyable and benefiting both; its sequel shows Aven's entering high school and continuing her full life.

These challenges and strengths are shown realistically, with readers reminded to accept those with physical disabilities as the individuals they are, rather than questioning how an exceptionality occurred, how abilities are achieved, being overly helpful, or shocked at accomplishments. Exceptionalities can occur to anyone, regardless of race or location.

Conjoined twins are indeed rare (although Abigail and Brittany Hensel are MN teachers at the time of this writing), but both Crossan's *One* (2015) and Mukherjee's (2016) *Gemini* feature sisters purposely living in small towns. Their stories are similar and heartbreaking, as both sets are in high school and realizing dating, career choices, and other things typically involving teens may not include them, with both also facing life-threatening surgeries from weakening shared organs. These girls are portrayed as distinct individuals and should be viewed likewise by peers. Is it right to ignore friends once becoming involved with things they cannot share?

Quinn, who has alopecia and Nick, a former football star who lost his legs in a snowboarding accident in Friend's (2018) *How We Roll*, bond similarly to Aven and Connor above, both helping the other regain confidence while re-adapting to high school life. Likewise, readers should perceive approaching such students first and offering friendship, as those with new exceptionalities have less confidence than those born with them.

Terra from Headley's (2008) *North of Beautiful* despises her facial birthmark, but a male befriends her, later becoming a relationship, and challenges her assumptions of herself, another example of viewing the person, not a single attribute. Another teen questioning herself is Parker—in Lindstrom's (2015) *Not If I See You First*—who has been blind since age seven and is on the track team but is miserable from her father's death and a recent break-up.

She engages in pondering her life, not her blindness, to determine what she wants and needs, with Cadence, having severe memory loss in Lockhart's

(2014) *We Were Liars*, remembering little of a fateful island summer and returning to discover events occurring then.

Elyse in Ockler's (2015) *The Summer of Chasing Mermaids* leaves town from her inability to cope once her dreams of being a professional singer are shattered by an accident damaging her vocal cords. She moves to a friend's small town, finds acceptance, and becomes involved, soon understanding she has a valuable life ahead.

Yancy from Alonzo's (2010) *Riding Invisible* similarly runs from home, being unable to handle his brother's violent mental illness, but finding a mentor. Their friendship allows his returning home, now better prepared. Another frightened teen is Vanni in Zodos's (2017) *Like Water*, who is enjoying her life until her father's Huntington's diagnosis; fear regarding her 50/50 chance of contraction leads to destructive behaviors until aided in reconciliation.

In tandem, Troy from Gomez's (2021) *List of Ten* can no longer accept his Tourette's, intending suicide, but as friendships and circumstances change, he reconsiders, seeing a better life ahead. How would these characters have fared if not accepted by peers and other residents?

Likewise, Gornall's (2018) *Under Rose-Tinted Skies* introduces Norah, a teen with such severe agoraphobia and OCD that she doesn't leave home, spurred to work harder on her problems upon meeting her new neighbor, Luke. He sees past her issues to her personality, liking her very much, and as Norah is without friends, surely readers would also enjoy her, as well as those in their town with similar conditions.

Sarah, with extensive burn scars from Crutcher's (1993) *Staying Fat for Sarah Byrnes*, becomes comatose with depression, literally saved by her best friend, Eric, similar to Luke and Norah, also demonstrating the power of a determined friendship.

Willie, from Crutcher's (1987) *The Crazy Horse Electric Game*, was a golden boy until a head injury, no longer accepted by friends and critical father. His leaving his small hometown and finding an alternative school save him, unlike peers who expected him to be exactly the same, an impossibility followed by harsher treatment. Willie's accident was traumatizing; surely, readers would have more compassion for their friends or others in similar situations.

Junior in Alexie's (2007) *The Absolutely True Diary of a Part-Time Indian* leaves his reservation for a better public-school education and accepted by neither; what is so unacceptable about remaining friends or making new ones? Many no longer wish to teach the novel due to Alexie's 2018 sexual misconduct allegations, but it won a National Book Award in 2007 and his personal life isn't included with its text.

Not to condone Alexie's actions, but an inability to separate an author's writing from personal life leaves many books shelved, with considering others also have secrets. Teens should decide for themselves whether they wish to read his works, but if not, are such standards required of actors, musicians, athletes, and others enjoyed?

In Naylor's (2016) *Going Where It's Dark*, Buck's profound stutter precludes friendships, his solitary hobbies further separating him. Buck is one many would enjoy as a friend; can readers really feel his stutter is so off-putting as to deserve their taunts and snubbing?

Harold from Lawrence's (2000) *Ghost Boy* has albinism and is an outcast; he runs to join the circus, finding acceptance (realizing there are distinct groupings there also), but remaining with those not caring of his appearance allowing his decision of where wishing to live. Could this not be achieved by peer friendships, rather than running from home?

Another teen needing understanding is Simone in Garrett's (2019) *Full Disclosure*, who is HIV-positive and changing schools from harassment once her diagnosis became known. Now at a new school and interested in a boy, she must decide whether to leave or announce her condition. Here, as elsewhere, readers can ponder whether any condition is an invitation to bully another.

Continually tormented are Calliope from Terry's (2017) *Forget Me Not* and Sam from Friesen's (2008) *Jerk, California*; both have Tourette's and Sam's friendship with an elderly man brings peace and friendship. Could this not be found in school with peers? More town and school torment are seen in Wood's (1992) *The Man Who Loved Clowns* and 1995s *When Pigs Fly*, both showing teens with an uncle and sister, respectively, with Down syndrome and angry regarding others' callous behaviors toward them.

Readers will benefit from seeing these protagonists' and family members enjoying one another and reflecting upon exceptionalities not precluding love, caring, or friendship. Yet again, readers are reminded of this fact and reminded these characters, and persons in real life resembling them are individuals, rather than a condition.

Perhaps the most egregious peer conduct is within Draper's (2010) *Out of My Mind*, in which Melody, extremely bright but speech-impaired by cerebral palsy, receives a Medi-talker, allowing her to speak. She leads her new social studies quiz team to the championships, an incredible achievement for any teen, with their qualifying to compete in the finals.

It requires much time and planning for Melody to fly with her team, something which she eagerly anticipates, feeling happiness and true belonging, excitedly arriving at the airport. At the gate, however, she learns she was given the wrong departure time, her team leaving earlier, not wanting to deal with her wheelchair and other disability accoutrements.

Melody is heartbroken and shocked, but must somehow reconcile and forgive, her grace also recognized by readers who may be sharing her classmates' views regarding traveling with one exceptional. Seeing its effect is sobering. Is there any reader not finding this inexcusable? Worse, why would it be condoned by an educator?

The 2019 sequel, *Out of My Heart*, portrays the above school year over and Melody thrilled for summer camp, eager to engage in activities not previously available, as horseback riding, flying on a zipline, or being on her own for the first time. The 2010 title is popular and frequently read by students, but its sequel was published long after the first and not necessarily as familiar to educators. While most prequels and sequels are published near one another, these extended dates are a reminder to always check for sequels, of if the author has featured a character in another title (much like Chris Crutcher's former protagonists now grown and often educators).

Some treat others badly because their peers do but examining these reactions more carefully and considering their effects upon exceptional peers, their reason for occurring, and importantly, so-called benefits, would doubtless bring new awareness and perhaps changes. Many teens are in situations mirroring these characters, with hearing their comments particularly persuasive.

Some teens' conditions are misunderstood, as Lucius from Covington's (1996) *Lizard*, placed in an institution for his facial deformity without testing his intelligence. When a man appears, falsely claiming to be his father, Lucius leaves with him, his only chance to escape.

A similar story is Mikaelsen's (1998) *Petey*, as in 1922 Petey's severe cerebral palsy was unrecognized, also placing him in a state facility. He suffered from caretakers continually leaving but taking another chance and befriending high school student Trevor memorably brightens both. Readers seeing Trevor's increased growth and happiness could consider working or volunteering in a similar facility, realizing interaction with those different beneficial and fulfilling.

Hardships to families are also relayed, as Culley's (2020) *These Things I Know Are True*, features Liv's brother's accidental shooting and his now necessary round-the-clock medical care, with Madden's (2007) *Louisiana's Song* showing Livy's family caring for their father after a car accident, his severe head injury causing their moving to another town for factory work to meet expenses.

Shawn, in Trueman's (2000) *Stuck in Neutral*, while not rural, has severe cerebral palsy, unable to make voluntary movements or communicate in any way. Needing total care, his father is unsure whether Shawn has a cognitive disability, or worse, in unrelenting pain, and considers a quick pillow death. Shawn, however, is extremely bright and cogent, aware of everything regarding his life, including his father's intention, something he's powerless to prevent.

Considering these novels, their teens and families would greatly benefit by assistance, as unrelenting care is more than a full-time job and even with insurance many needs remain unmet. Students need to be with those unlike them and presumably especially necessary and valued is relieving the caretaker from duties, allowing time to rest, another opportunity for peers' volunteering. How much could be accomplished by many spending just an hour or so each week in like households?

YOUNG ADULT LITERATURE CONNECTIONS WITH UNDOCUMENTED TEENS AND OTHER BIASES

Being undocumented is frightening in contemporary society (Speak English! Become an American! My taxes are paying for you!), with protagonists' stories assisting readers' understanding these complex situations and hardships, solutions neither quick nor easy. We cannot support or extend tolerance toward those of whom we're unfamiliar, and while free to choose whether becoming activists, friendship is easily and freely offered, and encouraged of readers.

Not all teens are aware that they are undocumented, as in de la Cruz's (2016) *Something In-Between*, with Jasmine being nine when coming to America and working hard to excel in school. During her senior year, she receives a prestigious scholarship funding four years of college and deciding to surprise her parents by announcing her news she is instead shocked to learn she isn't documented.

Similarly, Osmel, seventeen, in Dimmig's (2019) *Sanctuary Somewhere*, is told at a family cookout that he's undocumented, with his first thoughts fearing to tell friends (much the same as homeless students below), followed by why he wasn't told earlier and fears for his future. Can readers imagine being in such a situation, and how might they react by learning of their, or a friend's, undocumented status?

Others are aware of their status, with the ever-present fear of discovery and deportation dictating their every word. A heavy burden for anyone, especially teens and those younger, continually having to remember what to say and what not, and what was previously told to whom at all times.

Readers witness these and other negatives and complexities experienced in Andreau's (2015) *The Secret Side of Empty*. Here, MT begins panicking her senior year, as while friends are discussing college and dorm rooms, she makes excuses and changes the subject to avoid these conversations, knowing she's undocumented and too frightened and embarrassed to relay her secret.

Marquardt's (2015) *Dream Things True* portrays Alma, an undocumented star student with a large Mexican family, and Evan, a soccer player with influential parents. As Alma's father is gardener for Evan's family, the two meet and fall hard, but after Immigration and Customs officials appear in the community, their dreams of the future, individually and together, may be challenged.

Ursa is a firefighter and Rafi undocumented and working on a horse farm in Novgorodoff's (2008) *Slow Storm*, the two meeting after lightning strikes the barn Rafi calls home, setting it ablaze. Both dislike their situations, seeing no realistic way for change, but their friendship permits each to see life from a different perspective, and they eventually begin steps for improved lives.

Robbins Rose's (2015) *Look Both Ways in the Barrio* features twelve-year-old Jacinta, she and her sisters documented by her U.S. birth, her parents not. She feels somewhat out of place at school and home, but the youth center beckons, and she immerses herself in activities as swimming, learning another language, and gymnastics. All of this causes her to want more, and after her father is arrested and deported, realizes she might have been indiscreet regarding her situation, bringing enormous guilt.

Rebellion is also shown with fear, as in Ahmed's (2019) *Internment*, depicting the near future in which Layla's family and other Muslim American citizens are taken to internment camps, certainly an experience unnecessary for anyone. Layla and others plan to escape and lead a revolution against the camp's director and guards, all dangerous, and challenging readers to oppose contemporary society's complicit silence regarding such practices.

How would readers react, being taken and held elsewhere for their religious faith, and when has this occurred before? Why must others' beliefs be challenged or punished, rather than allowing all to worship as desired, and how is treating others reprehensibly for beliefs condoned as a religious practice?

Michal in Ayarbe's (2012) *Wanted* decides to use her redoubtable position as her high school's bookie when facing clashes between privileged White teens and poor Mexican ones by redistributing funds to those who are poorer. While a method not necessarily recommended, readers witness the many abuses from those with privilege upon those with lesser and ponder why necessary and why our economy is creating more upper and lower classes and fewer in the middle.

There are many ways to emigrate to America, with many more harrowing and complicated than portrayed or otherwise presented in various media. Few simply hop in their car and drive across the border to waiting family, jobs, or housing. Manuel's harrowing, years-long journey to the United States from Mexico begins when he is twelve in Johnston and Fontanot de Rhoads's (2019) *Beast Rider*, in which he rides on the tops of trains to reach the border.

He's routinely beaten, robbed, and left for dead, but also experiences goodness from fellow travelers or others helping along the way, his dangerous trek lasting several years. Upon arrival at his brother's however, he reviews his experiences and wonders whether worthwhile, something readers can also consider, along with the reasons, motivation, and drive for leaving one's home to live in another country.

While not all rural voices, Finney's (2011) *Head Off & Split: Poems* allows Black voices to describe their lives in the United States, its adversities, prejudice and biases, and progress, with readers viewing others' different treatment from race. How would their lives be changed, if being White meant having the same conditions as those portrayed? Why do race and skin color produce such hatred, prejudice, and unequal treatment, when people are essentially the same everywhere, and why hate those unknown to us?

YOUNG ADULT LITERATURE CONNECTIONS WITH HOMELESS TEENS

Like those undocumented, these teens are also frightened, most suddenly thrust in their situation, and attempting to quickly adapt to life without a home and greatly reduced, perhaps even not any, finances. Small towns don't have the numbers of homeless as larger cities, but rural areas and economies are no longer as secure as in the past.

Homelessness, too, is misunderstood (Just get a job! Stay with relatives! Why choose to be homeless?), complicated, and without quick and easy resolutions, but students must know these protagonists' stories too, with many having more in common with such characters than others know, also keeping situations as secret as those in YAL. As always, reading of these teens can initiate understanding, and understanding, tolerance, compassion, and perhaps assistance.

Homelessness is unexpected for many, as in Anns's (2013) *Tent City Princess*, in which Kennedy's father's job loss forces their move to a tent city outside of town. She keeps her situation secret, fearing loss of her prestigious internship that should lead to a scholarship, and certainly isn't going to tell her new boyfriend. After learning of plans to destroy the city, Kennedy slowly becomes an activist.

Like, Kennedy, Dan from Strasser's (2014) *No Place*, must also move to a tent city named Dignityville after both parents lose their jobs and eventually, their home. He is a popular senior, also worried of his new situation halting scholarships and other plans and finds it difficult adjusting to a completely new life. His friends now treat him with pity, disbelief, even cruelty, making things worse, but he's also drawn to residents and becoming an activist and advocate.

Other characters become homeless from dysfunctional families or other tragedies, as Linden from Rufener's (2018) *Where I Live* is keeping secret that her mother and grandmother have died, fearing foster care, and living inside the school at night when she can, in the baseball dugout when not. Although she believes she is keeping herself safe, living this way has multiple risks.

Mel in Sand-Everland's (2012) *A Tinfoil Sky* has moved eleven times in four years with her dysfunctional mother and then relegated to living in a car after the relatives her mother presumed would welcome them have the opposite reaction. Once her mother leaves one night without returning, Mel is left to fend for herself.

Andrea from Palmer's (2018) *All Out of Pretty* has nearly an identical story, living with her stable grandmother and unstable mother. Once her grandmother dies, her mother spends their small inheritance on drugs, eviction soon following. Now homeless, Andrea has additional fears after her mother becomes involved with a dangerous drug-dealing boyfriend.

Leonard's (2018) *Sleeping in My Jeans* features Mattie, similar to Mel and Andrea, also living in a car with her mother and younger sister. Like Mel, she too must care for herself and sister when her mother disappears.

Ansli isn't homeless in Moore's (2014) *The Sharp Sisters: Better Than Picture Perfect*, but as a photographer, she begins to doubt her parents and family as she looks so different from them in family portraits. Her boyfriend is homeless, however, and as she considers how to best help him, she also ponders what family and belonging mean. For these titles, students can also acknowledge what they might do in these situations, how they may support those living in them.

Connected to Layla's Muslim internment camp is Ember from Dooley's (2011) *Body of Water*, with her family's home destroyed by fire as a townsperson believes they are witches due to her mother's reading tarot cards for a living. Twelve-year-old Ember is sure the fire was set by her best friend, not meaning any damage, just a warning that his father was planning something terrible. Regardless, she too, is living in a tent, with the beginning of school nearing and without money for clothes and supplies.

Ember's story should have students questioning assumptions and checking facts before acting, or perhaps more importantly, why some religions are acceptable, and others not? What is so frightening about beliefs that one's home must be torched? Why must those with different religions be removed rather than allowing others to worship as they choose?

All these situations are of no fault of their protagonists, certainly not desired or particularly wanting to continue. If there is any group needing understanding, acceptance, and caring, it is the protagonists represented in the novels above and discussion will assist these positives.

DISCUSSION QUESTIONS AND SUGGESTED ACTIVITIES

Discussion Questions	Suggested Activities; Students Will . . .	Key Diversity Points
1. Is information regarding EXCP, undocumented, and homeless individuals interspersed throughout the school curriculum?	Students can easily list curricular mention of these and evaluate. How many notable EXCP persons/events are known to them? What more is needed for this often-overlooked group, and how may EXCP students assist with coverage/attention?	Are EXCP students represented at all, or even considered a minority? Is this the least represented group, as undocumented and homeless teens are often considered in a temporary situation?
2. Why are EXCP students frequently portrayed as high functioning, rather than representing those of all abilities, especially those lower?	What portrayals of middle- and lower-ability EXCP teens have students seen in the media or read in literature?	Medium and lower EXCP students are largely excluded from societal portrayals; what does this imply?
3. How are middle- or lower-ability EXCP students and adults treated in the community?	Students can consider and discuss various treatments and opinions regarding this group. What changes could be made that would be helpful to both?	How does such treatment benefit those EXCP and those not? Which group benefits more? What messages are being sent?
4. Why are minority LGBTQ+ students and EXCP LGBTQ+ students of color largely invisible, regardless of source? What role models do they have?	What novels or other information (including individuals) have featured this group? How may peers outside these groups assist, and what must they learn to be effective?	Why are these groups generally invisible? What does this imply?
5. Many cognitively disabled students are unlikely to understand YAL with protagonists like them. How may they receive the same benefits of YAL as others regarding seeing themselves portrayed positively?	Students could consider the differing levels of cognitive abilities for various conditions and determine what titles would be appropriate. Also discussed should be benefits of those non-EXCP reading such works.	YAL has few titles showing lower levels of ability, but others can be adapted. Needs can be met by bridging the disconnect between cognitive ability and novels, rather than not using YAL at all.

6. What supports are available in the public school(s) and community for undocumented and homeless students?	Supports may be available, but privately. Many smaller towns may not have either group, but regardless, how can students assist these peers?	What stigmas are associated with any supports? Do they prevent acceptance of assistances? What does this imply?
7. What social supports are available in the community for EXCP teens and adults?	As above, students can examine views and actions of the community regarding this group and their level of belonging. What is their opinion of these stances/actions, what changes could be considered for better inclusion, and why is this important for all?	How may these teens and adults consistently be truly welcome and enjoy community activities, or is this not desired? What does this mean?
8. Why is pity or avoidance of those EXCP, undocumented, or homeless individuals common, regardless of whether one knows individual members?	Students can ponder the ease of forming negative views regarding the abstract, but how does this change if knowing one from a particular group?	Must an acquaintance/relationship occur before acceptance, or can tolerance be extended to those unknown?
9. Many dislike entire groups based upon the negative actions of a few individual members. How is this amplified and continued, and by whom?	Students can consider how negative actions of an individual (or several) of any minority group forms opinions of the whole group.	Why are negatives more quickly applied to minorities than those not? What does this mean?
10. Are students and adults having more severe exceptionalities truly integrated into schools and the community?	Unfortunately, there is a divide between EXCP and non-EXCP students and residents. What are reasons and implications for this, and can changes be made?	EXCP students are often represented less than other minority groups; are they also the least valued?

REFERENCES

Anonymous. (personal communication, October 7, 2021).

Council for Exceptional Children. (2021). *Our policy agenda.* https://exceptionalchildren.org/policy-and-advocacy/policy-agenda

Davis, M. B. (personal communication, October 25, 2020).

Disabled World. (April 6, 2022). *LGBT and disability: Information, news, fact sheets*. Disabled World. Retrieved April 15, 2022, from www.disabled-world.com/disability/sexuality/lgbt/

Kosciw, J. G., Clark, C. M., Truong, N. L., & Zongrone, A. D. (2019). *The 2019 national school climate survey: The experiences of lesbian, gay, bisexual, transgender, and queer youth in our nation's schools*. GLSEN. https://www.glsen.org/research/2019-national-school-climate-survey

McMurry-Kozak, C. (Personal communication, November 30, 2021).

NPR, Robert Wood Johnson Foundation, & the Harvard T.H. Chan School of Public Health. (2018). *Life in rural America*. npr-rwjf-harvard-rural-poll-report-final_10_15_18-final-updated 1130

Sweeney, S. (Personal communication, April 25, 2022).

Sweeney, W. (Personal communication, November 15, 2021).

Sweeney, W., & Sweeney, S. (personal communication, November 15, 2021).

U.S. Census Bureau. (2018). *United States quick facts*. https://www.census.gov/quickfacts/fact/table/US

Wardlow, P. (personal communication, March 6, 2019).

Chapter 8

Rural Death and Grief

Death or other negative life-changing situations occurring to rural community members affect the entire town from their stronger ties and relationships to one another than others elsewhere. However, assisting adolescents and families through the grieving process is not always performed well, with methods for successfully navigation for all students discussed.

ABSENCE OF GRIEF EDUCATION

Although adolescents' U.S. mortality rate is approximately 49 deaths per 100,000 (Centers for Disease Control and Prevention [CDC], 2021), standards used and/or required of classroom educators including those from professional organizations, state education departments, regional/national accrediting agencies, national mandates (e.g., Common Core State Standards), or university/college curricula do not include grief/death education as a learning requirement, with such courses virtually nonexistent in post-secondary English language arts (ELA) programs.

ELA prospective and practicing educators may have a course including grief/death education, but presumably rare; these classes are generally in counseling and administration, both graduate programs. Regardless, all educators should have a course in this area as the unfortunate will occur in schools, and having prior preparation will positively affect all involved, most specifically the future well-being of grieving students.

RURAL ADOLESCENT AND ADULT MORTALITY RATES

Unsurprisingly, mortality rates are higher for rural residents as they tend to be older, poorer, and in worse heath than those suburban or urban. Further, their education levels, health behaviors/choices (higher rates of cigarette smoking, obesity, and blood pressure; less physical activity and lower seatbelt use) and decidedly less access to health-care services and fewer having health insurance all contribute. Rural opioid death rates have quadrupled among those aged 18 to 25, with falls and motor vehicle crashes about 50% higher than elsewhere (CDC, 2019; Noonan, 2017; Shipley, 2021).

The CDC (2019) stated heart disease, cancer, unintentional injuries, chronic lower respiratory disease, and stroke as the five illnesses/events with the highest mortality rates among all U.S. adults, with those rural more likely to succumb from them than their urban/suburban counterparts. While many are potentially preventable or better managed if diagnosed early, the above rural situations and choices doubtless partially contribute to higher mortality rates.

Rural children and adolescents also face health issues, with the CDC (2021) finding those with mental, behavioral, and developmental disorders having more community and family difficulties regarding treatment than peers elsewhere, also presumably from community situations and parental choices.

Predictably, rural adolescents are especially susceptible to agricultural injuries, with the Rural Health Information Hub (RHIHub; 2019) reporting that 33 children and adolescents are injured daily while living, working, or only visiting a farm or other like environment (e.g., grain bins, pastured animals). For those under age 20 and living/working on farms, transportation-related incidents (e.g., tractors/combines, motor vehicles, ATVs) cause the most deaths, followed by various accidents (especially falls bringing one in direct contact with machinery), and drowning.

The CDC (2021) and Forum on Child and Family Statistics (2020) reviewed mortality data for all U.S. children and adolescents, discovering unintentional injuries, cancer, suicide, birth defects, and homicide as their leading causes of death in that specific order. It was also found, however, that rural children and teens had higher death rates in all areas than suburban/urban peers. Again, rural lifestyle disadvantages and other situations uniquely rural were presumed for these larger numbers.

EFFECTS OF RURAL DEATH AND GRIEF

Anyone facing a death, terminal/chronic illness, or debilitating effects of an injury grieves, but the difference between rural communities and larger ones is the number of individuals affected. Put bluntly, a tenth-grade student's death within a school of 3,000+ will affect far fewer than one whose high school holds 35.

In larger schools, a student's death will affect his/her family, close friends/family, other classmates, and those regularly encountered in and outside the school community. Many educators and administrators from large cities/schools have not dealt with deaths (whether students or family members) directly as the individual involved may have been unknown to them, as not in their grade level or classes. Likewise, unless the student was a school star (e.g., headed the winning debate team, a leading athlete or musician), he/she may also be unfamiliar to many students.

Here, the grief/mourning process is the same but involving fewer individuals and frequently less personal. Some of these schools may utilize counselors, both from the school and elsewhere, and providing students time with them as desired. Others may routinely allow student shrines, dedicate a concert or game, or offer a ceremony in which a plaque is unveiled, a tree planted, and then continuing the school year as before. Those encountering a suicide may provide no formal remembrance at all, fearing additional such deaths.

However, rural grieving is different; a death here—whether child, teen, or adult—affects the school and town, as the individual was known to the community. Further, deaths of educators (or any associated with schools) will also be especially hurtful to students as these adults are considered family, not always true of larger places. Those rural experience often intense, or more, sorrow than those of larger areas from closeness to the individual and more openly grieving.

INEFFECTIVE COMMUNICATIONS WITH THE BEREAVED

Rural grieving is often more complex than elsewhere, with its smaller communities and residents known, friendly, and/or related to one another. Still, teens and adults everywhere grieve similarly and many offer condolences to losses that are nearly as hurtful as the death itself, attempting empathy in making comments presumed soothing (Branon, 2010).

Such remarks are common everywhere, included in funeral/memorial ceremonies and other events, printed on sympathy cards, and so ubiquitous as to be assumed acceptable and helpful. Many, having relayed them to others, don't recognize their upsetting content until also facing a tragedy and receiving themselves. Sadly, usually only those having experienced the same type of death (or recognize such remarks as unhelpful) are able to provide genuine comfort to one newly bereaved (Branon, 2010; The Dougy Center, 2020; NACG, 2012; Schonfeld & Quackenbush, 2010).

Those rural will likely receive more such condolences in shorter periods of time (and the smaller the town, the more commiserations) from community members. As these are also friends, family, or otherwise known to those with a loss, hearing their awkward expressions can be surprising and particularly jarring.

While most longer sympathies are directed to adults, children and teens are frequently accompanying them, also hearing. Naturally, special care should be taken in attempting to comfort anyone but especially children and teens, as aside from without adult maturity and experience, this may be their first personal experience of death. Commentary and the outward display of grief to children and teens must be carefully appropriate; words, regardless of content, will be remembered, even for a lifetime.

What are inappropriate and supportive comments to offer to those bereaved? The most helpful are heartfelt, showing genuine sympathy, understanding, and the willingness to listen to individuals discuss how they are feeling or what might be needed (Branon, 2010; The Dougy Center, 2020; NACG, 2012; Schonfeld & Quackenbush, 2010; Turner, 2010). Samples and short, and it is to be hoped, obvious, analyses for helpful and unhelpful remarks are below:

- The best response is *I am so sorry,* followed by *I can only imagine how difficult this is for you, Tell me how you are feeling?, How may I help?* (and doing so), *Many people have strong feelings of XXX when this happens. Has this been true for you?,* and *Please tell me how I may best honor XXX.*

These are simple and heart-felt; the speaker acknowledges both the other's pain and grief being individual, and aside from *I am so sorry,* directly prompts the listener to express their feelings, important as grief must be shared. Further, inviting one's expression of true thoughts without censure, embarrassment, or later gossip, allows realization of personal emotions, whatever they may be, are indeed common to all (illustrated if conversing with one different), with relaying and sharing bringing normality and relief.

While the last question is always appropriate, it's markedly so for mourners having grieving practices different from the majority, whether cultural or otherwise. It indicates the speaker's understanding and desire to engage in commentary most helpful, again allowing differences between others to lessen or disappear in grief's commonality.

Longer conversations are generally absent with first condolences and especially with teens, in lieu of quick, perfunctory comments while plunking a casserole on a table and hastily leaving, grief an awkward and frightening topic. A 10- to 15-minute exchange, however, can provide that desperately needed—and assist visitors in their own grief awareness and supportive abilities.

Unfortunately, inappropriate remarks are more common, and while seemingly mystifying how an otherwise stable, sound individual could possibly believe them helpful, those below are continually heard:

- Perhaps the worst is *Be thankful you just lost XXX, as losing a child is the worst loss of all,* followed by *Let me know if I can help!* (but not following through)*, I know exactly how you feel! My dog died last month, and I miss him so much, Well, my house burned, and we lost our belongings. At least you still have those! You're the man/woman of the house now* (to a child or teen), or *Oh, you must read XXX; those books were so helpful to me when my cousin died!* (to an older teen).

Additionally, those sharing the speaker's faith often find these uncomfortable, as *Remember, with God, all things happen for a reason, God never sends us more than we can handle,* and the supremely offensive to newcomers and those with differing beliefs and customs, *What practices do your people follow when someone dies?*

The difficulties of these are surely obvious, but while the statement of losing a child is a standard in society, grief cannot (and should not) be quantified. A new widow/widower, for example (or anyone not losing a child), will feel substantial pain hearing this, which also negates the loss, insinuating it of lesser importance and secondary to one worse.

Further, commonsense comparison of situations should reveal the tastelessness of likening a pet's (or similar) death, to an individual's, with the remark of losing one's house similarly unhelpful, the speaker implying criticism of another's grief by subtly bragging his/her situation worse and reaction superior. Overall, comparing negative situations is irrelevant and unhelpful, and denies one's right to grieve.

Announcing a teen or child must assume a parental role sharply recalls the loss, placing a too heavy and frightening burden on the listener. In tandem, suggesting books (as with *offering* assistance rather than *providing*; *borrowing* titles wasn't mentioned), hints they quickly assuage grief. Of course, many are helpful, but only when aiding rather than causing additional pain.

The second remark set establishes those different from the majority, their beliefs/customs deficient and lesser. Even if those speaking share beliefs there are doubtless differences, making such comments uncomfortable, even frightening, as insinuating the death was planned by a deity, leaving mourners wondering what terrible event is next.

They also insinuate showing/feeling grief is unnecessary (unlike that portrayed in the Christian Bible), the loss managed with more faith and effort. We can and should provide better comfort and assistance to anyone grieving with statements, especially teens, presumably having less experience with loss. Certainly, such discussion is a greatly needed classroom topic.

MISAPPLICATION OF GRIEF STAGES

The Kübler-Ross stages of grief model (2014) is perhaps the most well-known theory of how people manage death, declaring individuals experience five different stages (denial, anger, bargaining, depression, and acceptance) during bereavement. These stages are frequently referenced by those consoling or otherwise speaking to one having had a loss, but as with non-supportive sympathies, their usual interpretation as hierarchical is also unaccommodating.

Any responsible counselor (or one having suffered a significant loss) will convey them as recursive, several may be experienced together, perhaps encountered backward, repeated, one stage lasting months, another a few days, and multiple other combinations dependent upon the individual. As grieving teens and families are already facing pain and awkward commiserations, they (and all students) and their families should be assisted/informed of them, particularly understanding there isn't a single correct way to grieve nor a specified timetable.

RURAL SCHOOL GRIEF MANAGEMENT PLANS

Grieving is especially personal and complicated in rural areas, as a death will affect more residents with their lesser populations. The smaller the town, the more personal the loss among and between residents and the family, all of whom have varied (and frequently long-standing) relationships with one another, both positive, negative, and anything in between.

Reactions to a loss can range from overwhelming to shockingly lacking; those supportive are naturally helpful, but adverse emotions of guilt, doubt, confusion, hurt, and shame in addition to grief can also be felt, often unexpectedly, by many. Most of these will be directly experienced by adults, but their children and teens will also be subjected to them with far less understanding.

Grieving is individual, but too intense or lengthy community reactions can extend the process, with those seemingly incomplete or lacking cause its stalling, both unhealthy and especially for impressionable teens and children.

Most rural deaths in smaller towns, especially of students, their families, or school personnel will deeply involve all within the school(s), with these communities depending upon educators to provide reassurance, stability, and demonstration of appropriate grieving behaviors.

Rural educators are community leaders and a substantial part of students' and families' lives, certainly able to manage reactions and responses to tragedies and positively assist, if not lead, in navigating all through the grieving process and toward healing. Of course, doing so requires prior preparation, and as student deaths and like tragedies will occur, these educators must have a school-wide general plan for them (i.e., a Grief Management Plan or GMP), first for cohesion among themselves, and then for providing consistency to students and families.

Although a GMP may sound dubious or robotic, as tornado or fire drills, they can meet the many needs of rural communities by providing immediate assistance, directing school commemorations and ceremonies, working with families, assisting with funerals and other services, and moving all through the grieving process to healthy acceptance. Perhaps most importantly, such prior planning assures all facing losses are treated respectfully and equally.

DEATH'S MINORITY STATUS AND THE NECESSITY OF RURAL SCHOOL GRIEF MANAGEMENT PLANS

As above, rural residents are intertwined, with such close relationships positive, negative, variable, or nonexistent, depending, as elsewhere, but more heavily expressed, and felt in smaller places and especially schools. Naturally, deaths are keenly felt by the community, especially those of children and teens, but nearly all grieve.

Families facing the loss of a teen, or teens losing siblings or parents, for example, are likely yet another minority, depending, and can encounter additional pain as grieving is often misunderstood. American society states and depicts various false mourning expectations and assumptions that are applied to others without comprehending the hurt they may cause the individual, whether teen or adult. A GMP will recognize grieving realities and fallacies and assist accordingly, an immeasurable comfort to those whose feelings are inaccurately presumed.

There are multiple examples of GMP benefits, with one considering that while teens doubtless feel sympathy and/or empathy for one deceased, those new to the area may not know, or know well, the individual but feel obliged, and uncomfortable, participating in remembrances.

Similarly, although presumed rural residents and classmates care deeply for one another, this is not necessarily true; everyone, regardless of location, encounters those more preferred than others. These students may find themselves expected to attend and participate in various ceremonies yet suppressing anger or resentment doing so for another disliked.

In tandem, not all parents and families are nurturing; the death of a father who is also an abuser or otherwise contentious situations will result in mixed and confusing feelings, heightened by others' varying awareness, not always realized. Teens and families will be subjected to different opinions of grieving displayed, as speakers' comments are based upon individual knowledge and beliefs regarding home conditions, also painful, and likely reviving or revealing more hurt and stigma. This group needs support and extended assistance, presumably not provided without prior expectations.

Suicides, whether they be teens or family members, also bring complexities; schools frequently differ whether to commemorate or not, and if so, how, all difficult with discussions bringing contention and other problems disrupting thoughtful decisions. These teens and/or families, as above, will face similar difficulties, also benefitting from counseling.

Decidedly needing guidance are antagonistic, or worse, situations, as a teen's car accident resulting in their survival but passenger injury/death. Even if the driver was without fault, he/she will doubtless be blamed or criticized; if injured and hospitalized, far less attention will be given with anger at survival lingering. If at fault, the teen and his/her family can easily become pariahs, the accident never forgotten.

Likewise, anything involving parental misjudgment or supervisory lack (taking teens boating without double-checking stored life preservers; reminding a group to remain clear of a section marked no entrance at an outdoor market but some surreptitiously ignore) causing injury/death will be viewed as above.

These teens and families will doubtless experience multiple conflicts regarding grieving, compounded by assumptions of participation in various planned memorials perhaps painful or uncomfortable. Declining appears churlish or craven, unpopular among many, all definitively unhealthy. Selecting among activities, determining which offered, and the ability to converse with counselors or other adults would be sustaining and invaluable to this group, available through a GMPs prior planning.

Without structure, observances can be unequal; some deaths/negative occurrences receive too much attention, too little, or none at all. Grieving easily becomes overwhelming, as the many shrines, candlelight vigils, or groups of overexcited, sobbing teens can expand and extend mourning (and create those vying for attention as most bereft) rather than assisting its ease. Parents and other adults may hold additional ceremonies, possibly unwise, without school permission. Teens, related to the deceased, will surely feel ceremonies are seemingly never-ending, painful by constant reminders or allowing their holding death's reality in abeyance, rendering it harder moving forward.

Students lesser known or those and families more unpopular may receive substantially less attention, with that given for the first group obligatory, school ceremonies are perfunctory, causing families newer to the community feeling more estranged and perhaps less welcome than believed. Teens and families may draw inward, complicating their grieving by feeling unable to share with others.

Controversial families may also see less attention, with some given tinged with disapproval regarding lifestyles or age-old disagreements resurfacing. Older teens long in the community usually know underlying issues; those younger or newer residents, may not. Ceremony focus may be more on family discord than the deceased, all upsetting, and teens from the family likely also feeling anger, shame, guilt, all of which are additional negatives. These teens, as newer community residents, may also feel renewed hopelessness regarding belonging and status and likewise withdrawing, further complicating grieving.

Minority families may be awkwardly recognized, appearing as intolerance where none exists. Some may be ignored due to status, hesitation regarding different (or unknown) mourning practices/traditions or presuming preferences would be grieving with family. These alternatives may be welcomed, expected, or devastating, but these teens and families need recognition and assistance the same as all other residents. A GMP will detail minority grieving practices, and if antipathy is felt by some, seeing the same memorials and remembrances, with their unique and meaningful tailoring, could have a positive effect on views.

Likewise, students and parents suffering immediate family losses become another minority, although not always so recognized; the U.S. percentage of children and teen deaths is approximately 8% (UNICEF, 2021) with the majority of widowed adults dage 65-plus (Gurrentz & Mayol-Garcia, 2021). The death of senior's boy/girlfriend and soon-fiancé is not the same as a break-up, nor is losing a husband/father hardly different from a divorce, although frequently these, and more ill-fitting, comparisons are made, all jarring and painful. Grieving plans consider such situations and provide needed assistance to those with specific losses often viewed differently by others.

Another minority of sorts is privacy; although rural deaths typically receive much notice, it must be remembered that grief and mourning are individual;

some families, whether majority or minority, prefer few to no school/public commemorations, fewer home visitations, private funerals, and overall less attention, with more, although well meaning, bringing pain. These families, too, should be able to choose the remembrances and ceremonies desired without repercussions; a GMP plan has prepared for such decisions.

A GMP's goal is assisting all students and families during their immediate loss, strengthening the affection and friendships among and between individuals as the community faces and shares their hurt and grief. Following familiar and accepted rituals provides comfort, assurance, and hope, but grieving differences are also recognized.

They gradually propel students and adults forward, guiding them through grief to acceptance and fond remembrance, while continuing applicable assistance to both throughout the school years when various events poise intense, and often unexpected pain (father/son/daughter banquets, graduation).

Plans recognize that those who have died were loved, should be mourned, and will be missed, with those outside the immediate family also bereaved. If students and families can experience more comfortable grieving, then that alone is surely successful. GMPs are utilized within schools, their goal creating standard protocol for addressing deaths and grieving practices particularly affecting them (i.e., a student, teacher/staff, parent, etc.) as stated above.

They provide the stability, consistency, and familiarity desperately needed, but usually currently missing within the home, and schools without protocol. Perhaps most importantly, they assure every student and their family, whether majority or minority, compassion and dignity, equal treatment, and productive, proven methods managing grieving and assisting its transition from sorrow to moving forward with hope.

The GMP is meant for all schools within a district, the same as a fire/weather or other protocol considered standard procedure. Topics seeming essential are below, but naturally individual districts decide what will be included, or not, and most applicable procedure/rationale.

For example, one may offer counseling within the building, another may require it for all students, and a third recommending it with resources posted on their website. It's also assumed the GMP is always in process, various revisions and updates made as appropriate, and reviewed yearly for currency and applicability.

A district-wide committee is formed to create a GMP, its members best representing the district/educators, parents, religious leaders/counselors, and other community members. Of course, members, timeframes, acceptance of revisions/suggestions from those outside the committee, and the final copy's presentation, explanation, and availability (presumably placed on the district's website for downloading) are individually established.

However formed and conducted, plan necessities include determining practices regarding death/grief for community religions/beliefs, whether majority or minority, and including practices for those unassociated with a church/religion or otherwise nonreligious. Those without community representation (e.g., a town without Buddhists) are noted for future accommodation.

A School Spokesperson (SS), and perhaps assistants, designated to speak for the district/school and serve as its contact for students and families, communicating their needs and wishes to educators/personnel also seems essential. Particularly vital is the continual consideration of the deceased's family and following their explicit wishes for various school practices, regardless of popularity or tradition (another valuable example of diverse practices).

Another recommendation is inclusion of quality YAL novels featuring grief/death that would be particularly helpful to grieving students. Selections could be managed by a standing committee or otherwise designated individual(s), who continue compiling representative titles. Student participation is valuable, as skills in locating and reviewing novels for quality, along with a better understanding of grief/loss/death and grieving, would be attained.

Specific topics, issues, and situations are many, with committees determining which to address and how. Seemingly important to all schools, and especially those rural, include the groupings below and beginning with the school's official death announcement and grief assistance.

The accurate and timely announcement quells the many rumors already rampant, and the type of death is also significant regarding responses; suicides remain controversial as do those from poor choices (e.g., teens driving and texting, parents allowing drinking during a party), or involving more than one individual with both deaths and serious injuries.

Another determination is whether an official mourning period will be observed and its length (ending after the funeral), and if a memorial (e.g., tree, plaque, pavement stone) will be offered and its subsequent ceremony. Presumably also here are graduation and later awards/honors involving the student and acknowledgments.

Likewise, guidelines for unofficial memorials (e.g., students' mini shrines, locker decorations, town candlelight vigils) will be needed, and similarly later commemorations, as dedicating an activity most enjoyed by the student, as a football game or concert, and subsequent ceremony.

Protocol is helpful for rarer uncertain situations, including community newcomers unfamiliar with the deceased, and sadly, when the deceased student is the new resident. Certainly challenging and contentious in rural communities (and occurring at some time) is working with those students or/families negatively viewed by the school and/or community, difficult on both sides. Of course, all students/families should be treated the same as others; regardless of acquaintance or reputation, death is equally painful.

Clearly appreciated is planning/scheduling family visitations, foods provided, other needed assistances (e.g., running errands, shoveling snow), and a time length for such family aids (two weeks after the funeral is common). Another should be determining the school's representation at the funeral, any preparation or support needed for students attending, and during.

Housekeeping considerations, as procedures for returning student school belongings, grade or standardized test recording, and name removal from various lists and other communications (piercingly painful is opening an email discussing an upcoming debate in which a child will certainly not be attending).

Vital to rural parents but frequently overlooked is continuing assistance regarding grieving, as they must reconcile to suddenly becoming outsiders on various clubs and activities (e.g., booster clubs, dance/prom planning, providing meals for the basketball team). Additional hurtful changes are seeing their child's long-standing friends' absence from the home, with their child's romantic partner dating another distinctly painful.

Similarly, former peers' new driver's licenses, first dates and proms, college acceptances, and other common events and activities not including their child are heartbreaking, regardless of years after a death. Likewise, parents often feel guilty when grief eases as progressing can be equated with forgetting or abandoning a child; assistance again desirable here, and perhaps leading to serving on a grief management committee (GMC), sustaining others with losses.

Of course, schools remain in session after tragedies with students affected differently, but stability and reassurance are necessary for all. Practices will vary but recommended are remaining in session as usual on the first day, educators taking cues from students regarding activities; most will likely discuss/share reminiscences, some may wish to write, listen to the teacher read aloud, or perhaps read/discuss appropriate YAL excerpts, stories, or novels. Meeting with counselors will also likely be offered, students allowed to return home, or parents arriving for lunch, gatherings, or simply comfort.

Classrooms resume normal procedures on Day 2, with students reminded one should best honors the deceased by continuing living *while* grieving. All, including the deceased's siblings if present, are expected to follow classroom guidelines regarding conduct, assignments, deadlines, etc. This isn't cruel, but allows focus upon the classroom and its normalcy, easing pain somewhat by attention elsewhere, with peer presence invaluable.

The funeral is likely during the week; if classes remain in session those not attending are expected to follow procedures as above, but regardless, all should learn of specific service/family rituals, a beneficial time to discuss differences/similarities and practice productive grieving.

After the funeral, if appropriate, its discussion may occur, perhaps using some YAL readings and comparing, another reminder of respectfully honoring their classmate by moving forward. Unfortunately, the deceased's desk remains, frightening for some; the teacher and class should decide its graceful retirement (e.g., receiving another, changing seating arrangements).

Classes then begin proceeding as usual, educators seeking signs of complicated grief for referral, with peers likewise. Grieving is intense and difficult for rural individuals, and it too, should be recognized as part of the curriculum; its effects will be beneficial to all, life-changing for others.

YOUNG ADULT LITERATURE CONNECTIONS

Everyone experiences grief and loss; all are important and recognizing and appropriately assisting is necessary. We all have varying experiences with losses and death, and while generally the older one becomes the more experienced, it must be remembered there are children and teens having suffered more than many adults. Grieving losses is also intensely individual, as feelings and reactions depend upon the person and their situation. One teen may hurt intensely upon moving to another town and leaving friends/family, another may view as exciting and knowing they can connect with others using social media. Both reactions should be recognized and respected, as with all losses.

Another teen may puzzle adults by grieving the loss of an uncle over a father; however, the father may have been abusive, continually preoccupied with little attention on family, consumed by drugs or alcohol, living elsewhere and seldom or never communicating, among others, with an uncle instead the beloved father figure. This same family may have a sibling feeling entirely differently, caring for the father far more than the uncle. Again, both views are equally importance.

A family may be working together to assuage a mother's grief over the loss of a brother, not knowing the two were never close for any number of reasons. Their mother is naturally grieving the death, but not nearly as intensely if another sibling. Again, individual reactions are for personal reasons not necessarily known to even those closest but should be respected.

We must all be able to grieve whom or what we wish, and in the way that is most helpful. Educators and parents may, or may not, be aware of a teen's situation as much is hidden, but no one can necessarily know of that student's feelings regarding what or who was lost, nor can reactions be accurately predicted, parents likewise. Parents may not have expected to have one child deeply hurting from a pet's death, another not particularly affected or secretly glad the dog who loved to chew their belongings is gone. Reactions are not always foreseen, but all are normal.

Talking is vital for those reading, but YAL is also helpful. A teen can read of others experiencing their exact loss, including reactions. Teens chided for grieving too much or little can see similar characters, and for the same, or many of the same, reasons as themselves. All kinds of losses and grieving are portrayed in YAL, from losing a favorite belonging, a pet, moving, loss of friends and relationships, divorce, illnesses and debilitating conditions, all kinds of deaths, and more.

Not all teens are immediately eager to read of those also having a loss; educators should inform them that titles are available for when ready to read, and remember to follow through, as some teens may be ready in a week, while it may be months for others. It's also the situation that matters, not the protagonist, as attempting to locate YAL with rural settings having its main character exactly as the teen is rare. Any teen suffering the same loss as the reader is relatable, regardless of who they are.

Teens must also read of the losses peers face, understanding the issues above, and seeing characters hurt from other students in school or town residents is telling. YAL titles match the below discussion questions by dominant theme, with additional themes and subplots naturally extending titles to several questions and topics.

Discussion Question 1 speaks of euphemisms used in referring to death, with thirteen-year-old Sal's mother leaving in Creech's (1994) *Walk Two Moons*. Sal receives her postcards from across the United States for a short time, and her father becomes friendly with another woman, Margaret, and moves them to her town. Sal's unhappy over both and believes her mother will return if home for her birthday.

Sal and her grandparents begin a road trip to see her mother and she entertains with her friend's outrageous story, her own story soon unfolding, ending at her mother's tombstone. Her mother's death should surprise its younger readers as Sal's narration meanders through time with cryptic language and clever clues, as Margaret's last name is *Cadaver*, or grandparents saying they want to visit where Sal's mother was "resting peacefully" (p. 5).

The novel itself could be considered euphemistic as Sal's mother's fate isn't fully revealed until its end, hints used instead of direct statements. Aside from this discussion, noting euphemisms' positives and negatives and the novel's use of them, educators may also stress the importance of careful reading (why are quotation marks surrounding *resting peacefully*?) with students reconsidering interpretations, stating what was missed and why, connecting to pertinent text, and the ending's effect will be productive and entertaining talk.

The novel also relates to Question 4, difficulty accepting a death. Loss and grief are universal, and students should commiserate with Sal's imagining her mother simply away rather feeling enormous loss and pain. Rationalizing her reaction and why it occurred are important topics, as is whether allowing her belief is healthy, providing time for acceptance, or cruel by stalling grieving until facing a grave. Individuals may share stories that are similar and acknowledge death's pain, difficulties in acceptance, and coping methods; previous peer differences vanish here as death and pain are known by all.

Seemingly blasting euphemisms is Crutcher's (2007) *Deadline*, with Ben deciding to forgo treatment for his terminal illness and instead living fully and dying on his own terms, decidedly unpopular. It's important for teens to see they have choices regarding terminal illnesses, but also questioning them, as Ben.

Whether Ben's decision is realistic will be debated. If teens should have his choice, then what if later they want treatment, but it's too late for efficacy? Weighing if Ben is essentially committing suicide and the ethics of forcing grueling and ultimately unsuccessful treatments is another interesting discussion, as is the implication of denying medication for religious reasons, including teens desiring treatment but parents opposed.

March Ann, in Angle's (2008) *Hummingbird*, uses this tiny bird as a euphemism for her grandmother's impending death from heart disease, but realistically and effectively. Her grandmother loves hummingbirds, and after a nonmigrating one appears, March Ann works diligently, ensuring its winter survival so her grandmother can enjoy it at her window.

Her caring for the bird provides life for both, is symbolic of her love, a final gift, and proving that she can move forward when necessary. March Ann's grieves before her grandmother's death, time not necessarily allotted, with her illness not one with corresponding ravages, an important difference.

A special note is Louie from *Running Loose* (pp. 138–41), as Ben's teacher, but single, sad, and his tiny apartment uncomfortable. When last seen, he was gaining perspective regarding his girlfriend's death: What happened to him? Is he illustrating recovery from some losses impossible?

Readers can use these novels, and those following, to contemplate having time before a death, effects of various terminal illnesses, individual factors contributing to death's acceptance or denial, religious, cultural, and family beliefs and practices regarding death overall, all rich conversation points, responses doubtless varying, but its topic universal and enabling students to share and learn from one another.

Discussion Question 2 concerns grieving other losses; many students may not have experienced a death in their immediate family, but all should be familiar with this pain. Choyce's (2014) *Jeremy Stone*, features Jeremy, a First Nations teen, severely bullied at school and facing his father's desertion. After meeting troubled classmate Caitlan, their friendship grows, also problematic, but he can speak with his ancestors' spirits, their guidance allowing him strength to continue moving forward (also Question 8 and miracles, Question 9).

Native Americans should have much to share here, either by student or guest speaker, with other beliefs expressed. Whom do non-native students consult with overwhelming problems? Beverly in DiCamillo's (2019) *Beverly, Right Here* also needs someone to listen, as she's devastated by the loss of her dog and mother's inattention from alcoholism. Her travel is physical, moving to another town and befriended by an elderly woman, much like Jeremy's spirit guide, and finds solace from the ocean's waves. Readers can note (and probably experienced) the intense pain from a pet's loss, doubtless exacerbated from home problems. How would support from peers have assisted her?

Rufener's (2019) *Since We Last Spoke*, is a tangle of grief and loss; new couple Aggi and Max unexpectedly face a fatal car accident involving both their older siblings, with lawsuits and parents demanding the end of their relationship and any contact. They must grieve their siblings and relationship loss separately; others hurt by suddenly ended relationships can be vital here, and as these characters desperately need others for talk and sharing. How may peers assist each?

Grieving is difficult, and students must discover what assists them, another item shared in class and topic of Discussion Question 3, with Dillon from Crutcher's (1989) *Chinese Handcuffs* journaling to his brother who committed suicide. He finds comfort and strength in relaying his grief and guilt, analyzing and better understanding his brother's situation, discussing their relationship, and finally saying goodbye. Suicides are devastating, and teens should read of others navigating them, as if having experienced they are doubtless far from ready to share.

Lydia, from Shank's (2012) *Child of the Mountains*, has suffered the loss of her family and now living with her aunt and uncle, taunted in school and miserable. A teacher notices her writing talent, with his fiancé eager to assist, and Lydia begins talking with her and channels her grief through writing as Dillon and Lupita.

The appropriately named Wren, seen in Schröder's (2016) *Be Light Like a Bird*, is unable to discuss her father's shocking death from a plane crash with her too-distraught mother, but continues to birdwatch by a pond, a hobby formerly shared with him. She finds the water soothing and feels closer to her father, similar to March Ann's hummingbird or Davie's hiking in the hills. Like Lydia, she is also taunted and snubbed in her new school. How might teens have helped these two girls, rather than excluding from friendships? How many teens can join others in hobbies and other pastimes?

Lupita in McCall's (2011) *Under the Mesquite* is a poet, and upon learning her mother's cancer diagnosis begins writing poems to express her grief. Like Dillon, she writes, and as March Ann, has time to prepare, her poems similar to hummingbirds and perhaps reminiscent of Sal's postcards. Afterward, she finds solace in tossing them into the wind, releasing her feelings, symbolically sending them to her mother.

Almond's (2019) *The Color of the Sun* sees Davie beginning a hike, grieving his father's recent death and his friend's violent one. Along the way he meets those also wanting to remember and reminisce, surprising and helping him understand discussing others and cherishing memories is powerful, with students likewise encouraged to talk and savor.

Not all teens are able to grieve productively; some make bad choices or engage in negative behaviors in attempting to ease their pain. Beverly, again from DiCamillo's (2019) *Beverly, Right Here*, is a frequent runaway, the loss of her dog so intense she runs again. While finding solace, she wants permanence and feels uneasy, worried that her growing happiness won't last.

Sasha from Dooley's (2016) *Free Verse* also chooses to run; her mother left when she was five, her father died in the mines and now her brother's death sends her to a foster home. She's treated kindly and begins to write poetry as Lupita, but her sorrow is great and she impulsively bolts with a cousin, soon realizing grief accompanies one wherever traveling.

Serenity from Watson's (2010) *What Momma Left Me* resembles Sasha in having a supportive home, but her abusive father killing her mother causes her to make destructive choices. And, like Sasha, discovers she must reconcile her past before moving forward.

Emma, in Wiseman's (2015) *Coal River* doesn't run, but just like Sasha, she loses her parents. Unlike Sasha and Serenity, she must live with an aunt and uncle who treat her unkindly. Like Wren, she has no one to talk to, and becomes involved with working conditions of miners in their town. She considers joining a protest, although knowing this would alienate residents and certainly her relatives, which fits Question 7.

Further discussion with a friend would doubtless have made Emma's decision easier, with peers' friendship and attention (including educators, as with Lydia above, and as earlier, the question of bullying a new or any student having suffered a loss or tacitly allowing equally reprehensible) perhaps leading Beverly, Sasha, and Serenity to better decisions and a stronger sense of belonging, as in our classrooms and life.

Many teens feel intense guilt from a death, especially those occurring suddenly, as Tiger from Glasgow's (2019) *How to Make Friends With the Dark*. When last speaking with her mother they had an argument about a dress, with her mother's sudden death soon after. Tiger doesn't know her father or of any other relatives, and so bereft she's unable to move forward, considering suicide (also demonstrating unproductive grieving in Question 4).

Like Tiger and Cody below, Lowen, from Jacobson's (2018) *The Dollar Kids*, was trying to work on a project, but his younger friend, Abe, demanded too much attention. He sends Abe for licorice for quiet; when the boy is killed by a random shooter, his guilt is profound. He immerses himself in an extremely taxing housing project (Question 7) that is essentially his way of penance, although later he enjoys it and it allows him to channel his grief like other characters (Question 3). An important student lesson is that these teens weren't at fault; we cannot control others, another point of discussion.

Cody, in Foreman's (2015) *I Was Here*, is shocked by her best friend's suicide, unaware of her many issues and problems until finding her diary while packing her belongings. Still, she berates herself, feeling she should have known, intervened, been a better friend, something, but of course much was carefully hidden.

Likewise, teens from Morrissey's (2019) *When the Light Went Out* have been haunted by their friend's Marley's death by shooting five years earlier: Was it an accident, her cry for help, or suicide? Reuniting on its anniversary, their lives have stalled from guilt and uncertainty, but discussing the matter leads to their realization they'll never know Marley's intent. They bid farewell, allow her rest, and give themselves permission to move past her forever-age of fifteen to continue their lives.

Unfortunately, deaths and illnesses are viewed differently with varying expectations (or rather, the deceased and relatives) by others, depending upon personal views and beliefs as in Question 6. Paige within Lord's (2015) *The Start of Me and You* fits several categories: personal guilt, and also that of school or community responses (Question 7).

Known by her town as the girl whose boyfriend tragically died, it's been a year since his death, with Paige terribly guilty by never having revealed they'd only dated for a few weeks and weren't particularly close. She must tactfully inform others that she wants another relationship and move forward, but she's unsure how.

Scarlett's treatment is so cruel from her brother's overdose death in DeRiso's (2017) *All the Wrong Chords* from both her school and town she must move elsewhere to escape the relentless gossip. Naturally, actual events and situations become embellished with each telling and most where she is sure to hear, hardly justifiable treatment, with students considering its affect and prevention. Presumably teens would also have different perspectives that might help these protagonists, discussion could certainly present ideas, with Paige and Scarlett reminders of personal and school and community honesty, respectfully, rather than allowing false perceptions' growth until crippling.

Corey walks into a reenactment of *The Stepford Wives* (Levin, 1972) after returning home from some time away for her friend Kyra's funeral in Nijkamp's (2017) *Before I Let Her Go*. The friendly town she once knew has changed, especially regarding sharing circumstances of Kyra's death, with residents speaking strangely and using the same expressions. She's continually rebuffed from learning more, and although once close to Kyra's parents, they aren't interested in seeing her. Corey, as Scarlett would be helped by support; who in class would be unafraid to move from the crowd and offer assistance and friendship?

School and community responses fit nearly all of these titles, some positive, others not, with seventeen-year-old Grace from Blake's (2017) *How to Make a Wish* having spent her life nursing her ill mother. After her mother's death Grace has no idea how to proceed, as no other life was known. After Eva moves to town the two become friends, naturally noticed with disdain by residents, viewing Grace as a sainted caretaker. Grace's increasing romantic feelings toward Eva are unexpected but spur her to begin living her own life.

Similarly, Kingston from Callendar's (2022) *King of the Dragonflies* is devoted to his brother, Khalid. After Khalid's sudden death Kingston is so grief-stricken, he firmly believes his brother has turned into a dragonfly, with his family also transformed by sorrow. He needs someone to talk to, especially as he is also questioning his sexuality, something he wants to keep secret.

In tandem, Corrine, seen in Tyndall's (2020) *Who I Was With Her* is secretly LGBTQ+; when her girlfriend dies, she grieves alone, lest others discover her sexuality. She must be careful, not showing too much emotion or too little, not wanting to call attention to herself. These titles reminding teens of the many difficulties suffered by this group in all life's aspects, including death, and both also fitting Question 8.

Crutcher's (1983) *Running Loose* depicts Louie's immense grief and guilt over his girlfriend's death by car accident (Question 5); again, he couldn't have prevented it, and is soon unable to manage his grief. Dakota, his older friend, discusses his beliefs regarding life's events (pp. 138–41) gives him, and readers, valuable perspective (although somewhat strangely gone awry as above).

Best friends and lookalikes Maureen and Bridget had a devastating car accident with Maureen identified as having died, Bridget with debilitating injuries in Mitchard's (2008) *All We Know of Heaven*. After Maureen's funeral, a dental surgeon arrives for Bridget, soon discovering *Bridget* had died, not Maureen. Maureen's parents again have a daughter, with Bridget's facing a sudden, shocking loss. This causes immense guilt, as does the confusion and grief regarding the funeral and community, but all are supportive and remind students that being caring is always the best response.

Religion and culture affect grieving practices, offering comfort, or not, as in Question 8. Mystical traveling occurs in *Jeremy Stone*, above, and *Zane's Trace* (Wolf, 2007). Here, Zane's father is long gone, his mother committed suicide, and after his grandmother's death, he can no longer cope. He steals his brother's car to commit suicide (also Question 4; and miracles, Question 9), but as with Jeremy, spirits of his family and ancestors appear while traveling, allowing him to begin anew and accept his dysfunctional family.

More spirits are in Water's (2020) *Ghost Wood Song* (also miracles, Question 9) in which Shady inherited her deceased father's ability to call ghosts from the grave by playing his fiddle. Although doing so brings darkness and danger, once her brother is wrongly accused of murder, she must allow the dead to tell their long-held secrets.

Glorieta, as Shady, from Hamilton's (2018) *Days of the Dead* must also fight higher powers, as her mother tragically dies from becoming lost in her area's maze of lava caves, entering alone instead of with another as expected. Tia, the family's matriarch, considers her death a suicide from her being alone and denies her burial in consecrated ground. Glorieta knows she had no intention of suicide, working incessantly to change Tia's view.

All teens can benefit from learning of other's various beliefs and practices, including those of individual families. What practices, perhaps previously unknown or not considered, would be helpful to those suffering a loss?

There are multiple stories of miracle healings, presumably uplifting, although the same results are usually not seen in real life, adding to teens' guilt and grief, as in Question 9. Cam in Wunder's (2011) *The Probability of Miracles* has spent some seven years with cancer, now tired of her mother's constant traveling for cures—which were first legitimate, and then became local wonders. Their arriving in a town known for healing and witnessing some explainable events is intriguing, but Cam wants to use her remaining days to accomplish more satisfying goals and completing a personal milestone before dying.

After May's death in Rylant's (1992) *Missing May*, Summer and her uncle are so grieved they're uncertain how to continue, everything now so new and unfamiliar. They beg May to send them a sign, showing them how to proceed without her. They do receive an answer, but more from their doing a little more living each day and realizing she will always be present in their memories.

It should be noted and discussed that in all of the YAL titles considered here, the death occurs, with the miracle aspect arriving from characters essentially learning new ways of coping, accepting, and grieving. Death comes to all; Cam (and Ben from *Deadline*, above) illustrate the power of choice regarding how they wish their ending, an important choice that should be recognized. Likewise, others must also accept a death, naturally, a recurring theme for pondering.

One may have had a loss in the past, but a certain song, scent, film, or any event can trigger a remembrance of the event or person in seconds. These can be overwhelming for adults, and especially teens with a new loss. For most, they dissolve into fond memories or are no longer hurtful, but students can prepare for occurrences in many YAL titles.

Taylor and Willa in Doller's (2019) *Start Here* are losing their friendship but have long planned a post-graduation sailing trip to Florida with Finley, the friend who was to be their buffer of sorts. Finley makes most of the plans and arrangements, but she contracts leukemia, with her death unexpected and jarring. Not only must they decide if taking the trip will help their grieving or make it far worse by continually reminding them of Finley, they must also decide whether their friendship is worth saving and if an extended sailing vacation is the place to begin.

Sharples's (2013) *Running Lean* features opposites Stacey and Calvin. Stacey is from a large city, artistic, and free-spirited; Calvin a devout farm boy who enjoys his routines. After Calvin's mother dies, Stacey enjoys helping him, as it soothes her secret anorexia. Once he discovers her disorder, however, his efforts to assist her make both of their situations worse. They continue spiraling in silence until a threatening, yet positive, event occurs, bringing assistance.

As in so many titles, presumably, friends could have been helpful, rather than both character sets drawing inward rather than toward others, attempting to solve such overly large problems themselves. How might students have assisted these characters? Many of these titles have triggers, with students locating some, such as March Ann's hummingbirds or Lupita's poems bringing fond memories; certain dresses for Tiger or Lowen's licorice, far darker thoughts. What triggers do students already have regarding events in their lives?

Of course, there are more YAL titles featuring loss and death; grief is universal with none of these titles seeming dated, with Crutcher's 1983 *Running Loose* as captivating to contemporary teens as 2020+ titles, and those in between.

DISCUSSION QUESTIONS AND SUGGESTED ACTIVITIES

Discussion Questions	Suggested Activities; Students Will . . .	Key Diversity Points
1. Why are euphemisms frequently used to describe death, dying, serious illnesses, etc., and how are they harmful or helpful? What are some alternatives?	Teachers discuss euphemisms (common terminology for illnesses or death are "battling cancer," "passing," "went to heaven," etc.). Students locate examples from local paper obituaries and like sources and consider why euphemisms are used. Who prefers them? Which ones? For what reasons? Also pondered is effect of such terms, especially upon younger students who may not understand them. What other phrases might be beneficial? A famous euphemism is the 1996 Challenger space shuttle explosion designated a *major malfunction*; other common ones are those lacking food and funds as *underserved* or *food insecure*. What are these descriptions' effects?	Students comparing and discussing terms for illnesses and death used by different families and effects strengthen commonalities and understandings; likewise, perceptions of those from the media. Students labeled by euphemisms can discuss affects; peers realize power of words and labeling, perhaps viewing others with new understanding or compassion.
2. Death is not the only event causing grief. Many other losses are difficult, from moving to a different town, a relationship ending, a friend or family member moving, losing a championship game, and more. What are some non-death losses in your life, and how were you able to accept them?	Responses will vary, but discussion allows for understanding of all having many losses; a loss to one may not be to another. Discussing losses, coping skills, and acceptances is helpful, plus realizing it is acceptable, and necessary, to grieve hurts that aren't deaths. Those currently experiencing losses can be assisted by coping suggestions; students could create a handbook and continually revise. They might also help younger students.	Loss and grief are universal. Discussing non-death losses with others, especially those different in any way (males, females, teachers, students), reveals how similar we are with many shared experiences. Sharing losses allows new, stronger connections with others.

3. If having experienced a death in one's family, what was most and least helpful?

If not having a family death, most have experienced some loss and can imagine those more negative. Those having specific experience share views.
Death is frightening but discussion better prepares for its occurrence and assists the grieving process.
Considering how best to help others, especially younger students perhaps unable to articulate feelings and needs.
The above handbook could be extended to deaths, including helpful/unhelpful comments or actions.

We are one in grief regardless of differing beliefs/practices.
Also universal are commentary and actions deemed helpful, and not. Students better understand cultural/racial/religious differences and how best to assist others.
Those who have suffered a death can better help those grieving the same type of loss, regardless of formerly perceived differences.

4. Some teens are unable to grieve productively for various reasons and have difficulty accepting a death, and/or begin engaging in negative behaviors and choices. How may they be assisted?

Students can discuss reasons for such behaviors, such as an especially traumatizing death, having to relocate, or living with another family. Also considered is with whom to speak for professional guidance.

Nearly everyone needs assistance during grieving. Teens should watch for peer behavior changes, and those of new students to their communities and schools. Any teen can help another through friendship and notifying an adult regarding troubling behaviors.

5. Teens naturally experience guilt regarding some deaths as a suicide, arguing with a parent before their sudden demise, or having a sibling run errands, a fatal car accident following. How can such guilt be assuaged?

Students can discuss their numerous close calls, as almost being in a traffic accident, or narrowly missing a diving injury from not realizing a lake's depth change from drought. Most are quickly forgotten, but guilt is strongly felt when a death occurs. Unavoidability and forgiveness should be the focus.

Guilt and circumstances outside one's control occur to everyone, with sharing stories and learning how others forgave themselves beneficial to all.

Discussion Questions	Suggested Activities; Students Will...	Key Diversity Points
6. Does society expect us to care more about some deaths/illnesses more than others? Which ones, and what does this mean?	Students can discuss various expectations and reactions, as heavy smokers with lung cancer, drug overdoses, or an individual dying at age ninety-five. What assumptions may be made; is it presumed the first two caused their death, with the third having a long life with little grieving necessary? Discussions can consider rationales, damages caused, and necessary changes.	Are certain groups more prone to these reactions than others, and what do such reactions say about our society in general? How do they compare to personal experiences?
7. What are school and community responses and assists to those families coping with a death, serious illness, accident, and son? Are they helpful?	Students can list and discuss events and effectiveness, and any suggestions. Those with direct experience can share what was, or was not, helpful. Are some students treated differently by these, or are responses the same but individuals creating differences? Who, why, and what changes can be made?	Students may not have realized variances, but what would individuals feel receiving receptions of other peers? What do differences regarding treatments mean?
8. Religions and cultures have differing practices and attitudes toward death. What are those of others,' and what are positives and negatives?	Students can research and discuss practices different from their own and compare objectively.	We can learn from one another and incorporate others' practices into our lives, again lessening differences.

9. There are multiple stories of miracle healings achieved by prayer, both in the media and from individuals. While often heartwarming and uplifting, how are these also harmful and hurtful?

Students can discuss stories and conversation experienced and evaluate.
Hearing others' stories but without similar miracles eases guilt or other emotions. No one should feel that by doing something *better* would save another; we cannot control others' circumstances.
Discussion brings realization of only miracle stories published and are extremely rare. Their helpfulness, and reasons why, can also be considered.

All students have similar experiences, regardless of the loss.
Discussion is often the first time such hidden emotions were expressed, allowing realization of being shared by many. Talking strengthens commonalities.

10. Triggers are items/situations (e.g., song, scent, film) that suddenly remind one of past events, positive and negative, and can hurt deeply. What are some triggers experienced, and how can they be managed?

Various positive and negative triggers and effects of said triggers can be shared.
Students can discuss coping skills; not all have necessarily experienced triggers or understood them at the time. These peers and younger students can be assisted.

Sharing allows peer commonalities and realization of many different triggers but affects similar.

11. What YAL featuring characters facing illnesses, death, and other negative events has been helpful?

Educators and students can discuss and recommend positive YAL titles, including rationale for positivity. Titles considered negative should also be shared.
A bibliography could be created and updated.

Sharing titles, and by extension, personal experiences, is another way of becoming closer to others.

REFERENCES

Branon, D. (2010). *Beyond the valley: Finding hope in life's losses*. Discovery House.

Centers for Disease Control and Prevention. (August 3, 2021). *Adolescent health/mortality.* https://www.cdc.gov/nchs/fastats/adolescent-health.htm

Centers for Disease Control and Prevention. (November 7, 2019). *Leading causes of death in rural America.* https://www.cdc.gov/ruralhealth/cause-of-death.html

The Dougy Center. (November 12, 2020). *How to help a grieving teen.* https://www.dougy.org/resource-articles/how-to-help-a-grieving-teen

Forum on Child and Family Statistics. (2020). America's children in brief: Key national indicators of well-being, 2020 *child and adolescent mortality.* https://www.childstats.gov/americaschildren/child_mortality.asp

Gurrentz, B., & Mayol-Garcia, B. (April 22, 2021). *Marriage, divorce, widowhood remain prevalent among older populations.* U.S. Census Bureau. https://www.census.gov/library/stories/2021/04/love-and-loss-among-older-adults.html

Kübler Ross, E. (2014). *On death and dying*. Scribner/Simon & Shuster. (Original work published 1969).

Levin, I. (1972). *The Stepford wives*. Random House.

National Alliance for Children's Grief. (2012). *National poll of bereaved children & teenagers.* https://nacg.org/national-poll-of-bereaved-children-teenagers/

Noonan, R. (2017, November 28). *Rural America in crisis: The changing opioid overdose epidemic.* CDC. https://blogs.cdc.gov/publichealthmatters/2017/11/opioids/?platform=hootsuite

Rural Health Information Hub/RHIHub. (2019, August 29). *Rural agricultural health and safety* https://www.ruralhealthinfo.org/topics/agricultural-health-and-safety

Schonfeld, D. J., & Quackenbush (2010). *The grieving student: A teacher's guide*. Paul H. Brookes.

Shipley, A. (August 3, 2021). *Opioid crisis affects all Americans, rural and urban.* USDA. https://www.usda.gov/media/blog/2018/01/11/opioid-crisis-affects-all-americans-rural-and-urban

Turner, J. (2010). *Grief at school.* American Hospice Foundation. ahf@americanhospice.org

Unicef. (December 2021). *Mortality among children, adolescents and youth aged 5–24.* https://data.unicef.org/topic/child-survival/child-and-youth-mortality-age-5-24/

Appendix A
Bibliography of Rural-Themed YAL Titles by Single State

Alabama

- Nolan, H. (1996). *Send me down a miracle*. Harcourt. (Religion)
- Mendle, J. (2007). *Better off famous?* St. Martin's/Griffin. (Female relocates to NYC)
- Amateau, G. (2009). *A certain strain of peculiar*. Candlewick. (Female panic attacks)
- Forrester, S. (2009). *Leo and the lesser lion*. Knopf. (1930s female)
- Rumley, C. (2011). *Never sit down in a hoopskirt and other things I learned in Southern bell hell*. Egmont. (Female rebel)
- Glines, A. (2013). *While it lasts: A sea breeze novel*. Simon Pulse. (Romance)
- Key, W. (2016). *Terror at Bottle Creek*. FSG/Macmillan. (Male survival)
- Nijkamp, M. (2016). *This is where it ends*. Sourcebooks. (School shooting)
- Glines, A. (2017). *After the game: Field party, Book 3*. Simon Pulse. (Rape)
- West, K. (2019). *Maybe this time*. Point. (Romance)
- Hudson, G. (2020). *Boys of Alabama*. Liveright Publishing. (LGBTQ+, football)

Alaska

- Vanasse, D. (1997). *A distant enemy*. Lodestar Dutton. (Yup'ik male's family)
- Mikaelsen, B. (2001). *Touching spirit bear*. Scholastic. (Male survival)

- Giles, G. (2007). *Right behind you*. Little, Brown. (Male's terrible crime)
- Hill, K. (2007). *Do not pass go*. MKM/S & S. (Father's drug arrest)
- Frost, H. (2008). *Diamond willow*. FSG. (Female survival)
- Smelcer, J. (2016). *Stealing Indians*. Leapfrog. (Gov't. schools)
- Dirkes, C. (2017). *Sucktown, Alaska*. Switch/Capstone. (Male drug dealer)
- Nijkamp, M. (2017). *Before I let go*. Sourcebooks Fire. (Female friendship)
- Carter, A. (2019). *Not if I save you first*. Scholastic. (Female friendship)
- Lake, N. (2020). *Nowhere on Earth*. Knopf. (Female survival)

Arizona

- Carrillo, P. S. (2008). *Desert passage*. Arte Público. (Troubled cousins)
- Walls, J. (2009). *Half-broke horses*. Scribner's. (1901 frontier)
- Fichera, L. (2013). *Hooked*. Harlequin Teen. (Golf, Native American female)
- Bowling, D. (2017). *Insignificant events in the life of a cactus*. Sterling. (EXCP [exceptional student])
- Henson, S. F. (2017). *Devils within*. Sky Pony. (White supremacists)
- Dominy, A. F. (2018). *The fall of Grace*. Delacorte/PRH. (Embezzlement)
- Bowling, D. (2019). *Momentous events in the life of a cactus*. Sterling. (EXCP)
- Glasgow, K. (2019). *How to make friends with the dark*. Delacorte. (Grief)

Arkansas

- Draper, S. (2007). *Fire from the rock*. Dutton. (School integration)
- Hilmo, T. (2011). *With a name like love*. FSG/Macmillan. (Family of preachers)
- Anonymous. (2014). *The book of David*. Simon Pulse. (LGBTQ+)
- Hart, K. (2016). *After the fall*. FSG/Macmillan. (Romance)
- Brashear, A. (2018). *The incredible story of the making of the eve of destruction*. Soho Teen. (Filming Holocaust movie)
- Ha, R. (2020). *Almost American girl: An illustrated memoir*. B+B. (Korean female)

California

- Ryan, P. M. (2000). *Esperanza rising*. Scholastic. (Family financial troubles)
- Ritter, J. H. (2003). *The boy who saved baseball*. Philomel. (Baseball, 1880s)

- Patron, S. (2006). *The higher power of lucky.* Atheneum. (Abandonment worries)
- Korman, G. (2007). *Schooled.* Hyperion/DGB. (Living off the grid)
- Murphy, P. (2007). *Wild girls.* Viking. (Female, 1970s)
- Noël, A. (2007). *Kiss and blog.* Griffin/St. Martin's. (Female friendship)
- Soto, G. (2007). *Mercy on these teenage chimps.* Harcourt. (Males' growing pains)
- Smith, A. (2008). *Ghost medicine.* Feiwel and Friends/Macmillan. (Male's story)
- Bjorkman, L. (2009). *My invented life.* Henry Holt. (LGBTQ+)
- Jukes, M. (2009). *Smoke.* Frances Foster Books/Farrar, Straus & Giroux. (Male's story)
- Ritter, J. H. (2009). *The desperado who stole baseball.* Philomel. (Prequel)
- Alonzo, S. (2010). *Riding invisible.* Disney-Hyperion. (EXCP, violence)
- McNeal, L. (2010). *Dark water.* Knopf/Random House. (Migrant workers)
- Prinz, Y. (2010). *All you get is me.* HarperTeen. (Undocumented)
- Lupica, M. (2012). *True legend.* Philomel. (Basketball phenom)
- Demetrios, H. (2015). *I'll meet you there.* Henry Holt/Macmillan. (Friendship, romance)
- Broach, E. (2016). *The wolf keepers.* Henry Holt/Macmillan. (Female adopts wolves)
- Mukherjee, S. (2016). *Gemini.* Simon & Schuster. (EXCP)
- Stampler, L. (2016). *Little black dresses, little white lies.* Simon Pulse. (Female blogger)
- Demetrios, H. (2017). *Bad romance.* Holt. (Abusive relationship)
- Stone, P. (2018). *The perfect candidate.* Simon & Schuster. (Male DC intern)
- Dilloway, M. (2019). *Summer of a thousand pies.* Balzer + Bray. (Pie-making aunt)
- Garrett, C. (2019). *Full disclosure.* Knopf. (LGBTQ+)
- Morrissey, B. (2019). *When the light went out.* Sourcebooks Fire. (Grief)
- Parker, M. (2019). *Who put this song on?* Delacorte. (EXCP, sole Black teen in town)
- Elison, M. (2020). *Find Layla.* Skyscape. (Neglected female)
- Heagerty, M. (2021). *Martian ghost centaur.* Out Press. (Town economy)

Colorado

- Hobbs, W. (1989). *Bearstone.* Alladin. (Troubled Native American male)
- Hobbs, W. (1993). *Beardance.* Atheneum. (Sequel)
- Ault, S. (2008). *Wild inferno.* Berkley. (Wildfires, Native Americans)

- Abrahams, P. (2009). *Reality check*. HarperTeen. (Missing girl)
- Peters, J. A. (2011). *She loves you, she loves you not*. Little, Brown. (LGBTQ+)
- Novak, A. (2014). *My life with the Walter boys*. Sourcebooks. (Female orphaned)
- Flynn, L. E. (2020). *All eyes on her*. Imprint. (Male survival)

Connecticut

- Hughes, P. (2005). *Open ice*. Random House. (Hockey, head injuries)
- Fitzpatrick, H. (2014). *What I thought was true*. Dial/Penguin. (Romance)
- Black, T. B. (2018). *Girl at the grave*. Tor Teen/Macmillan. (Female, 1840s)
- Maldonado, C. (2021). *Fat chance, Charlie Vega*. Holiday House. (Body positivity)

Delaware

- Henriquez, C. (2014). *The book of unknown Americans*. Vintage/RH. (EXCP)

Florida

- Bloor, E. (1997). *Tangerine*. Houghton Mifflin Harcourt. (EXCP, family issues)
- DiCamillo, K. (2000). *Because of Winn-Dixie*. Candlewick Press. (Magical dog)
- Fogelin, A. (2000). *Crossing Jordan*. Peachtree Publishers. (Forbidden female friendship)
- Fogelin, A. (2006). *The real question*. Peachtree Publishers. (Studious male)
- St. James, J. (2007). *Freak show*. Dutton. (LGBTQ+)
- Lockhart, E., Mlynowski, S., & Myracle, L. (2008). *How to be a bad teen*. HarperTeen. (EXCP)
- Lupica, M. (2008). *The big field*. Philomel. (Baseball)
- Dalton, M. (2011). *Sixteenth summer*. SimonPulse/Simon & Schuster. (Romance)
- White, R. (2011). *A month of Sundays*. Farrar, Straus & Giroux/Macmillan. (Religion)
- Chappell, C. J. (2014). *More than good enough*. Flux/Llewellyn. (Native American male)

- Banks, A. (2015). *Joyride*. Feiwel & Friends/Macmillan. (Robbery, trauma)
- Pyron, B. (2015). *Lucky strike*. Arthur A. Levine/Scholastic. (Male's magical powers)
- de la Cruz, M. (2016). *Something in between*. Harlequin Teen. (Undocumented)
- Hoffmeister, P. B. (2016). *This is the part where you laugh*. Knopf. (Baseball)
- Self, J. (2016). *Drag teen*. Push/Scholastic. (College fund scheme)
- Curtis, M. L. (2018). *The leading edge of now*. Kids Can Press. (Female romance, grief)
- Gibaldi, L. (2018). *This tiny, perfect world*. HarperTeen. (Female's surprise scholarship)
- DiCamillo, K. (2019). *Beverly, right here*. Candlewick Press. (Grief)
- Aceves, F. (2020). *The new David Espinoza*. HarperTeen/HC. (Male body dysmorphia)
- Waters, E. (2020). *Ghost wood song*. HarperTeen. (Grief, magical powers)

Georgia

- Kadohata, C. (2004). *Kira-Kira*. Atheneum. (Japanese Americans, 1950s)
- Dudley, D. L. (2005). *Caleb's wars*. Houghton Mifflin Harcourt. (Black male, WWII)
- Dudley, D. L. (2005). *The bicycle man*. Houghton Mifflin Harcourt. (Female, 1920s)
- Jones, T. L. (2006). *Standing against the wind*. FSG/Macmillan. (Female yeans for college)
- Harazin, S. A. (2007). *Blood brothers*. Delacorte. (Males reminisce)
- Angle, K. G. (2008). *Hummingbird*. FSG/Macmillan. (Grief)
- Gilmore, S. G. (2008). *Looking for salvation at the Dairy Queen*. Shaye Areheart Books/Random House. (Female regrets leaving town)
- Hegedus, B. (2009). *Between us Baxters*. Westside Books. (Female, 1959)
- Coker, R. (2013). *Chasing Jupiter*. Zondervan. (Female, 1969)
- Dudley, D. L. (2013). *Cy in chains*. Clarion/Houghton Mifflin Harcourt. (Racial issues)
- Cocca, L. C. (2014). *Providence*. Merit Press. (Teen finds baby on train)
- Harkey, F. (2015). *Genuine sweet*. Clarion/Houghton Mifflin Harcourt. (Small-town life)
- Marquardt, M. (2015). *Dream things true*. St. Martin's/Macmillan. (Undocumented)

- Brown, J. R. (2016). *Georgia peaches and other forbidden fruit.* HarperTeen. (LGBTQ+)
- Deriso, C. H. (2017). *All the wrong chords.* Flux/North Star. (Grief)
- Poston, A. (2017). *Geekerella: A fangirl fairy tale.* Quirk Books. (Female's cosplay)
- Blake, A. H. (2018). *Ivy Aberdeen's letter to the world.* Little, Brown and Co. (LGBTQ+)
- Cartaya, P. (2019). *Each tiny spark.* Kokila. (EXCP)
- Courtney, N. J. (2019). *All-American Muslim girl.* FSG/Macmillan. (Muslim female)
- Poston, A. (2019). *The princess and the fangirl.* Quirk Books. (Sequel)
- Stone, N. (2019). *Jackpot.* Crown Books. (Lost million-dollar lottery ticket)
- Light, A. (2020). *The upside of falling.* HarperTeen. (Romance)
- Poston, A. (2020). *Bookish and the beast.* Quirk Books. (Sequel)
- Albertalli, B. (2021). *Kate in waiting.* HarperCollins/B+B. (Friendship, romance)
- Stone, N. (2021). *Fast pitch.* Penguin/Random House. (Female, softball)

Idaho

- Crutcher, C. (1983). *Running loose.* Bantam Doubleday Dell. (Grief, sports)
- Crutcher, C. (1987). *The Crazy Horse electric game.* Greenwillow/HarperCollins. (EXCP)
- Crutcher, C. (1989, 1991). *Athletic shorts: Six short stories.* Greenwillow/HarperCollins. (Sports)
- Crutcher, C. (1989). *Chinese handcuffs.* Greenwillow/HarperCollins. (Grief, sports)
- Crutcher, C. (1993). *Staying fat for Sarah Byrnes.* Greenwillow/HarperCollins. (EXCP, sports)
- Crutcher, C. (1995). *Ironman.* Greenwillow/HarperCollins. (EXCP, sports)
- Crutcher, C. (2001). *Whale talk.* Greenwillow/HarperCollins. (Sports)
- Crutcher, C. (2003). *King of the mild frontier: An ill-advised autobiography.* Greenwillow/HarperCollins. (Autobiography)
- Crutcher, C. (2005). *The sledding hill.* Greenwillow/HarperCollins. (Grief)
- Crutcher, C. (2007). *Deadline.* Greenwillow/HarperCollins. (Death)
- Richards, A. (2007). *Back talk.* Flux/Llewllyn. (Female's talk show internship)
- Tracy, K. (2007). *Lost it.* Simon Pulse. (Female, religious camp)

- Crutcher, C. (2009). *Angry management.* Greenwillow/HarperCollins. (EXCP, sports)
- Crutcher, C. (2009). *Stotan!* Greenwillow/HarperCollins. (Sports)
- Crutcher, C. (2013). *Period 8.* Greenwillow/HarperCollins. (EXCP, sports)
- Reardon, R. (2013). *The revelations of Jude Connor.* Kensington. (LGBTQ+)
- Hoffmeister, P. B. (2017). *Too shattered for mending.* Knopf/PRH. (Neglect)
- Crutcher, C. (2018). *Loser's bracket.* Greenwillow/HarperCollins. (Family, sports)
- Hand, C. (2019). *The how and the why.* HarperTeen/HarperCollins. (Female's family)
- Anderson, C. (2021). *What beauty there is.* Roaring Brook Press/Macmillan. (Trauma)

Illinois

- Peck, R. (1998). *A long way to Chicago.* Dial. (Great Depression)
- Peck, R. (2000). *A year down yonder.* Dial. (Sequel)
- Peck, R. (2009). *A season of gifts.* Dial. (Companion to above, 1958)
- Springer, K. (2011). *Just your average princess.* FSG/Macmillan. (Pageants)
- Polonsky, A. (2014). *Gracefully Grayson.* Hyperion. (LGBTQ+)
- Ruby, L. (2015). *Bone gap.* Harper/Balzer + Bray. (Female kidnapped)
- Belcamino, K. (2017). *City of angels.* Polis Books. (Homeless)
- Mills, E. (2019). *Famous in a small town.* Henry Holt. (Seeking funding for Rose bowl)
- Preston, N. (2019). *The lost.* Sourcebooks. (Murder investigation)
- Sass, A. (2020). *Surrender your sons.* North Star Editions. (LGBTQ+)

Indiana

- Tucker, T. (2008). *Over and under.* Thomas Dunne Books/St. Martin's. (Family issues)
- McKissack, F. (2009). *Shooting star.* Atheneum/Simon & Schuster. (Sports, steroids)
- Trigiani, A. (2009). *Viola in reel life.* HarperTeen. (Female films abusive home)
- Latham, I. (2010). *Leaving Gee's Bend.* Putnam. (Great Depression)
- Waltman, K. (2014). *Slump.* Cinco Puntos. (Sports, basketball)
- Lord, E. (2015). *The start of me and you.* Bloomsbury. (Grief)
- Keplinger, K. (2018). *That's not what happened.* Scholastic. (School shooting)
- Palmer, I. (2018). *All out of pretty.* Creston Books. (Homeless)

- Ellis, K. (2020). *Harrow lake*. Dial Books. (Female, mystery)
- Johnson, L. (2020). *You should see me in a crown*. Scholastic. (LGBTQ+)

Iowa

- Bauer, J. (1992). *Squashed*. Delacorte Press. (Pumpkin entry in state fair)
- Heynen, J. (1997). *Being youngest*. Henry Holt and Company. (Best friends' fun)
- Ripslinger, J. (2007). *Last kiss*. Flux/Llewellyn. (Male, murder accusation)
- Ylvisaker, A. (2007). *Little Klein*. Candlewick. (Male, 1949)
- Burd, N. (2009). *The vast fields of ordinary*. Dial. (LGBTQ+)
- Arntson, S. (2015). *The trap*. Houghton Mifflin Harcourt. (Time travel, 1963)
- Taylor, J. (2016). *Wandering wild*. Sky Pony. (Sibling hustlers)
- Hautman, P. (2017). *Slider*. Candlewick Press. (Competitive eating)
- Palmer, I. (2018). *All out of pretty*. Creston Books. (Homeless)
- Jahn, A. (2019). *The next to last mistake*. Light Messages. (Farm girl moves to city)

Kansas

- Paulsen, G. (1991). *The monument*. Dell. (Building war memorial)
- Ruby, L. (1993). *Miriam's well*. Scholastic. (Illness, religious issues)
- Uhlig, R. (2007). *Last dance at the Frosty Queen*. Knopf. (Male's life)
- Peck, D. (2008). *Sprout*. Bloomsbury. (LGBTQ+)
- Jennings, R. W. (2009). *Ghost town*. HMH. (Male's magical camera)
- Vanderpool, C. (2010). *Moon over Manifest*. Random House. (Great Depression, immigrants)
- Kadohata, C. (2013). *The thing about luck*. Atheneum/Simon & Schuster. (Female's summer in Japan)
- Adler, D. (2015). *Just visiting*. Spencer Hill/Contemporary. (Female friendship)
- Schantz, S. E. (2015). *Fig*. Margaret K. McElderry/Simon & Schuster. (EXCP, 1980s)
- Redgate, R. (2016). *Seven ways we lie*. Amulet/Abrams. (Seven deadly sins)
- Brashear, A. (2017). *No saints in Kansas*. Soho Teen. (Historical fiction, Clutter family)
- Dunn, P. (2017). *Girl on the verge*. Kensington. (Thai female's life)

- Smith, C. (2018). *Hearts unbroken*. Candlewick. (School play casting controversy)
- Henning, S. (2020). *Throw like a girl*. Little, Brown Books. (Sports)

Kentucky

- Covington, D. (1991). *Lizard*. Delacorte. (EXCP)
- Creech, S. (1994). *Walk two moons*. HarperCollins. (Grief)
- Holt, K. W. (2006). *Part of me: Stories of a Louisiana family*. Henry Holt. (Reading)
- Novgorodoff, D. (2008). *Slow storm*. Roaring Brook Press/Macmillan. (Undocumented)
- Wedekind, A. (2008). *A horse of her own*. F&F/Macmillan. (Female, riding camp)
- Napoli, D. J. (2009). *Alligator bayou*. Random House. (Sicilian immigrants)
- Naylor, P. R. (2009). *Faith, Hope, and Ivy June*. Delacorte. (Female friendship)
- Fawcett, K. P. (2010). *To come and go like magic*. Knopf. (Small-town life)
- Sherman, D. (2011). *The freedom maze*. Big Mouth House. (Female, time travel)
- McGarry, K. (2012). *Pushing the limits*. Harlequin Teen. (Romance)
- Elston, A. (2013). *The rules for disappearing*. Hyperion. (Female, witness protection)
- McGarry, K. (2013). *Dare you to*. Harlequin Teen. (Sequel)
- Elston, A. (2014). *The rules for breaking*. Hyperion. (Sequel)
- Going, K. L. (2015). *Pieces of why*. Kathy Dawson/Penguin. (Diverse choir)
- Holt, K. W. (2015). *Dear Hank Williams*. Henry Holt/Macmillan. (Female's letters, 1948)
- Allgeyer, A. (2016). *Dig too deep*. Albert Whitman Teen. (Female, underserved family)
- Wiechman, K. C. (2016). *Empty places*. Calkins Creek. (Female, 1930s)
- Armstrong, K. (2017). *Missing*. Random House. (Female dreams of being physician)
- O'Sullivan, J. (2017). *Between two skies*. Candlewick Press. (Female, Hurricane Katrina)
- Stevens, C. (2017). *Dress codes for small towns*. HarperTeen. (LGBTQ+)
- Elston, A. (2018). *The lying woods*. Disney/Hyperion. (Embezzlement)
- Thomas, L. (2019). *Wild and crooked*. Bloomsbury. (Female's father imprisoned)

- Callender, K. (2020). *King and the dragonflies*. Scholastic Press. (LGBTQ+, grief)
- Buford, C. (2021). *Kneel*. Harlequin/Inkyard Press. (Black player kneels during anthem)
- Callendar, K. (2022). *King and the dragonflies*. Scholastic. (Grief)

Maine

- Cooney, C. (1991). *The party's over*. Scholastic. (Friendship, romance)
- Schmidt, G. D. (2004). *Lizzie Bright and the Buckminster boy*. Clarion. (Friendship)
- Banghart, T. (2006). *What the sea wants*. Lizstar Books. (Female's coastal life)
- Lupica, M. (2007). *Summer ball*. Philomel. (Sports)
- Frank, H. (2010). *The view from the top*. Dutton/Penguin Putnam. (Female's summer)
- Jacobsen, J. R. (2010). *The complete history of why I hate her*. Atheneum. (Female's summer job)
- Wunder, W. (2011). *The probability of miracles*. Razorbill/Penguin. (Grief, death)
- Robinson, M. L. (2012). *Bright island*. Random House. (Female's beloved island)
- Wolf, E. (2012). *Camp*. Sky Pony. (Female's family purchases camp)
- Blagden, S. (2013). *Dear life, you suck*. Houghton Mifflin Harcourt. (Male's life)
- Blakemore, M. F. (2013). *The water castle*. Walker/Bloomsbury. (Male's scary house)
- Padian, M. (2013). *Out of nowhere*. Knopf/Random House. (Somali refugees, sports)
- Smith, J. E. (2013). *This is what happy looks like*. Poppy/Little, Brown. (Romance)
- Dalton, M. (2015). *Swept away: A sixteenth summer novel*. Simon Pulse. (Romance)
- Schmidt, G. D. (2015). *Orbiting Jupiter*. Clarion/HMH. (Eighth-grade father)
- Creech, S. (2016). *Moo: A novel*. HarperCollins. (Raising cow for state fair)
- Plourde, L. (2016). *Maxi's secrets*. Scholastic. (EXCP)
- Surrisi, C. M. (2016). *The Maypop kidnapping*. Carolrhoda/Lerner. (Teacher kidnapped)

- Tucholke, A. G. (2016). *Wink poppy midnight*. Dial/Penguin Random House. (Romance)
- French, G. (2017). *Grit: A novel*. HarperTeen. (Female sexuality)
- Dunbar, H. (2018). *Boomerang*. Sky Pony. (Male changes identity to run from mother)
- Drake, J. (2019). *The last true poets of the sea*. Little, Brown. (Coastal family)
- Culley, B. (2020). *Three things I know are true*. HarperTeen/HarperCollins. (EXCP)
- Moore, M. (2022). *Vacationland*. HarperCollins. (Female's coastal summer)

Maryland

- Fuqua, J. S. (2005). *King of the pygmies*. Candlewick Press. (EXCP)
- Bowers, L. (2007). *Beauty shop for rent . . . fully equipped, enquire within*. Harcourt. (Friends in beauty shop)
- Lyga, B. (2008). *Hero type*. Houghton Mifflin Harcourt. (Male hero, then traitor)
- Hahn, M. D. (2012). *Mister Death's blue-eyed girls*. Clarion/Houghton Mifflin Harcourt. (Mystery, 1950s)
- Ormond, V. (2012). *Believing in horses*. J.B. Max. (Female, horses)
- Sibson, L. (2019). *The art of breaking things*. Viking. (Female, abuse)

Massachusetts

- Cohn, R. (2004). *Pop princess*. Simon & Schuster. (Becoming a pop star)
- Wittlinger, E. (2007). *Parrotfish*. Simon & Schuster. (LGBTQ+)
- Parker, R. B. (2008). *The boxer and the spy*. Philomel. (Murder investigation)
- Lupica, M. (2009). *Million-dollar throw*. Philomel/Penguin. (Sports, town economy)
- Friend, N. (2010). *For keeps*. HarperTeen. (Family troubles)
- Paratore, C. M. (2011). *From Willa, with love*. Scholastic. (Romance)
- Lockhart, E. (2014). *We were liars*. Delacorte. (Female's summer trauma)
- Banks, K., & Sheldrake, R. (2015). *Boy's best friend*. FSG/Macmillan. (Male friendship)
- Hoffman, A. (2015). *Nightbird*. Wendy Lamb/Random House. (Family apple orchard)
- Stratton, A. (2015). *The dogs*. Sourcebooks Fire. (Mother and son running from father)

210   *Appendix A*

- Wittlinger, E. (2016). *Local girl swept away*. Merit Press. (Female's mysterious death)
- Messud, C. (2017). *The burning girl*. W.W. Norton & Company. (Female friendship)
- Wolk, L. (2017). *Beyond the bright sea*. Dutton/PRH. (Female, isolated island)
- Friend, N. (2018). *How we roll*. FSG/Macmillan. (EXCP)
- Thrace, M. (2018). *My whole truth*. Flux. (Female kills assailant)
- Barry, Q. (2020). *We ride upon sticks*. Pantheon/Penguin. (Sports)
- Lockhart, E. (2022). *Family of liars*. Delacorte. (Sequel)

Michigan

- Wood, J. R. (1992). *The man who loved clowns*. Hyperion. (EXCP)
- Wood, J. R. (1995). *When pigs fly*. Putnam & Grosset. (EXCP)
- Jones, P. (2008). *Cheated*. Walker. (Male's life-changing poor choices)
- Jones, P. (2008). *Stolen car*. Walker. (Romance)
- Potter, R. (2010). *Exit strategy*. Llewellyn. (Sports, steroids)
- Brewer, H. (2015). *The cemetery boys*. HarperTeen. (Male misfits)
- Mullen, D. C. (2015). *Tagged*. Charlesbridge. (Male graffiti artist)
- Schröder, M. (2016). *Be light like a bird*. Capstone. (Grief)
- Cook, E. (2017). *The hanging girl*. Houghton Mifflin Harcourt. (Religious prejudice)
- Madison, B., & Miller, S. (2018). *Losing brave*. Blink. (Female's twin missing)
- Allen, C. S. (2019). *Michigan vs. the boys*. Can/KCP Loft. (Female on male's team)
- Boulley, A. (2021). *Firekeeper's daughter*. Henry Holt/Macmillan. (Female, FBI)
- Couch, R. (2021). *The sky blues*. Simon & Schuster. (LGBTQ+)

Minnesota

- Paulsen, G. (1989). *The winter room*. Scholastic. (Male's farm life)
- Weaver, W. (1993). *Striking out*. HarperTrophy. (Sports, grief)
- Carter, A. (1995). *Between a rock and a hard place*. Scholastic. (Male survival)
- Weaver, W. (2007). *Defect*. FSG/Macmillan (Male can fly, fantasy)
- Friesen, J. (2008). *Jerk, California*. Speak/Penguin. (EXCP)
- Mitchard, J. (2008). *All we know of heaven: A novel*. HarperTeen. (Grief)
- Todd, P. (2008). *The blind faith hotel*. Margaret K. McElderry/S&S. (Female's life)

- Weaver, W. (2008). *Saturday night dirt*. Farrar, Straus & Giroux. (Stock car racing)
- Quigley, S. (2009). *TMI*. Dutton. (LGBTQ+)
- Sorrells, W. (2009). *Whiteout*. Dutton. (Female on run with mother)
- Weaver, W. (2009). *Super stock rookie*. Farrar, Straus & Giroux. (Stock car racing)
- Ellsworth, L. (2011). *Unforgettable*. Walker Books/Bloomsbury. (EXCP)
- Carlson-Voiles, P. (2012). *Summer of the wolves*. HMH. (Foster siblings, wolf cubs)
- Hoole, E. J. (2013). *Sometimes never, sometimes always*. Flux/Llewellyn. (Religion)
- Kadence, S. (2013). *On the right track*. Harmony Ink. (LGBTQ+)
- Mesrobian, C. (2013). *Sex & violence*. Carolrhoda. (Romance difficulties)
- Clark, C. (2014). *How to meet boys*. HarperTeen. (Friendship, romance)
- Petruck, R. (2014). *Steering toward normal*. Amulet/Abrams. (Male finds half brother)
- Sommers, J. L. (2015). *Truest*. Katherine Tegen/HarperCollins. (Small town life)
- Casanova, M. (2016). *Ice-out*. University of Minnesota Press. (Boy head of house, 1920s)
- O'Connor, S. (2018). *Until tomorrow, Mr. Marsworth*. Putnam/PRH. (Female's letters during Vietnam war)
- Biren, S. (2019). *Cold day in the sun*. Amulet. (Female on male hockey team)
- Bognanni, P. (2019). *This book is not yet rated*. Dial. (Male's troubled life)

Mississippi

- Murphy, J. (2018). *Ramona Blue*. Balzer + Bray. (LGBTQ+)
- Rees, D. (2018). *Elektra's adventures in tragedy*. Running Press/Perseus. (Divorce)

Missouri

- Kerr, M. E. (1995). *Deliver us from Evie*. Turtleback Books. (LGBTQ+)
- Crocker, N. (2007). *Billie Standish was here*. Simon & Schuster. (Rape)
- Katcher, B. (2009). *Almost perfect*. Delacorte. (LGBTQ+)
- Rudnick, P. (2013). *Gorgeous*. Scholastic. (Female becomes designer's muse)
- Brauning, K. (2014). *How we fall*. Merit. (Romance)
- Brown, J. (2014). *Torn away*. Little, Brown. (Female storm chaser)

- Katcher, B. (2014). *Everyone dies in the end*. Dark Continents. (Male journalist)
- Mackall, D. D. (2014). *The secrets of Tree Taylor*. Knopf/Random House. (Male's life)
- Halbrook, K. (2015). *Every last promise*. HarperTeen. (Sexual assault)
- Brandon, J. (2019). *Ziggy, Stardust, & me*. G.P. Putnam's Sons. (LGBTQ+)
- Cesare, A. (2020). *Clown in a cornfield*. HarperTeen. (Killer clown)

Montana

- Watson, L. (1993). *Montana, 1948*. Milkweed. (Family issues, 1940s)
- Mikaelsen, B. (1998). *Petey*. Hyperion. (EXCP)
- Collard, S. B. (2006). *Flash point*. Peachtree. (Conservation)
- Harmon, M. (2008). *The last exit to normal*. Knopf. (LGBTQ+)
- Chandler, K. (2010). *Wolves, boys & other things that might kill me*. Penguin. (Activism)
- West, S. G. (2011). *Blind your ponies*. Algonquin. (Sports)
- Larson, K. (2013). *Hattie ever after*. Delacorte/Random House. (Female in vaudeville)
- Warnock, C., & Schow, G. (2013). *Trouble's on the menu: A Tippy Canoe romp—with recipes*. Cedar Fort. (Friendship, romance)
- Hautman, P. (2015). *Eden west*. Candlewick. (Religious commune)
- Berkhout, N. (2017). *The mosaic*. Groundwood/Douglas & McIntyre. (PTSD)
- Ward, K. (2017). *Girl in a bad place*. Point/Scholastic. (Friendship)
- Russell, C. (2018). *Black bottle man*. Thistledown Press. (Trading souls for babies)
- Shrum, B. (2018). *The art of French ~~cooking~~ kissing*. Sky Pony. (Cooking school)

Nebraska

- Conrad, P. (1985). *Prairie songs*. The Trumpet Club. (Female's prairie life)
- Kehret, P. (2009). *Runaway twin*. Dutton. (Twins parted at age 3)
- Lieb, J. (2009). *I am a genius of unspeakable evil and I want to be your class president*. RazorBill/Penguin. (Eighth-grade cunning billionaire)
- Warren, A. (2009). *Pioneer girl: A true story of growing up on the prairie*. University of Nebraska Press. (Female's prairie diary)
- Portes, A. (2014). *Anatomy of a misfit*. HarperTeen. (Female's life)

- Fitzpatrick, B. (2015). *Dangerous lies*. Simon & Schuster. (Female, witness protection)
- Bowman, A. D. (2017). *Starfish*. Simon Pulse. (EXCP)
- Bahar, R. (2018). *The frontman: A novel*. SparkPress. (Israeli/Jewish romance)
- Vivian, S. (2018). *Stay sweet*. Simon & Schuster. (Female's summer before college)
- Rowell, R., & Hicks, F. E. (2019). *Pumpkinheads*. First Second Books. (Friends at work)

Nevada

- Ayarbe, H. (2012). *Wanted*. Balzer+Bray. (Undocumented)
- Cohn, R. (2017). *Kill all happies*. Hyperion. (Senior party goes awry)

New Hampshire

- Coman, C. (1995). *What Jamie saw*. Puffin. (Abuse)
- Bruchac, J. (1998). *The heart of a chief*. Puffin. (Troubled Native American male)
- Monninger, J. (2011). *Finding somewhere*. Delacorte/Random House. (Female friendship, horses)
- Knowles, J. (2012). *See you at Harry's*. Candlewick Press. (Female's family life)
- Moulton, E. E. (2014). *Chasing the Milky Way*. Philomel/Penguin. (Female, robotics)
- Farish, T. (2015). *Either the beginning or the end of the world*. Carolrhoda Lab/Lerner. (Female's family troubles)
- Monninger, J. (2017). *Game change*. Houghton Mifflin Harcourt. (Sports)
- Ostrom, M. (2018). *The beloved wild*. F&F/Macmillan. (Siblings traveling)

New Jersey

- Krumgold, J. (1959). *Onion John* (S. Shimin, illus.). HarperCollins. (Small-town life)
- Green, T. (2007). *Football genius*. HarperTeen. (Sports, illegal activities)
- Griffiths, S. (2007). *Thrown a curve*. Bancroft. (Female, sports)
- Green, T. (2008). *Football hero*. HarperTeen. (Sequel)
- Lecesne, J. (2008). *Absolute brightness*. HarperTeen. (Mysterious newcomer)
- Plum-Ucci, C. (2008). *Streams of babel*. Harcourt. (Mystery illness)

- Wilson, F. P. (2008). *Jack: Secret histories*. Tor. (Male friends solve mystery)
- Martino, A. C. (2009). *Over the end line*. Houghton Mifflin Harcourt. (Rape, sports)
- Meminger, N. (2009). *Shine, coconut moon*. MKM Books/S&S. (Harassment after 9/11)
- Griffiths, S. (2011). *Singled out*. Bancroft. (Sequel)
- Klass, D., & Klass, P. (2013). *Second impact*. Farrar, Straus and Giroux. (Sports)
- Wunder, W. (2014). *The museum of intangible things*. Razorbill/Penguin. (Friendship)
- Bloom, S. (2016). *The stand-in*. Carolrhoda. (High school male escort)

New Mexico

- Voorhees, C. (2008). *The brothers Torres*. Hyperion/DBG. (Male sibling difficulties)
- Stork, F. X. (2010). *The last summer of the death warriors*. Arthur A. Levine. (Illness, death)
- O'Connor, S. (2012). *Keeping safe the stars*. Putnam/Penguin. (Orphaned siblings)
- Tingle, T. (2013). *Danny Blackgoat, Navajo prisoner*. Seventh Generation. (WWII)
- Podos, R. (2017). *Like water*. Balzer + Bray. (EXCP)
- Crane, R. (2018). *The infinite pieces of us*. Skyscape. (Hidden pregnancy)
- Hamilton, K. (2018). *Days of the dead*. Sky Pony Press. (Undocumented, grief)
- Searcy, A. (2018). *Watch you burn*. Delacorte. (Troubled female)
- Mejia, T. K., & McLemore, A. M. (2020). *Miss Meteor*. HT/HC. (Beauty pageant)

New York

- Kerr, M. E. (1986). *Night kites*. HarperTrophy. (LGBTQ+)
- Hayes, D. (1991). *The trouble with lemons*. Fawcett Juniper. (Boy's dangerous discovery)
- Hayes, D. (1992). *The eye of the beholder*. Ballantine. (Sequel)
- Hayes, D. (1996). *Flyers*. Simon & Schuster. (Males and mysterious house)
- Bauer, C. (2000). *Harley, like a person*. Winslow. (Female's troubled family)

- Bauer, C. (2007). *Harley's ninth*. Knopf. (Sequel)
- Connor, L. (2007). *Waiting for normal*. HarperCollins. (Female's troubled family)
- Lipsyte, R. (2007). *Yellow flag*. HarperTeen. (Car racing)
- Bauer, J. (2008). *Peeled*. G.P. Putnam's Sons. (Female, town mystery)
- Griffin, P. (2008). *Ten mile river*. Dial. (Males living in abandoned house)
- Friedman, A. (2009). *The year my sister got lucky*. Point/Scholastic. (Sibling troubles)
- Going, K. L. (2009). *King of the screw-ups*. Houghton Mifflin Harcourt. (Male's life)
- Green, T. (2009). *Baseball great*. HarperCollins. (Sports, family troubles)
- Korman, G. (2009). *Pop*. HarperTeen. (Sports injuries)
- Suma, N.R. (2009). *Dani Noir*. Aladdin/Simon & Schuster. (Female sleuth)
- Demas, C. (2011). *Everything I was*. Carolrhoda/Lerner. (Female's troubled life)
- Schmidt, G. (2011). *Okay for now*. Clarion. (Male's family life)
- Giff, P. R. (2013). *Gingersnap*. Wendy Lamb/Random House. (Family life during WWII)
- Stewart, B. (2013). *The in-between*. St. Martin's. (Female's tragedies)
- Oliver, L. (2014). *Panic*. HarperCollins. (Senior survival contest)
- Airgood, E. (2015). *The education of Ivy Blake*. NP/Penguin. (Female's troubled life)
- Bruchac, J. (2015). *Walking two worlds: Pathfinders*. 7th Generation. (Seneca tribe)
- Crossan, S. (2015). *One*. Greenwillow. (EXCP)
- Storti, K. (2016). *Tripping back blue*. Carolrhoda Lab/Lerner. (Male, illegal drugs)
- Waas, E. (2016). *The Cresswell plot*. Hyperion. (Religious separatists)
- Firestone, C. (2017). *The unlikelies*. Little, Brown. (Friends' summer antics)
- Miller, M. (2017). *Little wrecks*. HarperCollins. (Beach town, 1970s)
- Silvera, A. (2017). *History is all you left me*. Soho Teen. (LGBTQ+, grief)
- Gansworth, E. (2018). *Give me some truth*. A.L/Scholastic. (Native American band)
- Herman, C. L. (2019). *The devouring gray*. Disney-Hyperion. (Teens, murder mystery)
- Ostrom, M. (2019). *Unleaving*. Feiwel and Friends. (Rape)
- Gansworth, E. (2020). *Apple (skin to the core)*. AALevine/Levine Querido. (Racism)
- Gomez, H. (2021). *List of ten*. Union Square & Company. (EXCP)

North Carolina

- Barkley, B., & Hepler, H. (2006). *Scrambled eggs at midnight*. Speak/Penguin. (Romance)
- Madden, K. (2007). *Louisiana's song*. Viking. (EXCP)
- Moses, S. P. (2007). *The baptism*. Margaret K. McElderry/S&S. (Religious issues)
- Herbsman, C. R. (2009). *Breathing*. Viking. (Romance)
- Leal, A. H. (2009). *Also known as Harper*. Henry Holt. (Female's underserved family)
- Dowell, F. O. (2011). *Ten miles past normal*. Atheneum. (Female's offbeat family)
- Myracle, L. (2011). *Shine*. Amulet/Abrams. (LGBTQ)
- Pyron, B. (2011). *A dog's way home*. Katherine Tiegen/HarperCollins. (Lost dog)
- Watkins, S. (2011). *What comes after*. Candlewick. (Family life)
- Calonita, J. (2012). *Belles*. Poppy/Little, Brown. (Family life)
- Jackson, C. (2012). *If I lie*. Simon Pulse. (Female's troubled romance)
- Turnage, S. (2012). *Three times lucky*. Dial/Penguin. (Female seeking mother)
- Fiore, K. (2013). *Taste test*. Walker/Bloomsbury. (Female, food contest)
- Sharples, D. L. (2013). *Running lean*. Zondervan. (Grief)
- Brown, J. R. (2014). *No place to fall*. HarperTeen. (Female, illegal drugs)
- Bliss, B. (2015). *No parking at the end times*. Greenwillow/HC. (Religion)
- Draper, S. (2015). *Stella by starlight*. Atheneum/S&S. (Racism, 1930s)
- Holmes, K. (2015). *The distance between lost and found*. HarperTeen. (Harmful rumors)
- Day, J. (2016). *The possibility of somewhere*. St. Martin's/Macmillan. (Valedictorians)
- Hostetter, J. M. (2016). *Aim*. Calkins Creek/Boyds Mills. (Male, WWII)
- Konen, L. (2016). *The last time we were us*. Katherine Tegen/HarperCollins. (Romance)
- Burt, J. (2017). *Greetings from witness protection!* F&F/Macmillan. (Family in hiding)
- Self, J. (2017). *A very, very bad thing*. Push/Scholastic. (LGBTQ+)
- Bliss, B. (2018). *We'll fly away*. Greenwillow/HarperCollins. (Males' different paths)
- Klare, S. (2018). *Surviving Adam Meade*. Swoon Reads/Macmillan. (Romance)
- Rufener, B. (2019). *Since we last spoke*. HarperTeen. (Grief)

- Smith, A. (2019). *Something like gravity*. Margaret K. McElderry. (LGBTQ+)
- Gonzales, S. (2020). *Only mostly devastated*. Wednesday Books. (LGBTQ+)
- Tyndall, N. (2020). *Who I was with her*. HarperCollins/HarperTeen. (LGBTQ+, grief)
- Gomez, H. (2021). *List of ten*. Union Square and Company. (EXCP)

North Dakota

- Saldin, E. (2018). *The dead eaters*. Simon Pulse. (Teens bound by past accident)

Ohio

- Lockhart, E. (2007). *Dramarama*. Hyperion/DBG. (LGBTQ+)
- Draper, S. (2010). *Out of my mind*. Atheneum/Simon & Schuster. (EXCP)
- Mlynowski, S. (2011). *Ten things we did (and probably shouldn't have)*. HarperTeen. (Female's family)
- Babbitt, N. (2012). *The moon over high street*. Hyperion. (Male adopted by billionaire)
- Beil, M. D. (2012). *Summer at forsaken lake*. Knopf/RH. (Sisters' summer at lake)
- Anns, L. (2013). *Tent city princess*. PageSpring Publishing. (Homeless)
- Green, T. (2014) *New kid*. HarperCollins. (Sports, family troubles)
- Hannah, A. (2014). *Of scars and stardust*. Flux/Llewelyn. (Female's troubled life)
- Green, T. (2015). *First team*. HarperCollins. (Sequel)
- Bacon, M. (2016). *Life before*. Sky Pony. (Male on run from murderer)
- Bauer, J. (2016). *Soar*. Viking/Penguin. (Sports)
- McGinnis, M. (2016). *The female of the species*. K. Tegen Books. (Troubled female)
- McBride, K. (2017). *The Bakersville dozen*. Sky Pony. (Female detective)
- Martin, M. M. (2017). *The big F*. Swoon Reads/Macmillan. (Female's school troubles)
- Simonet, A. (2018). *Wilder*. Farrar, Straus, & Giroux. (School pariah's romance)
- Henry, E. (2019). *When the sky fell on Splendor*. Razorbill. (Teen detectives)
- McGinnis, M. (2019). *Heroine*. HarperCollins/Katherine Tegen. (Female, illegal drugs)

- Draper, S. (2021). *Out of my heart*. Atheneum/Simon & Schuster. (Sequel)

Oklahoma

- Mccaughrean, G. (2011). *The glorious adventures of the sunshine queen*. HarperCollins. (Diphtheria epidemic, historical fiction)
- Zielin, L. (2012). *The waiting sky*. Putnam/Penguin. (Female storm chaser)
- Quinn, K. K. (2013). *Another little piece*. HarperTeen. (Missing female's sudden return)
- McGuire, J. (2018). *All the little lights*. Montlake Romance/Amazon. (Romance troubles)
- Nayeri, D. (2020). *Everything sad is untrue (A true story)*. A.A. Levine/Levine Querido. (Iranian teen in OK)

Oregon

- Watson, R. (2010). *What momma left me*. Bloomsbury Children's Books. (Grief)
- Noe, K. S. (2011). *Something to hold*. Clarion/HMH. (White female, reservation schools)
- Smith, K. (2013). *Trinkets*. Little, Brown. (Female shoplifters)
- Schroeder, L. (2014). *The bridge from me to you*. Point/Scholastic. (Sports, romance)
- Smith, K. (2013). *Trinkets*. Little, Brown. (Female shoplifters)
- Ockler, S. (2015). *The summer of chasing mermaids*. Simon Pulse. (EXCP)
- Asher, J. (2016). *What light*. Razorbill/Penguin Random House. (Romance)
- MacKenzie, J. (2016). *Spin the sky*. Sky Pony. (Female, talent show)
- Reed, A. (2017). *The nowhere girls*. Simon Pulse. (Female, mysterious house)
- Leonard, C. K. (2018). *Sleeping in my jeans*. Ooligan Press. (Homeless)
- Rufener, B. (2018). *Where I live*. HarperTeen. (Homeless)
- Saldin, E. (2018). *The dead enders*. Simon Pulse. (Resort town mystery)
- Wallenfels, S. (2018). *Deadfall*. Disney/Hyperion. (Brothers' adventures)
- Lundin, B. (2021). *Like other girls*. Hyperion/Freeform Books. (Sports, LGBTQ+)

Pennsylvania

- Spinelli, J. (1996). *Crash*. Scholastic. (Sports, bullying)
- Wallace, R. (1996). *Wrestling Sturbridge*. Alfred A. Knopf. (Sports, scholarships)

- Wallace, R. (1997). *Shots on goal*. Alfred A. Knopf. (Sports)
- Wallace, R. (2000). *Playing without the ball*. Alfred A. Knopf. (Sports)
- Plum-Ucci, C. (2002). *What happened to Lani Garver*. Harcourt. (Stranger in town)
- Althouse-Wood, J. (2007). *Summers at Blue Lake*. Algonquin. (LGBTQ+)
- Wallace, R. (2007). *One good punch*. Knopf. (Sports, harassment)
- Wallace, R. (2009). *Perpetual check*. Knopf. (Brothers in chess tournament)
- Connelly, N. (2010). *The miracle stealer*. Scholastic. (Boy seen as miracle)
- Gantos, J. (2011). *Dead end in Norvelt*. R.R. Donnelley and Sons. (Male's humorous 1962 summer)
- Lupica, M. (2011). *Underdogs*. Philomel. (Sports, town economy)
- Neri, G. (2011). *Ghetto cowboy*. Candlewick. (Male, abandoned horses)
- Weeks, S. (2011). *Pie*. Scholastic. (Famous pie baker leaves recipes to cat)
- Gantos, J. (2013). *From Norvelt to nowhere*. FSG/Macmillan. (Sequel)
- Smith-Ready, J. (2014). *This side of salvation*. Simon Pulse. (Religious issues)
- Wiseman, E. M. (2015). *Coal river*. Kensington. (Grief)
- Connelly, N. (2019). *Brawler*. Arthur A. Levine. (Male, illegal sports)
- King, A. S. (2019). *Dig*. Dutton. (Teens learn they share grandparents)
- Sibson, L. (2019). *The art of breaking things*. FSG/Macmillan. (Sexual abuse)

Rhode Island

- Cabot, M. (2007). *Pants on fire*. HarperCollins. (Romance)
- Hughes, M. P. (2007). *Lemonade mouth*. Delacorte. (Freshmen form band)
- Mackel, K. (2008). *Boost*. Dial. (Female on males' sports team)
- Robinson, M. L. (2011). *Bright island*. Random House. (Female's coastal life)
- Hughes, M. P. (2012). *Lemonade mouth puckers up*. Delacorte/Random House. (Sequel)
- Bennett, J. (2020). *Chasing lucky*. Simon Pulse. (Romance)

South Carolina

- Brande, R. (2007). *Evolution, me, and other freaks of nature*. Knopf. (Religious issues)

- Curtis, C. P. (2018). *The journey of Little Charlie*. Scholastic. (Male's family finances)

South Dakota

- Bennett, J. (1994). *Dakota dream*. Scholastic. (Female comes to U.S. to marry)
- Hobbs, W. (2008). *Go big or go home*. HarperCollins. (Meteor landing, life on Mars)
- Geisert, B. (2009). *Prairie winter*. Houghton Mifflin Harcourt. (Survival)
- Wendelboe, C. M. (2011). *Death along the spirit road*. Berkley Publishing. (Male returns to reservation home)
- Oppel, K. (2016). *Every hidden thing*. Simon & Schuster. (Rival paleontologists)

Tennessee

- Johnston, T. (2007). *Bone by bone by bone*. Roaring Brook Press. (Male, 1950s racism)
- Miller, K. (2010). *The eternal ones*. Penguin Young Readers. (Female seamstress)
- Kenneally, M. (2012). *Stealing Parker*. Sourcebooks. (LGBTQ+)
- McDaniel, L. (2014). *The year of chasing dreams*. DRH. (Female, troubled town)
- Allen, R. (2015). *The revenge playbook*. HarperTeen. (Females in male's scavenger hunt)
- Russo, M. (2016). *If I was your girl*. Flatiron Books/MacMillan. (LGBTQ+)
- Spears, K. (2016). *The boy who killed Grant Parker*. St. Martin's/Macmillan. (Male sent to small town for punishment)
- Zentner, J. (2016). *The serpent king*. Crown. (Religious issues)
- McDaniel, L. (2017). *Somebody's baby*. Delacorte/PRH. (Female learns of half-sibling)
- Tingle, T. (2018). *Trust your name: No Name, Book 4*. 7th Generation. (Sports, racism)
- Watts, J. (2018). *Quiver*. Three Rooms Press. (LGBTQ+)
- Russo, M. (2019). *Birthday*. Flatiron. (LGBTQ+)
- Bradley, K. B. (2020). *Fighting words*. Dial/Penguin Random House. (Sexual abuse)
- Vincent, R. (2021). *Every single lie*. Bloomsbury. (Female finds dead baby in boyfriend's gym bag)

- Zentner, J. (2021). *In the wild light*. PRH/Crown Books. (Male's unexpected scholarship)

Texas

- Paulsen, G. (1995). *The tent*. Harcourt Brace & Company. (Father/son religious hustlers)
- Ingold, J. (1998). *Pictures, 1918*. Harcourt Brace & Company. (Female photographer)
- Sachar, L. (1998). *Holes*. Farrar, Straus and Giroux. (Males, punitive summer camp)
- Charlton-Trujillo, E. (2007). *Feels like home*. Delacorte. (Female's troubled family)
- Cross, S. (2007). *Derby girl*. Henry Holt. (Female joins roller derby)
- Sanchez, A. (2007). *The god box*. Simon & Schuster. (LGBTQ+)
- Sáenz, B. A. (2008). *He forgot to say goodbye*. S&S. (Males' fathers' abandonment)
- Anderson, J. L. (2009). *Border crossing*. Milkweed. (Undocumented, EXCP)
- Volponi, P. (2009). *Homestretch*. Atheneum/S&S. (Male runs from abusive father)
- Toliver, W. (2010). *Lifted*. Simon & Schuster. (Female shoplifters)
- Heasley, G. (2011). *Where I belong*. HarperTeen. (Female's economic troubles)
- Kenneally, M. (2011). *Catching Jordan*. Sourcebooks. (Female on males' team)
- McCall, G. G. (2011). *Under the mesquite*. Lee & Low Books. (Grief)
- Osteen, N. (2012). *So the sign said*. Moonshine Cove Publishing. (Female, religion)
- Freeman, S. (2015). *The accident: A Port City High novel*. Saddleback. (Friendship)
- Loftin, N. (2015). *Wish girl*. Razorbill. (Friendship, romance)
- Murphy, J. (2015). *Dumplin.'* B+B/HarperCollins. (Curvy female, beauty pageant)
- Scanlon, L. G. (2015). *The great good summer*. Beach Lane/S&S. (Female's life)
- Honeyman, K. (2016). *Interference*. A.A. Levine/Scholastic. (Female, politics)
- Rae, K. (2016). *What you always wanted: An if only novel*. Bloomsbury. (Romance)
- Anderson, J. L. (2017). *Uncertain summer*. CBAY Books. (Female's family, friends)

- Mathieu, J. (2017). *Moxie*. Roaring Brook/Macmillan. (Male athletes harass females)
- Crossan, S. (2018). *Moonrise*. Bloomsbury. (Male's brother on death row)
- McCall, G. G. (2018). *All the stars denied*. Lee & Row. (Undocumented, 1930s)
- Johnson, A. (2019). *Even if I fall*. Ink Yard. (Male's false murder confession)
- Waller, S. B. (2019). *Girl on the verge*. Holt. (Female only Thai teen in town)
- Johnson, K. (2020). *This is my America*. Random House. (Racist imprisonment)
- Murphy, J. (2021). *Pumpkin*. HarperCollins/Balzer & Bray. (LGBTQ+)

Utah

- Smith, E. W. (2011). *Back when you were easier to love*. Dutton/Penguin. (Romance)
- Ellis, A. D. (2017). *You may already be a winner*. Dial/PRH. (Female's family troubles)
- Lauren, C. (2017). *Autoboyography*. Simon & Schuster. (LGBTQ+)
- Terry, E. (2017). *Forget me not*. Feiwel & Friends/Macmillan. (EXCP)
- Van Draanen, W. (2017). *Wild bird*. Knopf. (Female sent to wilderness camp)
- Glenn, S. (2018). *Beyond the green*. Charlesbridge. (Family relinquishes youngest child)

Vermont

- Hesse, K. (2001). *Witness*. Scholastic. (KKK arrives in town, 1920s)
- Belgue, N. (2006). *Soames on the range*. HarperTrophy Canada. (LGBTQ+)
- Wilhelm, D. (2007). *Falling*. Farrar, Straus & Giroux. (Male's family life)
- Hilton, M. (2015). *Full cicada moon*. Puffin/Penguin. (Japanese American female)
- Appelt, K., & McGhee, A. (2016). *Maybe a fox*. Atheneum/S&S. (Sisters' life)
- Harrison, M. (2016). *The killer in me*. Hyperion. (Female hunts killer)
- Logan, K. (2016). *True letters from a fictional life*. HarperTeen. (LGBTQ+)
- Oliver, L. (2018). *Broken things*. HarperCollins. (Females, murder mystery)

Virginia

- Staples, S. F. (1996). *Dangerous skies*. HarperTrophy. (Siblings of different races)
- Amateau, G. (2008). *Chancey of the Maury River*. Candlewick. (Female aids horse)
- Goetsch, L. (2008). *Back creek*. Bancroft. (Female's family troubles, 1970s)
- White, R. (2008). *Little Audrey*. FSG. (Female's family troubles, EXCP, 1940s)
- Hahn, M. D. (2009). *Closed for the season*. HMH. (Male's mysterious house)
- Erskine, K. (2013). *Seeing red*. Scholastic. (Grief)
- Lyne, J. H. (2013). *Catch rider*. Clarion/Houghton Mifflin. (Female's family troubles)
- Bauer, J. (2014). *Tell me*. Viking/Penguin. (Missing child)
- Bradbury, J. (2015). *River runs deep*. Atheneum/S&S. (EXCP)
- Tomp, S. (2015). *My best everything*. Little, Brown. (Female makes moonshine)
- Mittlefehldt, R. (2016). *It looks like this*. Candlewick Press. (LGBTQ+)
- Watkins, S. (2016). *Great falls*. Candlewick. (Sports, romance)
- Naylor, P. R. (2016). *Going where it's dark*. Delacorte/Random House. (EXCP)
- Smibert, A. (2018). *Bone's gift*. Boyds Mills Press. (Female, magical realism)
- McBride, A. (2021). *Me (Moth)*. Macmillan/F&F. (Black, Navajo romance)

Washington

- Trueman, T. (2000). *Stuck in neutral*. HarperTeen. (EXCP)
- Alexie, S. (2007). *The absolutely true diary of a part-time Indian*. (E. Forney, Illus.). Little, Brown & Company. (Reservation life, racism)
- Trueman, T. (2007). *7 days at the hot corner*. HarperCollins. (Sports, LGBTQ+)
- Deuker, C. (2007). *Gym candy*. Houghton Mifflin. (Sports, steroids)
- Mullen, T. (2007). *The last town on earth: A novel*. (1918 flu epidemic)
- Brouwer, S. (2008). *Thunderbird spirit*. Orca. (Sports, violence)
- Headley, J. C. (2008). *North of beautiful*. Little, Brown and Company. (EXCP)
- Kehm, M. (2009). *Suzi Clue: The prom queen curse*. Dutton. (Female sleuth)

- Deuker, C. (2010). *Payback time*. HMH Books. (Mysterious football player)
- Gurtler, J. (2011). *If I tell*. Sourcebooks. (Biracial female's struggles)
- Caletti, D. (2012). *The story of us*. Simon Pulse. (Large family life)
- Forman, G. (2015). *I was here*. Viking/Penguin. (Suicide, grief)
- Beaufrand, M. J. (2016). *Useless bay*. Amulet. (Quintuplets, coastal town)
- Deuker, C. (2016). *Gutless*. Houghton Mifflin Harcourt. (Sports, harassment)
- Dimmig, B. (2019). *Sanctuary somewhere*. West 44 Books. (Undocumented)
- Deuker, C. (2020). *Golden arm*. HMH Books. (Sports)

West Virginia

- Naylor, P. R. (1991). *Shiloh*. Bantam Doubleday Dell. (Male, abused dog)
- Rylant, C. (1992). *Missing May*. Dell. (Grief)
- Laskas, G. M. (2007). *The miner's daughter*. S&S. (Great Depression, miners)
- White, R. (2007). *Way down deep*. FSG. (Town finds abandoned toddler, 1940s)
- Slayton, F. C. (2009). *When the whistle blows*. Philomel. (Male's Halloweens, 1940s)
- Wyatt, M. (2009). *Funny how things change*. (Male reconsiders leaving town)
- Shank, M. S. (2012). *Child of the mountains*. Delacorte/Random House. (Grief)
- Gebhart, R. (2014). *There will be bears*. Candlewick Press. (Adventure)
- Wiersbitzky, S. (2014). *What flowers remember*. Namelos. (Alzheimer's)
- Dooley, S. (2016). *Free verse*. Putnam/Penguin. (Grief)
- Lemon, S. N. (2018). *Valley girls*. Amulet/Abrams. (Troubled female)

Wisconsin

- Carter, A. (1989). *Up country*. Scholastic. (Male's troubled life)
- Carter, A. (1994). *Dogwolf*. Scholastic. (Mixed-race male's troubles)
- Carter, A. (1999). *Crescent moon*. Holiday House. (Male's life, 1900s)
- Bauer, J. (2000). *Hope was here*. Puffin. (Running a diner)
- Murdock, C. G. (2006). *Dairy queen*. Houghton Mifflin. (Female's life in small town)
- Murdock, C. G. (2007). *The off season*. Houghton Mifflin. (Sequel)
- Cumbie, P. (2008). *Where people like us live*. HarperCollins. (Incest)
- Henkes, K. (2008). *Bird lake moon*. Greenwillow. (Lonely males, grief)

- Hijuelos, O. (2008). *Dark dude*. Atheneum/S&S. (Cuban American male, 1960s)
- Wroblewski, D. (2008). *The story of Edward Sawtelle*. Ecco/HarperCollins. (EXCP)
- Murdock, C. G. (2009). *Front and center*. HMH. (Sequel)
- McLoughlon, J. (2012). *At yellow lake*. Lincoln. (Teens' life-altering experience)
- Bick, I. J. (2013). *The sin-eater's confession*. Carolrhoda/Lerner. (LGBTQ+)
- Herbach, G. (2013). *I'm with stupid*. Sourcebooks. (Male's high school life)
- Anderson, J. L. (2014). *The vanishing season*. HarperTeen. (Friendship, romance)
- Eulberg, E. (2014). *Better off friends*. Point/Scholastic. (Friendship, romance)
- Hale, K. (2014). *No one else can have you*. HarperTeen. (Teen's murder mystery)
- Guhl, J. (2018). *Eleven miles to Oshkosh*. University of Wisconsin Press. (Teen investigates father's death)
- Eulberg, E. (2019). *Past perfect life*. Bloomsbury. (Female's family life)
- Herbach, G. (2019). *Cracking the bell*. Katherine Tegen Books. (Sports)

Wyoming

- Hubbard, K. (2011). *Like Mandarin*. Delacorte/RH. (Romance, friendship)
- Coel, M. (2013). *Killing Custer: A wind river mystery*. Berkley/Penguin. (Custer reenactment, mystery)
- Kronzer, N. (2020). *Unscripted*. Amulet/Abrams. (Female, improv. camp)

Appendix B

Bibliography of Rural-Themed YAL Titles by Multiple States/Areas

Note: Places in parentheses are listed in order of appearance within the novel.

- (LA, AK) Alsaid, A. (2014). *Let's get lost*. Harlequin Teen. (Female, Northern lights)
- (NH, NJ) Baldwin, R. (2017). *The last kid left*. Picador. (Teen's murder arrest)
- (IL, NY) Banash, J. (2008). *The elite*. Berkley Jam. (Female harassment)
- (CT, TX) Barnes, J. L. (2020). *The inheritance games*. Little, Brown. (Teens' mysterious inheritance)
- (CT, TX) Barnes, J. L. (2021). *The Hawthorne Legacy*. Little, Brown. (Sequel)
- (CT, TX) Barnes, J. L. (2022). *The final gambit*. Little, Brown. (Sequel)
- (Cuba, NY) Behar, R. (2017). *Lucky broken girl*. Penguin. (Female's family life)
- (Across U.S.) Brooks, B. (1986). *Midnight hour encores*. HarperCollins. (Female prodigy)
- (Northeast) Bruchac, J. (2007). *The way*. Darby Creek. (Male Native American harassment)
- (IL, MT) Burks, B. (1997). *Soldier boy*. Harcourt Brace. (Battle of Little Bighorn)
- (Chisholm Trail) Burks, B. (1999). *Wrango*. Harcourt Brace. (Black cowboy)
- (U.S.) Carpenter, N. C. (Ed.). (2020). *Rural voices: 15 authors challenge assumptions about small-town America*. Candlewick Press. (Short stories)

- (MA, UK) Cusick, J. M. (2013). *Cherry money baby*. Candlewick. (Female befriends famous actress)
- (CA, Mexico) De La Peña, M. (2009). *We were here*. Delacorte. (Male criminal)
- (Canada, U.S.) Dimaline, C. (2021). *The marrow thieves*. Amulet/Abrams. (Futuristic, hunting Native American bone marrow)
- (Canada, U.S.) Dimaline, C. (2021). *Hunting by stars*. Amulet/Abrams. (Sequel)
- (OH, FL) Doller, T. (2019). *Start here*. Simon & Shuster/Simon Pulse. (Grief)
- (WA, NM) Flores-Scott, P. (2018). *American road trip*. Henry Holt/Macmillan. (Male road trip, PTSD)
- (NY, Haiti) Farrar, J. (2013). *A song for Bijou*. Walker/Bloomsbury. (Romance)
- (WA, OR) Geiger, J. C. (2017). *Wildman*. Hyperion. (Male's unexpected road trip)
- (IL, IA) Hart, J. (2014). *Undead with benefits*. HarperTeen. (Teen zombies)
- (NC, TX, Mexico) Hobbs, W. (2011). *Take me to the river*. HarperCollins. (Survival)
- (TN, NY) House, S., & Vaswani, N. (2012). *Same sun here*. Candlewick. (Romance)
- (Mexico, CA) Jiménez, F. (1997). *The circuit*. Scholastic. (Migrant family)
- (OK, CA) Lacko, R. (2019). *A song for the road*. SparkPress. (Male seeks father)
- (Oregon Trail) Lawrence, I. (2000). *Ghost boy*. Dell Laurel Leaf. (EXCP)
- (N. Plains) Marshall, J. M. (2004). *The journey of Crazy Horse*. Viking. (Crazy Horse)
- (NC, TN) McGinnis, M. (2020). *Be not far from me*. HarperCollins. (Female survival)
- (Oregon Trail) McKernan, V. (2009). *The devil's paintbox*. Knopf. (Orphaned siblings)
- (NY, MA) McManus, K. M. (2020). *The cousins*. Delacorte Press/PRH. (Strange island)
- (AK, WA) Medema, D. (2020). *The truth project*. HarperCollins/Quill Tree Books. (Female's family troubles)
- (Guatemala, U.S.) Mikaelsen, B. (2002). *Red midnight*. HarperTrophy. (Male survival)
- (WY, MT, ID) Mullin, M. (2011). *Ashfall*. Tanglewood Press. (Yellowstone survival)
- (Appalachia, NY) Nolan, H. (2003). *When we were saints*. Harcourt. (Male's quest)

Bibliography of Rural-Themed YAL Titles by Multiple States/Areas

- (Across U.S.) Oaks, J. A. (2009). *Why I fight*. Atheneum/S&S. (Homeless)
- (OH, OR) Paulsen, G. (1994). *The car*. Harcourt Brace. (Male-built car)
- (WI, MT) Perkins, L. R. (2010). *As easy as falling off the face of the earth*. Greenwillow. (Survival)
- (UT, MA) Plummer, L. (1991). *My name is Sus5an Smith. The 5 is silent*. Dell. (Female's coming of age)
- (OR, TN) Rapp, A. (2009). *Punkzilla*. Candlewick. (Male travels to dying brother)
- (AK, WV) Rylant, C. (2006). *Ludie's life*. Harcourt. (Female's life)
- (SD, MN) Scaletta, K. (2009). *Mudville*. Knopf. (Baseball curse)
- (WY, MT, ID) Thebo, M. (2017). *Dreaming the bear*. Wendy Lamb/Penguin Books. (Female helps injured bear)
- (NY, Japan) Thompson, H. (2011). *Orchards*. Delacorte/Random House. (Grief)
- (Haiti to FL) Wagner, L. R. (2015). *Hold tight, don't let go*. Amulet/Abrams. (Female moves to FL)
- (AL, UK) Weiss, B. J. G. (2017). *Kit meets Covington*. Candlewick. (Horseback riding)
- (MD, OH) Wolf, A. (2007). *Zane's trace*. Candlewick. (Grief, spirits)
- (SC, NY) Yeh, K. (2015). *The truth about Twinkie Pie*. Little, Brown. (Female wins lottery)

Appendix C
YAL Bibliography of Settings Outside the United States

Arctic

- Hautala, B. (2015). *Waiting for unicorns*. Philomel/Penguin. (Female moves to Arctic)

Australia

- Abdel-Fattah, R. (2009). *Ten things I hate about me*. Scholastic. (Female Muslim)
- Hartnett, S. (2016). *Golden boys*. Candlewick. (Male friendships)

British Columbia

- Acheson, A. (2006). *Mud girl*. Coteau Books. (Female's troubled family)
- Kyi, T. L. (2013). *Anywhere but here*. Simon Pulse. (Male's family troubles)

Canada

- Paulsen, G. (1987). *Hatchet*. Simon & Schuster. (Male survival)
- Paulsen, G. (1991). *The river*. Bantam Doubleday Dell. (Sequel)
- Paulsen, G. (1996). *Brian's winter*. Bantam Doubleday Dell. (Sequel)
- McMahen, C. (2007). *Klutzhood*. Orca. (Males' antics)
- Schmidt, R. (2008). *Leaving Fletchville*. Orca. (Town's sole black family)
- Walters, G. (2008). *Fouling out*. Orca. (Sports, male friends)

- Yee, P. (2008). *Learning to fly*. Orca. (Chinese American male's struggles)
- Hoban, R. (2012). *Soonchild*. Candlewick.
- Ryan, T. (2012). *Way to go*. Orca. (LGBTQ+)
- Ellis, D. (2013). *True blue*. Pajama Press. (Male arrested, mob mentality)
- Nelson, C. (2015). *250 hours*. Coteau. (Male's community service)
- White, T. (2015). *Where I belong*. Tradewind Books. (Female activist, immigrants)
- Florence, M. (2016). *The missing*. Lorimer. (Missing indigenous women)
- Johnston, E. K. (2016). *Exit, pursued by a bear*. Dutton/Penguin. (Rape)
- Ozkowski, J. (2016). *Watching traffic*. Groundwood Books. (Female's tragic past)
- Camlot, H. (2017). *Clutch*. Red Deer. (Father's death)
- Körner, M. (2017). *Yellow dog*. Red Deer. (Sled dogs)
- Marshall, K. A. (2018). *I am still alive*. Viking/Penguin Random House. (Survival)
- Deen, N. (2019). *In the key of Nira Ghani*. Running Press. (Sole brown-skinned student)
- Hicks, F. E. (2019). *Comics will break your heart*. Roaring Brook. (Needs college funds)
- Bruchac, J. (2020). *Found*. 7th Generation. (Male survival)

England

- Rosoff, M. (2004). *How we live now*. Ember. (Female, WWII)
- Kelley, A. (2007). *Bower bird*. Luath Press. (EXCP)
- Crow, M. (2017). *Another place*. Atom/Little, Brown. (Female depression)
- Almond, D. (2019). *The color of the sun*. Candlewick. (Grief)

France

- Scott, E. (2011). *Between here and forever*. Simon Pulse/Simon & Schuster. (Grief)

Mexico

- Johnston, T., & Fontanot de Rhoads, M. E. (2019). *Beast rider*. Harry N. Abrams. (Undocumented)

Newfoundland

- MacLean, J. (2010). *The present tense of Prinny Murphy*. Fitzhenry & Whiteside. (Underserved female)

Northwest Territory

- Hobbs, W. (1996). *Far north*. Avon. (Male survival)

Pacific Islands

- Venkatraman, P. (2011). *Island's end*. Putnam/Penguin. (Female living as ancestors)

Philippines

- Ribray, R. (2019). *Patron saints of nothing*. Kokila. (Male cultural identity)

Sweden

- Vivian, S. (2016). *The last boy and girl in the world*. Simon & Schuster. (Romance)
- Backman, F. (2017). *Beartown*. Simon & Schuster. (Sports, troubled town, family)

Appendix D

YAL Bibliography of Titles From Unidentified State or Unidentified State With Named Area/Region

Unidentified State

- Woodson, J. (2007). *Feathers*. G.P. Putnam's Sons. (White male in Black school)
- Coy, J. (2009). *Top of the order*. Feiwel and Friends. (Sports, female on male team)
- Hepler, H. (2009). *The cupcake queen*. Point/Scholastic. (Small-town life)
- Dooley, S. (2011). *Body of water*. Feiwel and Friends/Macmillan. (Homelessness)
- Walker, M. (2011). *Small town sinners*. Bloomsbury. (Religious issues)
- Green, T. (2012). *Unstoppable.* HarperCollins. (Sports, troubled male)
- Pearce, J. (2012). *Purity*. Little, Brown. (Female's purity club)
- Sand-Eveland, C. (2012). *A tinfoil sky*. Tundra. (Homelessness)
- Grisham, J. (2013). *Theodore Boone: The activist*. Dutton/Penguin. (Male's life)
- Kirby, J. (2013). *Golden*. Simon & Schuster. (Female unsure of life after high school)
- Andreau, M. E. (2014). *The secret side of empty.* Running Press. (Undocumented)
- Choyce, L. (2014). *Jeremy Stone*. Red Deer. (Grief)
- DeWoskin, R. (2014). *Blind*. Viking/Penguin. (EXCP)
- Strasser, T. (2014). *No place*. Simon & Schuster. (Homelessness)
- Hepler, H. (2015). *Frosted kisses: The cupcake queen, Book 2*. Point/Scholastic. (Sequel)

- Jayne, H. (2015). *The escape*. Sourcebooks. (Missing students)
- Knowles, Jo. (2015). *Read between the lines*. Candlewick. (Short stories)
- Lindstrom, P. (2015). *Not if I see you first*. Poppy. (EXCP)
- Lynch, C. (2015). *Killing time in Crystal City*. S&S. (Male running from troubles)
- Robbins Rose, J. (2015). *Look both ways in the Barrio Blanco*. Candlewick. (Undocumented)
- Summers, C. (2015). *All the rage*. St. Martin's/Macmillan. (Rape)
- Turner, H. (2015). *Ask the dark*. Clarion/Houghton Mifflin Harcourt. (Troubled male)
- Dinan, K. (2016). *Don't get caught*. Sourcebooks Fire. (Male's prank goes awry)
- Fiore, K. (2016). *Thicker than water*. HarperTeen. (Female's troubled life)
- Alene, C. (2017). *The sky between you and me*. Sourcebooks Fire. (Female anorexia)
- Jacobson, J. R. (2018). *The dollar kids*. Candlewick. (Grief)
- Dugan, J. (2019). *Hot dog girl*. G.P. Putnam's Sons. (LGBTQ+)
- Kann, C. (2019). *If it makes you happy*. Swoon Reads. (LGBTQ+)
- Kemmerer, B. (2019). *Call it what you want*. Bloomsbury. (Male's troubled family)
- McAdam, T. (2021). *Sink or swim*. Orca. (Survival)

Midwest

- Underdahl, S. T. (2008). *Remember this*. Flux/Llewellyn. (Family troubles)
- Cheaney, J. B. (2014). *Somebody on this bus is going to be famous*. Sourcebooks. (Mysterious bus stop)
- Gottfred, B. T. (2015). *Forever for a year*. Henry Holt/Macmillan. (Romance)

Northeast, New England

- Preller, J. (2008). *Six innings*. Feiwel and Friends/Macmillan. (Sports, males)
- Marino, P. (2009). *Magic and misery*. Holiday House. (LGBTQ+)
- Abrahams, P. (2010). *Bullet point*. HarperTeen. (Male's criminal father)
- Emond, S. (2011). *Winter town*. Little, Brown. (Changing female friendships)
- Northrop, M. (2011). *Trapped*. Scholastic. (Survival)
- Altebrando, T. (2012). *The best night of your pathetic life*. Dutton/Penguin. (Senior scavenger hunt)
- Blake, A. (2017). *How to make a wish*. HMH. (Grief)

- Frick, K. (2018). *See all the stars*. MKM/S&S. (Female's past tragedies)
- Mele, D. (2018). *People like us.* Putnam/PRH. (Female, sports, mystery)
- Allen, J. (2019). *The lonesome era*. Iron Circus Comics. (1990s comics)

Northwest, West Coast

- Sloan, H. G. (2011). *I'll be there*. Little, Brown. (Brothers abducted by father)
- Nickerson, S. (2015). *The secrets of blueberries, brothers, Moose & me*. Dutton/Penguin. (Small-town life)
- Adrian, E. (2018). *The foreseeable future*. Dial/PRH. (Female's life after high school)
- Purcell, K. (2018). *This is not a love letter*. Hyperion. (Racism, suicide)

About the Author

Lisa A. Hazlett is a professor of secondary education at the University of South Dakota, where she teaches middle/secondary English language arts education courses, specializing in young adult literature regarding presentations and publications. She also serves and provides leadership for numerous NCTE assemblies, special interest groups, and committees, especially ELATE, and is an avid reviewer of young adult literature and manuscripts for various journals and publishers.

www.ingramcontent.com/pod-product-compliance
Lightning Source LLC
Chambersburg PA
CBHW032035300426
44117CB00009B/1074